# Praise for *Trans\* in College*

"Z Nicolazzo offers a powerful analysis of trans* collegian's experiences honors their voices. Z delivers a thoughtful and provocative book about resilience, kinship, and social justice, requiring readers to think more critically about safety, outness, engagement, and identity. Nicolazzo's book draws much needed attention to trans* oppression in higher education, how we are all implicated, and calls for us to rethink our approach to practices that shape our campus environments."

—**Chase Catalano**, *Assistant Professor, College Student Personnel,*
*Western Illinois University*

"In a society and educational system that repeatedly marginalizes trans* people, Z Nicolazzo has done what few higher education scholars attempt; that is, Z not only centers the experiences of trans* college students but also presents their stories in a way that brings visibility to their lives and wonderfully humanizes them as whole people. *Trans\* in College* is an amazingly thoughtful and introspective examination of what it means to both navigate and transgress the exclusive structures, policies, and cultures of post-secondary institutions. Readers will appreciate Z's approach in this book, particularly hir capacity to complicate existing trans*-related research and the liminal space that trans* persons have occupied in gender and sexuality discourses. This book is a necessary read for anyone, particularly cisgender people, seeking to understand trans* lives and experiences in college. While the emphasis is on trans* students, this book has larger implications for facilitating social justice on college and university campuses. This book should be required classroom reading and would be an outstanding resource for professional development programs. Lastly, this book should serve as inspiration to prompt future research which centers trans* lives."

—**Lori D. Patton**, *Professor, Higher Education and Student Affairs,*
*School of Education, Indiana University Bloomington*

"A timely and persuasive contribution to the literature on communities on the margins of higher education, Nicolazzo offers deep insight into the multiplicity of intersectional and systemic barriers faced by trans* collegians. But this book goes far past the expected story of trans* suffering to powerfully center trans* resilience and voice. The trans* students at the heart of this work demand better from all of us. A must-read for all concerned with true inclusion and change in the academy.

For every higher education administrator and change agent, this book offers a clarion call to consider how the collegiate environment continues to be shaped without trans* students in mind."

—**Sumun L. Pendakur**, *Associate Dean for Institutional Diversity,*
*Harvey Mudd College*

"Z Nicolazzo's first book, *Trans\* in College* is a beautifully written, rigorous, and masterful insight into the lives of nine trans* collegians at City University [a pseudonym] and how postsecondary educators can do better to support the education, resilience practices, and life chances for trans* collegians. Through the use of critical theoretical frameworks and methodologies that begin from the experiences and needs of the participants, Nicolazzo also demonstrates new possibilities for both the doing and reporting of research in higher education. As a scholar, I look forward to sharing this book with future graduate students as an example of how we can proliferate possibilities through and for scholarship. As a trans* parent of a trans* child, I am unspeakably grateful to the nine trans* collegians who have collaborated with Nicolazzo to create together this beautiful reflection of us."

—**Dafina-Lazarus Stewart**, *Higher Education and Student Affairs,*
*Bowling Green State University*

"With recent estimates of the trans* population in the United States showing three to six times as many trans* people under the age of 18 as there are over the age of 18, the work Z Nicolazzo undertakes in this book should be required reading for educators at every level of instruction. Gender is changing in ways we can scarcely comprehend, and millions of students already live lives that break the gender binary and contest what Nicolazzo calls 'compulsory heterogenderism.' We owe it to those students to acknowledge their reality and reflect it in our pedagogy, curriculum, and institutional practices."

—**Susan Stryker**, *Associate Professor of Gender and Women's Studies,*
*University of Arizona; and founding coeditor of* TSQ: Transgender
Studies Quarterly

TRANS* IN COLLEGE

# TRANS* IN COLLEGE

## Transgender Students' Strategies for Navigating Campus Life and the Institutional Politics of Inclusion

## Z Nicolazzo

### Foreword by
### Kristen A. Renn

### Afterword by
### Stephen John Quaye

1996–2016  20TH ANNIVERSARY

Stylus
PUBLISHING, LLC.

STERLING, VIRGINIA

Published by Stylus Publishing, LLC.
22883 Quicksilver Drive
Sterling, Virginia 20166-2102

**Library of Congress Cataloging-in-Publication Data**
Names: Nicolazzo, Z, author.
Title: Trans* in college: transgender students' strategies for
navigating campus life and the institutional politics of inclusion /
Z. Nicolazzo; foreword by Kristen A. Renn ; afterword by Stephen
John Quayle.
Description: Sterling, Virginia : Stylus Publishing, LLC, [2017] |
Includes bibliographical references and index.
Identifiers: LCCN 2016016797 (print) |
LCCN 2016029461 (ebook) |
    ISBN 9781620364550 (cloth : alk. paper) |
    ISBN 9781620364567 (pbk. : alk. paper) |
    ISBN 9781620364574 (library networkable e-edition) |
    ISBN 9781620364581 (consumer e-edition) |
    ISBN 9781620364574 (library networkable e-edition))
Subjects: LCSH: Transgender college students. |
College student orientation.
Classification: LCC LC2574.6 .N52 2017 (print) |
LCC LC2574.6 (ebook) |
DDC 378.1/98--dc23
LC record available at https://lccn.loc.gov/2016016797


13-digit ISBN: 978-1-62036-455-0  (cloth)
13-digit ISBN: 978-1-62036-456-7  (paper)
13-digit ISBN: 978-1-62036-457-4  (library networkable e-edition)
13-digit ISBN: 978-1-62036-458-1  (consumer e-edition)


Printed in the United States of America

All first editions printed on acid-free paper
that meets the American National Standards Institute
Z39-48 Standard.

Bulk Purchases

Quantity discounts are available for use in workshops and for
staff development.
Call 1-800-232-0223

First Edition, 2017

10   9   8   7   6   5

*For all the bois, girls, and folks like us,*
*this is my love letter to us.*

*And especially for T.J.,*
*for saving me more times than I can count.*

# CONTENTS

# FOREWORD

In our lives as scholars, we are not always in the right place at the right time and for the right reasons to bring forward knowledge inherent in the lived experiences of others. In the case of the book you are about to begin, it is clear that Z Nicolazzo was, and continues to be, exactly there: working with nine trans* collegians to illuminate their experiences and resilience. The recent increase in trans* visibility through celebrities, fictional story lines (e.g., the series *Transparent* from Amazon Studios), and media has not seen a parallel increase in visibility of ordinary trans* people, such as youths and college students, who continue to be socially positioned as impossible beings as a result of trans* oppression (Pitcher, 2015, 2016a, 2016b; Spade, 2015). *Trans* in College* defies this impossibility and brings us as readers into the possible and, I suggest probable, lives of nine undergraduates and Z hirself. There has never been a more important time for a book like this to help readers know that trans* college students not only are possible but also face the seemingly impossible task of speaking their stories and, in the tradition of minoritized peoples, writing themselves into existence.

I wrote a few years ago that there was a need for scholarship on trans* people in higher education (Renn, 2010). Since then, and as documented in the second chapter of this book, a modest amount of literature on trans* students (and even more modest on faculty; see Pitcher, 2015, 2016a, 2016b) informs policy and practice. This literature bears witness to the possibility, indeed the probability, of heretofore impossible people living, studying, and working among those of us who have for a longer time been possible in higher education: White people, cisgender men and women, people of color, enabled students and scholars, and so forth. Even those of us who identify as queer but not trans* (in my case, a White cisgender lesbian woman) have been possible for decades longer than our trans* students and colleagues have been able to be imagined. And yet, they (as we) have been here all along, as this book and several other publications (e.g., Bilodeau, 2009; Catalano, 2014, 2015b; Marine & Nicolazzo, 2014; Nicolazzo & Marine, 2015) make sometimes joyfully, sometimes painfully, and often poignantly in their everyday-ness clear.

Z elected to center this book in and on scholarship and lived experiences of trans* people in higher education. Early in Chapter 1, Z refuses to define *sex* and *gender* for the reader to not confine or limit these concepts. Z leaves them open, as exponential, entropic understandings of individual genders and societal categories of genders. This rhetorical decision invites us as readers to see gender and its manifestations like ripples in a pond. When Z or students choose to "come in" to community, or perhaps choose not to pass or cover their gender, they set off a similar reaction of shock waves emanating, multiplying, and amplifying out from individuals, their identities, and experiences, and the ways they are read by others.

The creativity and resilience necessary to be at the center of such a disturbance in the trans* oppressive norm—a particularly heightened, violent version of the forces of genderism (Bilodeau, 2009) that constrain people of every gender and that Z writes about in Chapter 1—come through in the stories in this book. Neither heroes nor victims (another false binary like gender), these students develop ways through, around, over, and beside the societal, family, and campus forces that would have them conform to prescriptive, ascriptive senses, and presentations of self. And through this resistance and resilience, they create counterspaces in analog and virtual relationships that provide glimpses into the possibility of trans* collegians. No longer possible for us as readers to unimagine, we are left to consider our own campuses and the ways we are complicit in the ongoing erasure of the possibility of trans* students and colleagues.

So how are we in higher education to respond to what we learn here? Z invites readers to consider Spade's (2015) notion that "social justice trickles up" (p. 137). This notion of social change, centered on an analysis of trans* lives, requires "participatory resistance led from the bottom up" (p. 138). What might a trickle-up approach to social justice look like in higher education? For one thing, it might look like the book you are holding, which began as a dissertation study by a trans* academic who came into hir trans* identity only a few years before beginning this project. It might also look like the self-formed "T* Circle," a group of trans* academics who have come together as scholars and colleagues, in contrast to the masculinist, competitive, individualist culture in many academic fields, to support one another and their work. Trickle-up social justice in higher education might look like cisgender readers of this volume doing our own work without seeking approval or rewards (known pejoratively as *cookies* among some social justice educators) from our trans\* students and colleagues. When we challenge what Z calls compulsory heterogenderism in all its forms, including those that lurk among other oppressive forces (e.g., racism, sexism, ableism, anti-Semitism, anti-Islamism), we may begin to make some inroads that will make our campuses possible places for more trans\* students and colleagues.

As is so clear throughout this book, trans\* students are not impossible people in higher education. For centuries, higher education has constructed itself to be an impossible place for trans\* people to be themselves, to be safe, to be seen. We with power in higher education (e.g., tenured and tenure-stream faculty, administrators, majoritarian students) have allowed it to be so, and we have benefited from it. We can change it. We can read the stories presented in this book, and we can make higher education live up to its best image of itself as an institution that provides opportunity. It's time we see and let them be seen on their terms, not ours: Adem, BC, Derek, Jackson, Kade, Megan, Micah, Raegan, Silvia, and Z.

Kristen A. Renn
Professor
Michigan State University
East Lansing, Michigan
March 3, 2016

*Some people have asked me what is the use of increasing possibilities for gender. I tend to answer: Possibility is not a luxury; it is as crucial as bread.*

—Judith Butler, *Undoing Gender*

*I am deliberate and afraid of nothing.*

—Audre Lorde, *The Collected Poems of Audre Lorde*

# ACKNOWLEDGMENTS

The writing of this book would never have happened were it not for a cadre of committed and loving people in my life. First of all, I need to thank D. Chase J. Catalano and his partner, Stephanie. Chase was the first person I came out to as trans*, and in a fitting turn of events, I began writing this book in Chase and Stephanie's house. Their hospitality, love, and care know no bounds. Next, I am completely indebted to T.J. Jourian. There are no words to describe what T.J. means to me, or how many times he has saved me, so any attempt to explain this seems to miss the mark. T.J., it sounds so very inadequate, but from the depths of my being, thank you, and I love you.

D-L Stewart has also become not only a fast and dear friend but also an intensely trusted colleague. It was ze who introduced me to my editor, and ze who has continually pushed me to do some of my best thinking and writing. As qualitative researchers, we discuss ourselves as being our own research instruments, and it has been D-L who has fine-tuned me as a qualitative researcher. Thank you, D-L, for being so many things at so many times. I am because we are together.

This book was largely written in the company of fellow trans* kin. Thanks to T.J. Jourian, D-L Stewart, and S Simmons for being my company and for motivating me with your words, laughter, commitment to increasing trans* scholarship, and loving hugs. Thanks also to finn schneider, Heather Lou, and Dan Tillapaugh for your encouragement and love along the way. Distance has always separated us, but your support feels like home.

Thanks also to my readers, Shannon Jolliff-Dettore, Alex C. Lange, and D-L Stewart, who helped me make this book even better than the dissertation study from which it was developed. Along with my original dissertation committee of Elisa Abes, Susan B. Marine, Lisa Weems, Stephen John Quaye, Peter Magolda, and Madelyn Detloff, these folks have made me think deeper, write clearer, and conduct research more holistically than I ever thought I was capable of doing. I still doubt my own abilities as a researcher and writer, but with the support and careful, patient reading of these people, I know I am developing a unique voice as a critical scholar and educator.

While I am on the topic of my dissertation committee, I must again publicly thank my adviser and dissertation chair, Elisa Abes. I moved to Oxford, Ohio—halfway across the country from where I had been living, and still another half a country away from my family—to work alongside her, and I could not be happier with this decision. Elisa is one of the humblest, most caring, and most brilliant people I have had the pleasure of knowing. She is also the very model of educator I hope to be one day. Thank you, Adviser, for always filling my cup and for showing me what care looks like in the academy.

Thank you also to my editor, John von Knorring, and the staff at Stylus. I appreciate your willingness to take a chance on my work, and for your endless patience with me as a first-time writer. Also, thank you to Kristen A. Renn and Stephen John Quaye, who wrote the foreword and afterword for this book. Both of you fell into my life at just the right time, and I could not be more pleased for our enduring relationships.

No acknowledgments section would be complete without thanking my family, especially my mother. You continue to be my biggest supporter, Mom. I love you to the moon and back. And although she passed away during the time I was collecting data for this book, I must acknowledge my late grandmother, Josephine Nicolazzo. My only regret in life is that I could not work fast enough for her to see me receive my PhD. However, I trust she knew I loved her and that every day I strive to make her proud.

Finally, thank you to the nine participants who journeyed with me for this book: Adem, BC, Derek, Jackson, Kade, Megan, Micah, Raegan, and Silvia. No matter where we are across this world, I continue to carry you in my heart. This book is truly for you all, and for us as a kinship network. Thank you for showing me what resilience, community, and love looks like in practice.

# INTRODUCTION

I can still remember the first time I told someone out loud, "I am transgender." The memory is forever etched in my mind as if it happened yesterday. I was sitting outside a coffee shop along a busy thoroughfare in Tucson, Arizona. In my right hand was my phone, pressed to my ear, and in my left hand was a cigarette, shaking because of my nerves. I sat staring at my iced coffee, condensation beading up and dripping off the plastic cup in the dry desert heat. I felt alone. I felt nervous. I paused midsentence, momentarily worrying that my words would be met with resistance, with the comment, "No, I don't think you are" from the other end of the line. It was a silly worry, but it was present nonetheless, which then made me wonder what it meant to be transgender. Did I want to biomedically transition? What would that mean for me? What would that mean for my job? What would that mean for my family, for my friends, and for my life? And what if I did not want to transition? The few transgender people I knew were all transitioning, so I did not have a sense of what it meant to be transgender and not transition. That pause seemed to stretch out interminably. I brought the cigarette to my lips, took a drag, let out my breath, and said into the receiver, "Chase, I think I am trans*."

I start with my own coming out, my own trans* becoming, not to be self-indulgent. I start with my own story because it is a moment every trans* person I have talked with is able to pinpoint. Or if we cannot pinpoint a particular moment, we are able to tap into a general feeling or sentiment when we noticed for the first time that we were different, that we were not like the other people with whom we shared playgrounds, classrooms, workplaces, coffee shops, and sports fields. Collectively, these moments, feelings, and stories act in two specific ways. First, they set up a world in which we recognize our difference. In these moments, through these feelings and in recovering these stories, we uncover how our trans* becomings—or the ways we are always already coming into our unfolding trans*ness (Garner, 2015)—cast us as outside and other than the perceived norm of gendered living. Although many of us—myself included—lack the words in the moment to name this phenomenon, this is the first time we bump up against transgender oppression, or the systemic presumption that there are two immutable,

1

fixed genders (i.e., man and woman) that frames those of us who do not fit this norm as abnormal, abject, wrong, or otherwise less than our cisgender peers (Catalano, McCarthy, & Shlasko, 2007). Although we may not know what this means, we know that it means we are somehow different from our normatively gendered peers, and that because of this difference our lives will be changed in a variety of ways.

The second way these stories operate is to bring forward a new "us" into which "we" enter. In effect, our coming out as trans* acts as a *coming in* of sorts. For example, when I came out to Chase, I chose him specifically, as a trans* man, as a form of coming into a trans* community. In response to my coming out/in, Chase, who at the time was working at a college in upstate New York, told me to find and read trans* memoirs. He suggested a couple of titles, which I remember scribbling on a napkin and then going home to purchase online. Throughout the next few months, I remember devouring these texts, hungry to learn about myself and my people. As I discuss later in this book, through these memoirs and historical texts I began to develop my own trans* community. Through these texts I began to develop a sense not only of who I was as a trans* person but also of who we were as a trans* people. And through these texts I found and began to come into a new community, my new community.

This particular moment, the notion of coming into community, is what I have been particularly consumed with over the past five years, personally and professionally. This text represents how I have tried to understand and make sense of trans* community. Moreover, I undertook this investigation in one of the few ways that made sense to me, and that was to conduct my research alongside other trans* people, specifically trans* collegians. As I thought when I began the research study that undergirds this book—and as I still think now—there was no better way I could understand trans* community than by exploring it alongside my fellow trans* kin. And yet, even as I sit here now, typing these words at Chase's dining room table, it seems only fitting that I would cycle back to a central question of this book: Who is the *we* trans* people come into? To describe what exactly I mean by this, it may be helpful to share another story.

In my current life as an assistant professor, I have taken an interest in disability studies. Partially born from the research that follows in this book, and partially from the ways I continue to understand myself and the world I live in, I have become fascinated by the ways trans* and disability identities, rhetoric, and discourse become enmeshed. According to many scholars, these are not easy connections and could perhaps be better understood as fault lines that detail the rough, jagged, and complicated nature of the terrain between, along, and among trans* and disabled bodies (of knowledge). Although I delve into more detail about the overlaps of trans* and disabled identities and lives throughout this book, one notion from the disability rights movement is important to discuss in this introduction, and that is, "Nothing About Us Without Us!" (Inckle, 2015, p. 44). This phrase was—and still is—a powerful reclamation of control by disability rights activists, scholars, and educators. Essentially, it means that the nondisabled (or whom Clare [2015] termed *enabled*, focusing on the ways environments enable certain lives and bodies over others) could no longer assume control over the narrative about disabled people. Quite literally, there could and should be nothing about disabled people that did not emanate from the disabled community.

This sort of "for us, by us" mentality—originally conceived and popularized in the Black community by Keith Perrin, Daymond John, Carl Brown, and J. Alexander Martin, the cofounders of the clothing brand FUBU (Dunn, 1999)—has been replicated in other movements, including the trans* movement (Richards, 2016), and this mentality has caused me to pause, wondering just who is the "us" being called to the fore? Who are "we" joining to coalesce and connect with? And, what do these questions about what is meant by "us" and "we" mean about the very community "we" create? For example, is there one trans* community? Or should "we" talk about ourselves in pluralities, discussing instead "our communities"? For example, when I tell people, as I often find myself doing, that my work is ultimately about writing trans* collegians and the trans* collegiate community into existence, what sort of community is it exactly that I am tracing?

I understand these are theoretical questions; however, they are also deeply existential. In other words, I have come to recognize that these questions about "us," who "we" are, and what it means to come home into the trans* community are more than just a matter of semantics. These questions uncover important considerations regarding trans* livelihoods, kinship, and self- and group understandings about gender. These questions allow trans* people to unlearn the self-hatred and internalized oppression we experience when we first recognize that we are different and that our difference somehow masquerades as our being undesirable. In essence, thinking deeply about "us," about who "we" are, and about what community means is the very stuff that allows us as trans* people to reclaim our bodies, minds, genders, and lives in ways that are expansive, liberatory, and full of self-affirmation and love. It is here that the theoretical rubs up against the lived, and where who we are and what community means provide clues to the very possibilities of trans* existence on college campuses. In the context of this book, these questions about us, who we are, and about what community means permeate the text and highlight the various ways postsecondary educators might reimagine their work environments to proliferate possibilities for new, varied trans* becomings.

In contrast to the disruption that thinking about trans* identities causes binary notions of gender, this book is organized in a logical pattern. In Chapter 1, I introduce various words and concepts that may be unfamiliar to readers but are critical to understanding trans* collegians, and as such, serve as a basis for the empirical study for this book. I also spend time discussing my own positionality as a trans* researcher and scholar and outline the aims and scope of the book in detail.

Between chapters, I have inserted interludes. Mirroring the use of this rhetorical device by Jones and Abes (2013), these interludes allow readers to understand better my process and approach to research and writing. Because we as qualitative researchers are the instruments through which our research occurs (Corbin & Strauss, 2008; Jones, Torres, & Arminio, 2006; Stewart, 2010), these interludes are especially important, as they allow me to provide an ongoing sense of who I am and how I undertook the research that grounds this book. The interludes also serve to bring me into a closer relationship alongside participants, our research project, and the ensuing findings and implications. Because this research was framed as a collaborative endeavor, I use the interludes as a way to bring myself into closer conversation with participants and the research process itself. In this way, the interludes allowed me a way to reflect my theoretical perspective and study methodology beyond the collection of data, and throughout the writing of this book (see the appendix for more information on my overall study design).

In Chapter 2, I explore literature germane to trans* people and, more specifically, to trans* collegians. In doing so, I explore the reality that although research in higher education and student affairs has grown regarding lesbian, gay, and bisexual (LGB) students, there is still a paltry amount of empirical research related to trans* students. By exposing this disconnection, I call upon Renn's (2010) commentary that sexuality (i.e., LGB identities) and gender identity (i.e., trans* identities) continue to be conflated in dangerous ways throughout higher education research and practice. In other words, although sexuality and gender do overlap, they are also discrete identities, which is often missed by the regular (mis)use of the LGBT (lesbian, gay, bisexual, and trans*) acronym to discuss research that either primarily or exclusively focuses on sexuality. I also discuss the multiple understandings of gender, the conceptions of oppression and intersectionality, and the use of resilience theory as a framing device for the research that guides this book.

Chapters 3 through 7 discuss data specifically from the study I conducted for this book. These data were gathered during an 18-month ethnographic study I performed alongside nine trans* collegians at City University (CU; a pseudonym). As an ethnographic study, these data elucidate not just the particularities of trans* collegians' lives but also illustrate the ways gender regulates the lives of all people at CU. As a result of gender as a regulatory system—which I discuss as occurring through the twin realities of the *gender binary discourse* and *compulsory heterogenderism*—trans* students are forced to develop skills and strategies for navigating a collegiate environment that continues to be shaped without them in mind. These strategies, which I refer to as practices of resilience, provide possibilities for trans* student liberation alongside the very real problem of causing various forms of exhaustion. They also require trans* students to develop what I refer to as kinship networks, which occur in physical and virtual spaces alike.

After exploring data from the study, I discuss the implications for practice for educators in higher education and student affairs in Chapter 8. These implications should be understood as guides for practice rather than a prescribed list of best practices. In fact, I suggest moving beyond best practices because, despite the necessity of best practices related to trans* students, these practices do little, if anything, to change the actual ethos regarding gender that persists throughout higher education environments. In other words, I suggest that best practices may do little to disrupt the oppressive realities of the gender binary discourse and compulsory heterogenderism that exist in collegiate contexts. In the words of one participant, Adem, in Chapter 8, these best practices operate as "caution tape," detailing where educators should not go but perhaps doing little to increase life chances for trans* students.

I conclude the book with the participants sharing what they want college faculty, staff, and students to know about trans* students. It strikes me that in a book about trans* community, and in a context where trans* people are often erased—physically, through the curriculum, and otherwise—ending with participants' own words is particularly important. In other words, the years participants and I spent conducting, analyzing, and writing this research study mark a rather vexing reality. On the one hand, there was a dramatic increase in the visibility of (some) trans* lives. People like Laverne Cox, Janet Mock, CeCe McDonald, and Chelsea Manning (among others) have brought discussions of (some) trans* people into a greater number of homes and families across the country. On the other hand, the increased visibility of (some) trans* lives was juxtaposed with an increase in violence against the trans* community, particularly trans* women of color who were murdered at appalling rates in 2015 (Gossett, 2015). The conundrum of increased visibility and increased violence and threats underlines the very nature of what is meant by the trans* community, which I discussed earlier. In other words, who is the "we" being discussed when media outlets suggest that as a nation we have arrived at a supposed transgender tipping point, as *Time* magazine did when Laverne Cox graced its June 9, 2014 cover (Steinmetz, 2014)? Essentially, ending the book with the participants exposes and expands just who is understood to be trans* and, as a result, increases the possibilities and life chances for trans* collegians on their own terms and through their own words.

One of the main lines of questioning I have continued to encounter in relation to trans* students has been about vocabulary and terms. Because I do not want this to be an impediment to further action regarding trans* equity, I have included a glossary. Additionally, for those interested in doing research with and alongside trans* students, my hope is the appendix provides a useful sketch for working alongside a marginalized population in a manner that foregrounds ethics, care, and reciprocity.

In essence, I hope this book is practical and can be used in a variety of ways by a variety of people. For the practitioner, I hope the book provides some concrete ways to shift and change student affairs policy and practice in relation to trans* students. Finally, it is my hope that this book may also prove useful to trans* students themselves. Just as I went first to books to find myself and my trans* communities when I first came out/in, I hope this book can help welcome trans* students into a varied set of trans* communities.

I know many trans* people and students across the country who, just like me, are shaking with the realities that our genders mark us as different and are feeling the full weight of that difference. Therefore, I hope this book can be of some use for my trans* kin who, like me, are still trying to read, write, research, and learn our people into existence. To all of you who may pick up this book, I want you to know I see you, I hear you, I feel you, and I am with you. Indeed, we are, and always will be, together in community.

# 1

## SITUATING THE STUDY

Although the term *transgender* has been in use less than 40 years (Ekins & King, 2006), many scholars and researchers have documented the numerous definitions regarding trans* identities (e.g., Currah, 2006; Hill, 2003; Stryker, 2008) along with the various tensions (e.g., Valentine, 2007), debates (e.g., Halberstam, 1998; Hale, 1998; Rubin, 2006), and conflations (e.g., Renn, 2010) that arise because of these definitions. Even my use of the asterisk, which symbolizes the multitude of identities and identity categories used to refer to those of us who are trans* (Tompkins, 2014), represents a relatively new—and contested—turn in how the community is understood and represented textually. This rocky terminological terrain mirrors Sedgwick's (2008) provocative statement, "The relations implicit in *identifying with* are, as psychoanalysis suggests, in themselves quite sufficiently fraught with intensities of incorporation, diminishment, inflation, threat, loss, reparation, and disavowal" (p. 61; emphasis in original). Language and categories are insufficient to capture the fluid nature of the various permutations of gender identities, expressions, and embodiments that show up in various spatial and temporal locations. However, despite their seeming inadequacy, such categories are in many ways necessary in their ability to make individuals and populations culturally intelligible (Butler, 2006) as well as to help individuals find communities of support. According to E.C. Davis (2008),

> Controversy over academic representations of transgender lives centers on and reiterates false dichotomies of stable/fluid, hegemonic/subversive, and oppression/empowerment. . . . Neither the emphasis on stability nor the postmodern framing of fluidity can completely account for the ongoing, everyday practices and experiences of (trans) gender identity construction. Attempts to create and present a coherent self may coexist with diverse ways of exhibiting and explaining this self. (p. 99)

Valentine (2007) extended this point, saying that although language and categorization are both necessary, they are far from neutral. If the language and the categories of identification one uses are never neutral, then one must recognize overarching matrices of power and privilege as influencing the ways individuals and groups invoke such discourse and categorization. I agree with E.C. Davis's (2008) and Valentine's (2007) commentary and can mark points in my history when the language and categories I have used to self-identify have been seen—and not seen—as intelligible based on my privileged and subordinated identities.

Despite the contingency of language and the inadequacy of categories, both are still necessary to promote an understanding of trans* students. For the purposes of this book, I use the term *trans\** when discussing this student population. As previously mentioned, the use of the asterisk is a relatively new development, one that has yet to receive widespread acceptance and use, especially in educational research and scholarship. The asterisk refers to the way computer search functions allow one to search for any words attached to the prefix *trans-* (e.g., transgender, transsexual, trans* woman). Thus, it provides a textual representation of the malleability of gender identities, expressions, embodiments, and performances (Tompkins, 2014). The term is consistent with Stryker's (2008) definition of *transgender*, which, she stated, "Refer[s] to people who move away from the gender they were assigned at birth, people who cross over (*trans-*) the boundaries constructed by their culture to define and contain that gender" (p. 1; emphasis in original). The asterisk also provides a visual disruption for readers, severing the conflation often made by educational researchers of the words *transgender* and *transsexual*, to signify "a person who identifies as the opposite *sex* of that which he or she was assigned at birth" (Teich, 2012, p. 136; emphasis in original). The asterisk also serves as a reminder that categories, while seemingly expressing a solitary identity, are sites of fractious, contested, and varied meanings.

Regardless of my preference and use of the word *trans\**, I allowed research participants to define and use their own terms regarding their gender identity. I honored their choices by using their terms and definitions when referring to them throughout this book. I also did not change the quotations of those scholars I cite throughout this text. If an author's use of terminology is unclear in relation to my own, I clarified this discrepancy. However, I did not modify their original text as a way to honor their voice, perspective, and the context of their writing. I have also taken care to create as broad a definition as possible for the term *trans\**, making sure to discuss it in terms of proliferating possibilities for who we are as trans* people rather than setting boundaries on who is or is not trans*.

The next definition I address is for the word *cisgender*. Schilt and West-brook (2009) defined this as "[replacing] the terms 'nontransgender' or 'bio man/bio woman' to refer to individuals who have a match between the gen-der they were assigned at birth, their bodies, and their personal identity" (p. 461). By defining *cisgender* as replacing the term *nontransgender*, Schilt and Westbook suggested one should not understand there to be a cisgender/trans* binary in relation to gender identity, a point other scholars have also been keen to emphasize (e.g., Enke, 2012). In fact, some people may iden-tify as cisgender but have an outward gender expression others may read as transgressing gender boundaries. For example, metrosexuals, or males who pay particular attention to their appearance, are one population that illus-trates the slipperiness of the cisgender/trans* binary. A metrosexual man may be cisgender, despite his expressing traits culturally marked as feminine (e.g., having well-groomed hair and nails, wearing feminine clothing such as scarves and deep V-neck T-shirts). Thus, the indicators of metrosexuality may be some of the same trans* people use to express their gender.

Here, it is clear the line separating the cisgender metrosexual from the trans* person who transgresses gender boundaries by employing some of the same outward cues is, at best, thin. In fact, one may argue the main thing separating these two people is the way they self-identify their gender. Although cisgender metrosexual men enjoy a certain amount of cultural cachet in the United States, trans* people—and specifically trans* women and trans* women of color—still face widespread social ostracism (Grant et al., 2011). So, while a cisgender metrosexual man may express himself similarly to a trans* individual, the social response, including the policing and enforcement of gender norms, may affect these two people differently, with the individual who self-identifies as trans* being punished for hir[1] gender identity and expression (Dusenbery, 2013). Even if the social response is the same, and the cisgender metrosexual man faces social stigma, this will have been because of systemic trans* oppression and the perception that he is transgressing the gender binary in a way that he should not be.

This extended example shows the complexity of individual understand-ings of gender identity, expression, embodiment, and experiences of trans* oppression for cisgender and trans* people alike. Although one could argue metrosexual men are more often mistaken as gay rather than trans*, the fact remains that the negative reaction to these individuals is rooted in their gender transgression or their presenting their gender in a way that is insuf-ficiently masculine. Namaste (2006) referred to this as *genderbashing*, sug-gesting that although individuals may be ostracized because of the perception of their being gay or lesbian, such ostracism—and the potential violence that accompanies such ostracism—is mainly a result of their transgressing gendered social norms. Therefore, this is a salient example to uncover the pervasiveness of trans* oppression—and homophobia—as well as its potential effects on all people who transgress the gender binary, regardless of if one self-identifies as trans*. This example also underscores that one cannot view the terms *cisgender* and *trans** as always wholly dichotomous.

A final definition that requires immediate attention is the term *trans* oppression*, or a system of oppression that places at a disadvantage "people whose gender identity or expression do[es] not conform to binary cultural norms and expectations" (Catalano & Griffin, 2016, p. 183). As Catalano and colleagues (2007) noted, "Someone need not be connected with a transgender community or movement in order to experience transgender oppression. In fact, one need not even necessarily appear to transgress gender at any given moment" (p. 221). Thus, trans* oppression reflects the wide variety of gender identities, expressions, and embodiments that encompass the trans* community. Additionally, Catalano and colleagues wrote:

> Like any form of oppression, transgender oppression works in conjunction with other manifestations of oppression such as racism, ableism, and classism. Whether people are reinforcing gender norms through everyday words or actions or through more overt policing behaviors such as harassment or violence, transgender oppression is experienced in many contexts. (p. 221)

Here, Catalano and colleagues connect trans* oppression to various other forms of systemic oppression (e.g., racism, ableism, classism). They also mark trans* oppression as overt and tacit, conscious and unconscious. Thus, trans* oppression acts as a term that reflects not only the diversity of trans* lives and experiences but also the various (and interlocking) ways that trans* oppression is felt by those who transgress, defy, and resist gender norms in numerous ways.

Some scholars have used the word *genderism* to discuss this form of oppression, even locating this practice in higher education. Although genderism as a term critiques normative and binary social discourses of gender, it does not rely on or center trans* people in its operation. Put another way, genderism critiques gender broadly, whereas trans* oppression requires one to recognize and center trans* people and our needs in understanding that these needs are not met as a result of systemic trans* oppression. To be clear, I find *genderism* to be a useful concept; I myself have used the term, as have other trans* people, in previous scholarship (Jourian, 2015a, 2015b; Nicolazzo, 2015); however, it does not center trans* people in its definition and operation. Therefore, I use the term *trans* oppression* exclusively in this book, making sure to primarily cite those trans* scholars who have written about this concept. My doing this is a way to (re)center trans* people and trans* scholars. In this sense, then, this citational practice is yet another way for me to attempt to focus on and amplify the critical work being done about trans* people by us as trans* people. A hope of mine is that readers who are interested in learning more about trans* collegians, trans* oppression, and trans* resilience may be drawn to other trans* scholars' work as a result of my citing them in this book. Moreover, for trans* readers, I find it especially important to (re)center trans* voices, because although we are often unexpected or unacknowledged in higher education and student affairs (Jourian, Simmons, & Devaney, 2015), we are present and continue to do important, critical work to promote scholarship about our trans* kin. Therefore, for a population that rarely sees itself reflected throughout higher education (i.e., trans* people), citing trans* scholars is a way to resist the very trans* oppression that makes us invisible.

Although it may seem antithetical for a book that revolves around expanding conceptions of gender, I have intentionally chosen not to provide concrete definitions of the words *sex* or *gender* at this time. As I discuss in the next chapter, Butler (2006) suggested that providing normative definitions for such terms delimits the possibilities for how one understands oneself and others, stating that such definitions may "determine in advance what will qualify as the 'human' and the 'livable'" (p. xxiii). Similarly, Henderson (2015) wrote that "as soon as you subject a [definition] to a statement of what it 'is,' you more or less cut off other versions of what they are, or what they could be" (p. 35). Because this book focuses on proliferating possibilities for who trans* students are, how trans* students come to know themselves, and how others come to understand trans* students, I am choosing to not define *sex* and *gender* at this point. If readers feel these definitions are necessary, I have included them in the glossary. However, I would caution readers against using these definitions as anything but starting points for how they can be— and often are—used and (re)shaped by trans* people for our own needs.

Other terms are likely to be unfamiliar to some readers at this point. As a way to focus readers' attention on the trans* collegians who are central to this book, I have decided not to begin with an exhaustive list of definitions. However, to increase the accessibility of this text, I have defined certain terms in the glossary as they appear throughout the book.

## My Positionality as Author

Qualitative researchers act as the instrument through which data collection and analysis happens (Corbin & Strauss, 2008; Jones, Torres, & Arminio, 2006; Stewart, 2010). As a result, I am implicated in this book as a trans* researcher and educator. Speaking specifically of ethnographers (whose methodology I used for the research guiding this book), Bochner and Ellis (1996) wrote, "It's dishonest to pretend we're invisible. We've left traces of our convictions all over this text. Instead of masking our presence, leaving it at the margins, we should make ourselves more personally accountable for our perspective" (p. 15). For this book, I used a methodology called *critical collaborative ethnography* to collect data (Bhattacharya, 2008; for more detail on this, please refer to the appendix). This meant that I worked to situate myself *alongside* and *with* the trans\* collegians with whom I was in community. This brief description, however, belies the complex, asymmetrical, and shifting distribution of power between the study participants and me throughout the time of our working together. In other words, power was continually negotiated between the participants and myself, as no one held ultimate authority over the entirety of the study. For example, although I had power over the final written text of this book, participants also had power in granting me access to information, experiences, and their perspectives of trans\* oppression on campus. Additionally, the participants and I had power over determining the nature of the relationships and friendships we formed throughout the research process (de Laine, 2000).

Simply put, as a critical scholar and educator, I claim that neither objectivity nor neutrality is possible, let alone desirable (Madison, 2012; McBeth, 1993). Therefore, rather than presuming that power does not have an impact on my study because my methodology is collaborative, I continued to question, interrogate, and struggle with the notion of power and its effects on the research process openly with research participants. Therefore, an exploration of my own positionality as I entered the research process—as well as how my positionality has changed between collecting data and writing this book— is essential (Fine, Weis, Weseen, & Wong, 2003; Kincheloe & McLaren, 1998). Far from being self-indulgent, exploring my own positionality provides an opportunity for me to reflect on how my experiences, identities, and relationships have formed who I am and, thus, how they influence the very way I wrote this book.

I first realized I was trans\* during the spring of 2011. At the time, I was living in Arizona and finishing my last semester as an entry-level fraternity and sorority adviser at the University of Arizona. Coming out felt liberating and dangerous; I was excited to explore my gender identity more, but I was scared of doing this in Arizona, which was becoming an increasingly dangerous place for subaltern populations to reside because of contentious laws such as the Support Our Law Enforcement and Safe Neighborhoods Act, the Ethnic Studies Ban, and Proposition 107.[2] I was also overwhelmed in thinking about coming out, especially to my family and those who had known me for a long time. In my final months living and working in Arizona, I came out to several close friends and went out in public several times in what many may define as women's clothing. Despite the support I had from the queer network of friends I had established, I was always nervous about running into coworkers, students, or other acquaintances I did not feel safe with in disclosing my gender identity. In this sense, I framed my leaving Arizona and moving to the Midwest to pursue my doctoral degree as liberatory, providing me with an opportunity for a fresh start in a new area where many people did not yet know me. I understand this was a liberty many trans* people do not have, including the trans* college students I worked with to write this book. In a sense, then, my privilege of being able to have a fresh start led me to writing this book because it gave me a chance to explore how one's coming out as trans* in a place where one has lived for some time and developed significant relationships (e.g., trans* collegians) may differ from my own experience and, thus, affect how one defines and makes sense of resilience.

Since leaving Arizona, I have grown exponentially as a trans* scholar, educator, and person. The effect of experiences that previously infuriated me, such as the disavowal of my trans* identity by colleagues and peers, have since dampened, and I find I am better able to cope with the negative impacts of trans* oppression. This is not to say these experiences do not cause deep emotional harm, nor is it an indication that they have ceased to occur. Instead, like the trans* students I worked with, I have developed my own practices of resilience that allow me to navigate the omnipresence of gender binary discourse and rhetoric, which I confront daily on individual, organizational, and systemic levels. Part of my ability to cope with these realities is directly related to the cultivation of a supportive queer and trans* community. Together with these people, whom I refer to as my queer and trans* kin, I have created a microclimate in which I can find sanctuary from the consistent assaults of trans* oppression. It does not mean these incidents occur any less frequently, but when they do occur, I am better able to process through them in community with my fellow queer and trans* kin, who remind me that I should not use cisgender (il)logics to measure my own self-worth as a trans* person. Similar to the trans* collegians whom I worked with for this book—and, in fact, in large part because of my work with these students—I have also become much more connected to trans* people in virtual spaces such as Facebook, Twitter, and YouTube. These outlets have given me another landscape where I can see my identity as a trans* person represented as well as a unique way to reach out to others in a way that my physical location had prevented me from doing.

I am also well aware that my being an out trans* faculty member places me in a peculiar position where I vacillate between experiences of privilege and oppression. For example, although my gender identity is often flattened by those assuming I am an effeminate gay man (an experience I term *compulsory heterogenderism* and discuss at length later in this book), I also have realized a level of affirmation as a trans* person in various professional venues that I know many may never find. I also know that my experiences of affirmation and validation are inherently linked to the dominant identities I have as a White, middle-class, abled assistant professor in a tenure-track position. In other words, my experiences as a queer, femme, culturally Jewish trans* person are always mediated by the privileges accorded to me by my race, class, disability, and employment statuses.

My epistemological grounding as a critical scholar and educator means that my identities are always already personal and political. Specifically speaking of my gender identity, my active denial to abide by gender norms not only resonates with how I choose to identify and express my gender but also operates as a way for me to openly resist, push back, and call into question these very norms themselves. I have also chosen not to take hormones, voice lessons, or seek other medical interventions to alter my body. Although I often change my own physical appearance by wearing makeup, what are traditionally coded as feminine clothing and accessories, and prosthetics, I want to reduce the level that others (e.g., medical or psychiatric professionals) regulate my ability to present my gender on my own terms. Although this does not preclude me from seeking these options in the future, my choice has been a comfortable one for now and reflects my current desires related to my own trans*ness.

My experiences as a trans* person led me to writing this book, in which I explore the experiences of trans* college students. In particular, my preoccupation with thinking about the ways trans* students are successful despite the trans* oppression they face in college signals why I framed this book around the notion of resilience. As I discuss in the next chapter, approaching the lives of trans* students from an affirmative standpoint—one that positions trans* success as a reality from the start—has been an embarrassingly uncommon practice throughout previous educational research. Although this practice is starting to change based on the work of a small number of trans* scholars, the cisgender higher education community continues to control the narrative of who trans* students are, what trans* students need, and how educational policy regarding gender should be crafted. Because of my experiences, identities, and epistemological grounding as a critical trans* educator, this book reflects my desire—and indeed the urgent need—to create a rich, complex, and practically useful text about trans* students that problematizes systemic trans* oppression and the individual and institutional practices that emanate from it rather than promoting the continuation of practices that seek to accommodate trans* students. Although necessary, these accommodations only serve to propagate an environment where trans* oppression flourishes. Instead, I propose throughout this book ways to unlearn the deeply entrenched (mis)understandings of gender that continue to harm, erase, and sometimes violently ensnare trans* college students. With this in mind, I move now to a discussion about the purpose and content of this book.

## Aims and Scope of the Book

In the foreword to *The Transgender Studies Reader*, Stephen Whittle (2006) wrote,

> Communities of transgender and transsexual people . . . offer new challenges to politics, government, and law, and new opportunities to broaden the horizons of everyone who has a trans person as their neighbor, coworker, friend, partner, parent, or child. (p. xi)

Trans* identities have entered the mainstream in many ways (Whittle, 2006). Although there is a growing body of positive research and media depictions (e.g., Halberstam, 2005), there is also a long litany of negative portrayals that depict trans* people as either tragic or deceptive individuals (Bornstein, 1994; Halberstam, 2005; MacKenzie, 1994; Serano, 2007; Sloop, 2000), which contributes to the ongoing marginalization of the trans* community.

The marginalization of trans* individuals has been widely demonstrated in the research literature (e.g., Beemyn & Rankin, 2011; Bornstein, 1994; Catalano et al., 2007; Catalano & Shlasko, 2013; Grant et al., 2011; MacKenzie, 1994; Marine, 2011b), including the literature specifically related to trans* college students (e.g., Dugan, Kusel, & Simounet, 2012; Rankin & Beemyn, 2012; Rankin, Weber, Blumenfeld, & Frazer, 2010; Seelman et al., 2012). The trans* oppression trans* students face has a negative impact on their health (Mulé et al., 2009), safety (Grant et al., 2011; Rankin et al., 2010), personal well-being (Haper & Schneider, 2003), experience of their campus culture and environments (Nicolazzo, in press), and persistence in higher education (Rankin et al., 2010). Despite this growing body of literature, a distinct lack of studies focusing on trans* student resilience signals a gap in the literature (Marine, 2011b). Therefore, not only are trans* students vastly misunderstood but also a majority of the research on this population focuses on the myriad forms of risk, violence, and harassment they face. The deficit language and models constructed from this research have the effect of portraying trans* students as problems for whom administrators must make accommodations. It also promotes the notion that trans* students need protection rather than focusing on trans* student resilience or the positive coping strategies and approaches trans* students call on as they successfully navigate the gendered college contexts where they find themselves.

As Marine (2011b) succinctly stated, "Few or no examples of transgender [college] students' resiliency are noted" (p. 73) throughout the research literature. Therefore, the aim of this book is to elucidate how trans* college students navigate their gendered cultural context, paying particular attention to how these narratives align with notions of resilience. My focusing on resilience has the benefit of recognizing the agency of trans* college students as well as providing a platform from which they could talk back to the trans* oppression in their environment. In doing so, trans* students would no longer be situated as problems for whom one must make accommodations, echoing Marine's (2011a) emphatic statement that "transgender students are not a problem to be solved" (p. 1182). Instead, I flip this illogical reasoning, making the college environment the problem by detailing how trans* students are resilient individuals capable of developing supportive communities and navigating the gendered cultural context of college life.

The scope of this book centering on trans* student resilience, however, does not suggest that all trans* students consider themselves resilient. In fact, the trans* participants who collected data with me for this book sometimes questioned their own capability to maintain a sense of resilience, which I discuss in detail later in this book. Despite the uneven ground on which trans* students did (not) immediately self-identify as resilient, I contend that their persistence and ability to thrive on their own terms in highly gender-dichotomous collegiate environments suggests otherwise. As Adam (1978) stated, "Dominated peoples develop a range of behavior patterns to cope with their recalcitrant social environment" (p. 1). It is these resilience-based attitudes, behaviors, and strategies trans* students possess and call upon—which I call practices of resilience—that I explore and uncover throughout this text. In other words, I am more concerned with the process by which trans* students demonstrate and practice resilience, not whether they used this particular—and highly subjective—term as an identifier.

For a more detailed discussion on the study design for the research this book draws on, including theoretical perspective, research questions, methodology, and methods, please refer to the appendix.

# Notes

1. *Ze* and *hir* are pronouns some trans* people use instead of normatively gendered pronouns. For more information on pronouns, refer to the glossary on page 165.

2. The Support Our Law Enforcement and Safe Neighborhoods Act (SB 1070) granted "state and local law enforcement officials the responsibility to detain persons whom they have 'reasonable suspicion' to believe are unlawfully present" (Campbell, 2011, p. 1). Predicated on the fallacious rhetoric that migrants, specifically individuals crossing the Mexico-U.S. border, were dangerous criminals who were attempting to steal U.S. citizens' jobs and gain free access to health care and education, SB 1070 has continued to cause an unsafe environment for Latinx Arizona residents.

   HB 2281, commonly referred to as the Ethnic Studies Ban, effectively ended teaching ethnic studies courses in the Tucson Unified School District (Soto & Joseph, 2010). Originally intended for the Tucson school district, this bill is being promoted as an effective strategy for dismantling similar programs offered in higher education by the former Arizona superintendent of public instruction and ex-officio regent on the Arizona Board of Regents, John Huppenthal (Planas, 2012).

   Proposition 107 was an anti–Affirmative Action ballot initiative that passed with a 60% majority. The wording of the initiative claimed Affirmative Action was a method of giving members of marginalized communities preferential treatment, thus promoting the myth of meritocracy as a strategy for passing the initiative (Ganesan & Swenson, 2010).

# INTERLUDE
## INTRODUCING MY COMMUNITY

I will always remember the exact moment I realized I was trans*. I was watching television on a weekend and kept seeing a detergent commercial. In the commercial, a young girl was bouncing around her room, trying on all different kinds of tights, jumping on her bed, and looking in the mirror. The commercial insisted that to keep this girl's tights clean, bright, and vibrant, one should use this particular brand of detergent. After seeing this commercial repeatedly, I said to myself, "Gosh, I wish I had those tights." And then the panic set in.

"Shit," I thought. "I wish I had those tights."

What did this mean for me? Who was I? Whom could I turn to? I felt alone, lost, and confused. I also began to worry for my safety. Living in Arizona at a time when xenophobic laws targeting oppressed groups were increasingly being passed, I immediately felt a need to keep whatever feelings I was having under cover. I started pacing in my studio apartment, realizing the next four months—the time I had left in Arizona before I moved— would be tough. I had already found and developed a queer community of support, but how would these people, the queer students I advised, my loving friends and colleagues, and my extended national network of friends and family, take the news that I was trans*?

I began searching the Internet trying to find out about myself but soon became exasperated. I had no idea where to start. Did I want to transition biomedically? Did I want to wear women's clothing? Did I want to come out to my family? What if friends decided they no longer wanted to be close to me? And where was I to start learning more about this new revelation? I began to get frustrated that I had more questions than answers; I needed someone to guide me, something to root me in place, but I had neither. Quickly, I sent off a cryptic e-mail to Chase, a trans* friend, asking if we could talk soon.

When I spoke to Chase on the phone the next week, I was still nervous. I was sitting outside a coffee shop in the Arizona sun, cigarette in hand, peeking around to see if anyone was in earshot and would find me out. I spoke in a hushed tone and remember trying hard not to say something that would reveal my ignorance. The truth was I felt guilty and ashamed of the fear and anxiety I had around my new identity and was worried this shame would come across as transphobic. My friend was gracious and kind, reminding me I should be patient with myself. He told me that when he first realized he was trans*, he started reading trans* memoirs. Because he knew I learned best by reading, he suggested I do the same. He told me a few titles to check out, and over the next couple of weeks, I devoured these books and more. Without a community of people in my local area to explore my new identity with, I created a community through literature. These people, whom I became closer to with every turn of the page, helped me feel more comfortable and get to know myself better. They helped me feel less alone, and although they may never know it, I am forever indebted to their words. Their writing increased my ability to be resilient in a threatening geographic area and at a time in my life when I was struggling to understand and feel good about myself, to say nothing of remaining safe and comfortable in a place that had grown increasingly hostile to marginalized populations. These people—writers, theorists, poets, intellectuals, and trans* memoirists—continue to be a community for me. In a sense, I have been reading myself into existence; the more I read, the better I understand myself. The chapter that follows represents my community, the people who helped me and many other trans* people learn about and feel comfortable with ourselves. Welcome to my community; welcome to my people.

# 2

---

# A REVIEW OF
# TRANS*-RELATED RESEARCH

There is little doubt the investigation and detailing of trans* individuals, embodiments, and communities has a robust legacy throughout various disciplines, including psychiatry, medicine, law, English, and philosophy, among others. In fact, the study of gender variance has even generated its own field of study: transgender studies (Stryker & Whittle, 2006). Regardless of the venue, the wealth of theoretical and research-based interdisciplinary scholarship suggests two themes. First, gender as an organizing principle for trans* individuals to make meaning of their lives is not a passing fancy. As stated by Jennifer Finney Boylan (2003), "Gender is many things, but one thing it is surely not is a *hobby*. Being [trans*] is not something you do because it's clever or postmodern, or because you're a deluded, deranged narcissist" (p. 22; italics in original). Second, although many have written about trans* identities from a variety of perspectives and in multiple academic disciplines, there remains a dearth of such research emanating from the field of higher education. Furthermore, most of the scant amount of scholarship on trans* college students in higher education and student affairs is nonempirical and/or centers on a deficiency discourse that situates trans* individuals as victims of violence, harm, harassment, ostracism, and/or performing worse than their cisgender peers across various measures and indicators.

With this in mind, the following review of literature moves from exploring the myriad—and contested—understandings of the term *trans** to situating trans* students on college and university campuses. From here, I examine the common nodes of discussion in relation to trans* college students: marginalization and accommodation. Finally, I review the existing literature on resiliency, suggesting this as a framework one can apply to understanding how trans* students navigate their rigidly gender-dichotomous environments. As I plan to show throughout the literature review, the current gap in the literature surrounding trans* resiliency in gender-dichotomous collegiate environments informs the necessity of the present study.

## Understanding Trans*

> We differ in terms of political praxis: some feel we should assimilate into the mainstream culture; others celebrate the creation of separate "queer" space. We're variously gay, post-gay, queer, bi-queer, butch, femme, top, bottom, feminist, masculinist, intersexual, genderfuckers, trans, pre-op, post-op, confused, certain, ambivalent, and generally awed by the diversity of our ranks. We are obviously not all the same (nor have we ever been), and we do not all configure our desire in the same way. (Alexander & Yescavage, 2003, p. 3)

As the preceding passage indicates, and as I wrote in the previous chapter, the trans* community is vast. In fact, although some have tried to capture the number of people who identify as trans*, which etymologically stems from the prefix *trans-* (meaning across), they invariably run into several pitfalls. Alexander and Yescavage's (2003) words note three important points germane to gaining an understanding of the trans* population: specifically, trans* is not synonymous for transsexual; the term captures a wide array of identities, expressions, and embodiments that continue to grow and expand; and although there is a common thread among trans* individuals in their transgression from gender norms and expectations, there are many differences among us as well. However, before discussing these points in detail, I provide an answer for (re)thinking the desire to determine how many trans* people there are in the United States.

## Answering the Question, "Just How Many Trans* People Are There?"

Despite the use of the word as an identifier of a seemingly unified identity, there has been fierce discussion and debate over who counts as *trans**. From the trans/butch border wars (Halberstam, 1998; Hale, 1998; Rubin, 2006) to the tensions inherent in the asymmetrical use of the term among activists and those they define as *trans** (Valentine, 2007), the category of trans* remains an open question.[1] Indeed, there is wide variance when attempting to determine just how many trans* people there are. Figures for the adult U.S. trans* population range from 0.3% (Gates, 2011) to 2% (Conron, Scott, Stowell, & Landers, 2012), and even these numbers suffer from what Gates called "substantial limitations" (Chalabi, 2014, para. 6).

Whether methodological, conceptual, or pragmatic, the difficulties researchers have encountered in pinning down just how many people identify as trans* in the United States are numerous. Of particular note, determining this number necessitates adherence to a certain stable notion of what it means to be trans* and, by extension, who counts as being "trans* enough" (Catalano, 2015b, p. 411). Currah and Stryker (2015) discussed this problem as "the proverbial square peg in a round hole," whereby "one makes (i.e., compels) trans count by forcing atypical configurations of identity into categories into which they do not quite fit" (p. 4). Counting trans* people is not only a process of forced categorization but also an insinuation of gender policing and violence. For example, Spade (2010) discussed how counting and categorizing trans* people has led to increased surveillance and policing of gender, particularly as it relates to race and nationality (Beauchamp, 2013; Puar, 2007). Furthermore, there is no reliable way to quantify how many trans* students there are in higher education (Nicolazzo & Marine, 2015) and the question about numbers is often used to suggest trans* people are rare, oddities, or may not be a population worthy of time, attention, and resources. Additionally, although some educational researchers and practitioners have attempted to collect demographic information about incoming college students' sexuality and gender (Stainburn, 2013), this belies that these identities shift over time, as do the markers people use to describe their various gendered senses of self.

## Trans* Is Not Synonymous With Transsexual

Stryker (2008) defined *transsexual people* as individuals "who have a strong desire to change their sexual morphology in order to live entirely as permanent, full-time members of the [sex] other than the one they were assigned at birth" (p. 18). Given Stryker's definition of *transgender* as representing "any and all variation from gender norms and expectations" (p. 19), it is clear the terms *trans** and *transsexual* are not synonymous. Despite this difference, however, conflation of the two terms is widespread throughout writing and conversation as trans* people who biomedically transition are attracting more attention and visibility in the United States.

Although the visibility of all trans* individuals needs to be increased, there have been calls for additional research and writing regarding trans* individuals who are not seeking to change their body morphology (Bilodeau, 2005; Califia, 2003; Feinberg, 1998; Mattilda, 2006b). The exact reasons are unclear, but several rationales are possible regarding why most of the scant amount of writing and research regarding trans* individuals centers on those who have undergone gender confirmation surgery, of whom some but not all identify as transsexuals. Some have suggested it relates to a societal adherence to the gender binary, or the cultural assumption that individuals must fit into one of two gender categories, that is, man and woman (Serano, 2007). Therefore, discussion of those who transgress gender only becomes culturally intelligible (Butler, 2006) insofar as these individuals make the transition from one identifiable gender (e.g., woman) to the other (e.g., man). Others have even suggested the foregrounding of transsexual narratives could be because of their economic privilege (S. Marine, personal communication, October 17, 2012). Gender confirmation surgeries are costly, and although some health insurance companies have revised their policies to cover transition-related expenses (Pérez-Peña, 2013; Transgender Law Center, 2014), at the time this book was written, they remain uncovered by most health insurance plans (Spade, 2015). Even if this changes and health insurance providers are required to provide trans*-inclusive coverage, which seems possible given a recent announcement from the U.S. Department of Health and Human Services (National Center for Transgender Equality, 2016), not all trans* people have and/or can afford health insurance because of the increased job insecurity and levels of poverty trans* people face (Grant et al., 2011). This means only those with significant financial capital can have these surgeries performed. Of course, not all transsexual people have undergone—or may ever undergo—gender confirmation surgery (e.g., individuals who identify as preop, or preoperative, transsexual people; transsexual people who are unable for one reason or another to undergo gender confirmation surgeries). However, the intersection at which gendered bodies become culturally intelligible and one's ability to pay for gender confirmation surgeries provides possible insight into the heightened level of cultural capital (Bourdieu, 1977/2002) needed to have one's identity socially recognized and, thus, why transsexual narratives are foregrounded largely through current literature.

The privileging of transsexual narratives also unintentionally occludes the wide variety of gender transgression among trans* individuals, including individuals with various other salient social identities (e.g., race, class, disability, age). To counteract this phenomenon, Califia (2003) stated, "The best we can do is speak our own truth, make it safe for others to speak theirs, and respect our differences" (p. 2). In many ways, Califia's words ground my rationale for writing this book: so we as trans* people can speak our truths, make it safer for others to speak theirs, and work toward having our differences recognized and respected.

## Trans* as a Constantly Growing Array of Identities, Expressions, and Embodiments

Stryker (2008) and E.C. Davis (2008) both portray *trans** as a category with porous and constantly expanding boundaries. Rather than being restrictive, the definition allows individuals to self-identify as trans* regardless of their desire to biomedically transition, to be recognized as another sex or gender (i.e., to pass), or to be seen as existing within the false constructs of the gender binary. Here, one is able to tease apart the differences between gender identity, gender expression, and one's embodiment of hir gender. *Gender identity* relates to one's internal understanding of hir own gender. Conversely, *gender expression* relates to one's outward expression of gender through cultural forms (Kuh & Whitt, 1988) such as language, gestures, and artifacts (e.g., clothing, makeup). Furthermore, one's *embodiment* of hir gender relates to the ways one may choose to morph hir bodily representation—either through biomedical modes or otherwise—to mirror hir internal gender identity or outward gender expression (e.g., someone born female taking testosterone injections; a drag king wearing a prosthetic penis to appear more masculine). Therefore, being trans* may have little to do with others being able to define an individual as such. For example, someone assigned male at birth who chooses not to wear clothing typically ascribed as feminine (e.g., a dress) out of fear of harm may still identify as trans*, regardless of the individual's lack of outward feminine expression and not being read as trans* by others.

Disentangling the ways individuals may identify, express, and embody their gender, and understanding them as fluid constructs, increases understanding of the plethora of combinations and permutations of what it means to be trans*. Moreover, it becomes clear that one's trans* identity, expression, or embodiment is not something one can ascribe to someone else; instead, the identity must be personally assumed by the individual hirself. For example, although a female may dress in clothes that have been traditionally understood as masculine (e.g., cap, leather jacket, flannel shirt, jeans, no makeup), that individual may not identify as trans*. The potential rupture between how others read an individual and how that individual chooses to self-identify foregrounds the reality that despite the overarching similarity of transgressing gender norms and expectations, there are many differences in self-identification among trans* individuals. However, this realization exposes the precariousness with which one can understand notions of community and alliances made among trans* people.

## Communities of Difference

Writing about blending critical and postmodern theory to address the problems facing higher education in the twenty-first century, Tierney (1993) sought to "offer a definition of community based on the concept of *difference*, rather than similarity" (p. 3; emphasis in original). Trans* people challenge the notion of what is assumed to be absolute (e.g., the gender binary). Furthermore, some trans* individuals actively seek—and readily embrace—cultural *un*intelligibility. An example of this would be individuals who identify, express, or embody genderfuck (Alexander & Yescavage, 2003; André & Chang, 2006), which consists of a gender performance that is intentionally contradictory and confounding to others.

A microcosm of the various identities, expressions, and embodiments captured within the constantly expanding notion of trans*, genderfuck elucidates how "the idea of difference becomes an organizing principle" (Tierney, 1993, p. 5) when attempting to understand the possibilities—and tensions—of a cultural analysis of trans* individuals. Despite the overarching similarity of defying gender norms and expressions, trans* people remain highly varied and distinct from one another. There is widespread intragroup divisiveness about the identification, expression, and embodiment of trans* subjectivities (Califia, 2003; Sedgwick, 2008). Because trans* individuals represent a wide array of identities, expressions, and embodiments, we are always already in and out of community with one another based on the multiple and shifting ways we identify our trans*ness.

Rather than needing a definitive definition for the term *trans**, I contend it is at its most powerful when held as an open question pointing toward the instability of the assumed gender binary, recognizing trans* people as constituting a community of difference. However, although this analysis tends to proliferate different trans* identities, expressions, and embodiments, it does little to address how connections are made between and among trans* individuals and others with whom they interact. If trans* people do not make up a coherent community and yet develop relationships with others, how should one refer to these groupings? There is likely no definitive answer to this question. However, for the purposes of this study, I refer to the relationships between and among trans* students, faculty, and staff on college campuses as kinship networks.

Although the notion of kinship is often mistaken for being synonymous with *family of origin*, several scholars have written about queer kinship (e.g., Rubin, 2011; Weston, 1991), thereby extending visions of kinship to include trans* and queer populations. Furthermore, the notion of kinship, and specifically kinship-building, provides a way of understanding the relationships trans* students make within a resiliency framework. Put another way, the notion of kinship offers a way to view relationships as meaningful to how trans* students develop individual and group-based coping strategies and behavioral skill sets to confront trans* oppression. I write more about trans* kinship in Chapter 7.

I now move from discussions about group identity (e.g., communities of difference, kinship, and kinship-building) to individual identity. Specifically, I address the literature regarding what causes, if any, may be a foundation for the development of one's trans* identity. Although many have framed the argument mostly through a nature/nurture binary, I elucidate in the following section how these seemingly opposite positions may also converge.

## The Biological and Social Construction(s) of Gender

Stephen Whittle (2006) stated, "This . . . is perhaps the most controversial issue in sex and gender theory. Is the basis of gender identity essential and biologically based or is it socially constructed?" (p. xiii). This question has prompted a wealth of studies from a wide range of disciplines (Serano, 2007), illuminates deep personal insecurities (e.g., Ablow, 2011), and exposes rifts within the trans* community regardless of the answer. However, Whittle's assessment of the debate between the biological essentialism and social construction of gender presents the issue as a false dichotomy (Lane, 2009, 2016). In addition to these perspectives, another exists, which proposes biology as diversity. Lane (2009) said, "While arguments for a biological role in gender development need careful scrutiny, they should not be rejected out of hand, especially when they stress nonlinearity, contingency, self-organization, open-endedness, and becoming" (p. 137). I explore these perspectives—gender as social construction, gender as biological determinism, and biology as diversity—and the influential role they have in shaping the ways trans* individuals understand their gender identities in the following sections.

### Gender as Social Construction

The notion that gender is socially constructed is seemingly innocuous; however, there are two nuanced ways to come to understand this concept. These two perspectives are captured through the work of Riki Wilchins (2002a, 2002b), who suggested individuals had individual control over their genders, and Judith Butler (2006), who proposed gender as a sociocultural phenomenon with an ongoing genealogical trajectory. In this section, I discuss the thinking of both scholars, siding with Butler's conceptualization as a more complete and precise understanding of how people come to know—and come to be known through—gender.

*Riki Wilchins and Gender as Private*
According to Riki Wilchins (2002b),

> The way in which we think—and especially the way we "think the body"—has too often become an off-the-rack, one-size-fits-all approach. One that favors that which is universal, known, stable, and similar. But my experience of my body and my place in the world is exactly the opposite: mobile, private, small, often unique, and usually unknown. (p. 38)

Wilchins hinted at the tension between the biological determinism and social construction of gender, landing squarely on the side of social construction. Wilchins was not alone in her thinking (Barnett & Rivers, 2004; Gagné, Tewksbury, & McGaughey, 1997). This idea also has traction on college campuses. Students who have had previous exposure to discussions on gender often make the statement that "gender is a social construct." These students say this as if it were axiomatic, with little regard to any alternative understanding of gender. Furthermore, the idea that gender is something one *does* rather than something one *is* (Wilchins, 2002a) seems to be an appealing idea for many trans* college students, granting them agency over their own gender identity and expression.

*Judith Butler and Gender Performativity*
The work of Judith Butler (2006) has become foundational to how scholars understand gender. Although it shares a faint similarity with the notion of gender as a social construction based on her refusal of gender being a biological truism, Butler's conception of performativity offers a vastly different approach to the concept of gender as an organizing principle. For Butler, Wilchins's (2002b) claim regarding the malleability of gender is somewhat limited. In elucidating this point, Butler (2006) wrote, "If gender is [socially] constructed, could it be constructed differently, or does its constructedness imply some form of social determinism, foreclosing the possibility of agency and transformation?" (pp. 10–11). For Butler the notion of gender as socially constructed implies that a society is acting on one's gender rather than, as Wilchins suggested, one having full autonomy and agency to determine one's own gender presentation. The dynamic interplay between self and society as it relates to gender brings Butler to her notion of *gender performativity*, or the idea that how one expresses one's gender is mediated

by one's social milieu and also produces effects in the world to which others respond.

Gender performativity suggests a link between one's understanding of hir gender identity—an internal self-conception—and the perceptions others may have based on hir gender expression—an outward articulation that may or may not align with one's own internal gendered self-concept. Butler (2006) stated, "Assuming for the moment the stability of binary sex, it does not follow that the construction of 'men' will accrue exclusively to the bodies of males or that 'women' will interpret only females" (p. 9). Here, Butler uncouples the perceived unity of sex as an embodied biological construct and gender as a social concept. She went further, suggesting this splitting of sex and gender revealed further questions, including the very notion of what sex is. In addressing this question, Butler (2006) suggested that throughout history, hegemonic discourse in various social institutions (e.g., psychiatry, medicine, law, education) formed the concept of sex as biological, natural, and binary as a way to regulate individuals' lives, a notion Foucault (1976/1990) termed *bio-power*. Extending this line of thought, Butler (2006) claimed, "Perhaps, this construct called 'sex' is as culturally constructed as gender; indeed, *perhaps it was always already gender* [emphasis added], with the consequence that the distinction between sex and gender turns out to be no distinction at all" (pp. 9–10). In other words, Butler suggested that because gender and sex are both mapped onto bodies rather than being innate, embodied facts, the two terms may in fact be defining the same social phenomenon. Thus, the need to define *sex* and *gender* is unnecessary; as Butler suggested, there may not be a distinction between the terms.

Beyond calling into question the supposed naturalization of sex as a category and intimating that sex may have always already been gender, Butler's (2004, 2006) theoretical work is also important because of her focus on increasing what she discussed as the livability of lives for people who exist on the margins of sexuality and gender. Butler's decision not to define *sex* and *gender* is not just a rhetorical or linguistic trick; instead, she makes this choice as a way to resist the ways definitions normalize, and thereby delimit, possibilities for how one understands hir gender. A main thrust of Butler's work is the expansion of which bodies and genders are deemed culturally intelligible, thereby increasing the chance for those with marginalized genders (e.g., trans* people) to lead livable lives. Her efforts to denaturalize sex and not provide definitions of *sex* or *gender* "was done from a desire to live, to make life possible, and to rethink the possible as such" (Butler, 2006, p. xxi). Far from suggesting that the performance of gender is a form of false consciousness (Rubin, 2003), Butler (2006) stated, "The giddiness of the performance is in the recognition of a radical contingency in the relation between sex and gender in the face of cultural configurations of causal unities that are regularly assumed to be natural and necessary" (p. 187). Once the rigid schemas linking certain sexed bodies (e.g., female) to certain gendered performances (e.g., feminine) are exposed as flawed, as Butler (2006) indicated, the number of legible gender possibilities increases. Thus, trans* subjects move from being culturally unintelligible to being culturally intelligible.

Because of the similar starting places for Butler's and my work (e.g., the expansion of understandings about people on the margins of gender and, thus, the promotion of livable lives), I have also decided not to define *sex* and *gender* in this book for fear it may delimit the possibilities of how trans* students are understood. As I have stated previously, I do provide definitions in the glossary, but I caution readers to read these as a starting point for how to understand the terms as they relate to their genealogical histories. In other words, the definitions in the glossary should be seen as socially constructed in and of themselves, not constitutive of natural, innate borders and binaries that prelude the possibilities for how people can live and define their own sex and gender experiences.

In addition to Butler's (2006) theorizing on gender performativity and Wilchins's (2002a, 2002b) argument regarding gender as a social construction, another group of theorists claim that gender (and sex) are innate, immutable, and biologically determined realities. I now explore scholarship suggesting gender is biologically determined and follow this with an alternative way to understand biological literature regarding gender, namely the notion of biology as diversity.

## *The Biological Determination of Gender*

A leading scholar in the fields of biology and gender studies, Fausto-Sterling (1985) claimed the debate between the biological versus social determinism of gender was far from resolved, and in fact stated, "Children show a great deal of (albeit not total) flexibility in the development of a gender self-concept" (p. 89). However, if this is the case, why are some individuals consumed with the notion of gender being completely biologically determined?

Barnett and Rivers (2004) chronicled the litany of books published in the early years of the twenty-first century dedicated to the notion that men and women represented biologically discrete, gendered categories; were by nature distinct; and therefore had certain predilections and predispositions. Addressing the arguments for the biological foundations of gender, Lane (2009) discussed a later line of thinking in neurology that attempts to connect phantom limbs with transsexuals' image of their bodies. Lane detailed research indicating that "trans women have a much lower rate of phantom penis after [gender confirmation surgery]—30%—than men who have had their penis amputated due to cancer—60%" (pp. 149–150). Additionally, Lane stated, "An astonishing 60% of trans men report a phantom penis prior to [gender confirmation surgery] and only 10% report a phantom breast after [surgery] compared with 30% of women after mastectomy for breast cancer" (p. 150). This finding, Lane claimed, has been used as evidence of a biological link between one's material sexed body and gender identity.

Despite the attempts to claim gender as natural and innate through fields such as biology and psychology, some (e.g., Fausto-Sterling, 2000) cite methodological errors that render the findings inaccurate. Lane (2009, 2016) also criticized some scientific and psychiatric disciplines for forwarding oversimplified and reductionist views of gender as an innate human trait. However, what is one to make of gender if it is neither a social construction nor a biologically determined trait?

## The Danger of Dichotomies and the Turn Toward Biology as Diversity

Although people make strong claims in support of both sides of the nature/nurture divide—and even stake their identities on them, as illustrated by the "Born This Way" campaign taken up by Lady Gaga (Born This Way Foundation, n.d.; Halberstam, 2012)—such either/or thinking can be dangerous. For example, although some find comfort in the biological claim that trans* people are "born this way," it opens the door to the notions of reparative hormone treatments and eugenics-based interventions, as has happened in terms of the possible treatments for "girl[s] born with what looks like a small penis" (Schaffer, 2012). Additionally, for those who agree gender is purely a social construction, conversion therapy is still socially present (Steigerwald & Janson, 2003). First championed by Nicolosi (1997), who designed the intervention as "an attempt to reorient gay, lesbian, and bisexual clients to heterosexuality" (Steigerwald & Janson, 2003, p. 56), some have alluded to or written about the need for similar psychiatric interventions for people who transgress gender norms (e.g., Ablow, 2011). Seen in conjunction with the continued pathologizing of trans* identities (MacKenzie, 1994) throughout the medical and psychiatric communities, some claim these identities can—and should—be treated as a way of "curing" trans* people.

Sedgwick (2008) highlighted the dangers implicit on either side of the nature/nurture argument, along with the clear lack of epistemological grounding to support fully one stance over the other, stating, "Every step of this constructivist nature/culture argument holds danger" (p. 42). Specifically, if trans* people are born trans*, then the institutions of medicine and psychiatry (among others) can help steer parents in the direction of only giving birth to cisgender children. However, if trans* identities are entirely socially constructed, then being trans* could be construed as merely a choice, which assumes someone could just as easily not make that choice and lead a happy, healthy, and fulfilling life as cisgender. Thus, one arrives at an existential dilemma. If trans* people are neither born this way nor have a gender that is socially constructed, then how can one understand trans* identities? Butler (2004) suggested this paradox reflects the "limits of the discourse of intelligibility" (p. 74) rather than casts trans* people as problems in their inability or lack of desire to fit neatly into either framework. However, if trans* identities point to the limits of discourse—a point that is further crystallized in my previous commentary on the slipperiness of trans* identities, categorizations, and definitions—then how can researchers represent the breadth of such claims without falling into the pitfalls and half truths that go along with the narrowness of an either/ or perspective?

Lane (2009) suggested another way out of the difficulties of such an either/or perspective, suggesting there are "approaches [in which] biology produces sex and gender diversity in processes that are nonlinear, chaotic, dynamic, and indeterminate. . . . Biology is [therefore] no longer figured as constraint, but as capacity" (p. 146). Lane claimed one should not overlook the field of biology as a site for understanding gender as a complex phenomenon extending beyond a scientifically determined relationship. However, Lane was not alone in this line of thinking. Adding to the discourse on biology as a site of complexity and diversity, Bonchev and Rouvray (2005) stated, "In complex systems 'the whole is greater than the sum of the parts.' What is more these systems possess the properties of emergence, adaption, and self-organization" (p. xii). Here, Bonchev and Rouvray advanced the possibility that one may be unable to understand how the complex systems of sex and gender operate for individuals. This admission signals the potential connections between scientific and socially based discourses of gender. Moreover, it recognizes the sheer complexity of sex and gender as categories, opening up a variety of possibilities for how one identifies, expresses, and embodies one's gender at any given moment.

The previous discussion about natural and social foundations of trans* identities is far from conclusive but raises important questions about how certain lines of thought influence how trans* students make sense of their gender. Similarly, the concepts of oppression, intersectionality, and the social imperative to "pass" or "cover" influence trans* students' ability to navigate their college environments successfully. I now elucidate these concepts and their relation to trans* oppression to explore the complexity of the trans* college student experience.

## Oppression, Intersectionality, and the Social Imperative to Cover

Hardiman and Jackson (2007) defined *oppression* as "an interlocking, multileveled system that consolidates social power to the benefit of members of privileged groups and . . . consists of three levels: (a) individual, (b) institutional, and (c) social/cultural" (p. 39). People carry out trans* oppression on an individual level through person-to-person acts such as hate crimes and bias-related incidents (Catalano & Griffin, 2016). Institutions perpetuate trans* oppression through policies, such as the maintenance of dress codes that delineate appropriate dress based on gender norms and practices, such as the inability to easily change (or exclude) one's sex on many forms of identity documents (Spade, 2015).

These individual acts and institutional practices of trans* oppression also resonate with Hardiman and Jackson's (2007) discussion of oppression as a set of "values that bind institutions and individuals, [including] philosophies of life, definitions of good and evil, beauty, health, deviance, sickness, and perspectives on time, just to name a few" (p. 40). This form of oppression is structural (Young, 1990), meaning it does not require an active participant to engage in oppressive behavior or create and maintain oppressive policies. Instead, structural oppression is woven into the very fabric, or structure, of society. For example, as I and others have written about elsewhere (Catalano & Griffin, 2016; Jourian, Simmons, & Devaney, 2015; Nicolazzo, 2015; Nicolazzo & Marine, 2015), the cultural norm and unstated assumption of the gender binary create a culture in which those who transgress, resist, or deviate from the binary are deemed less than those who do not.

Gilbert (2009) demonstrated the impossibility of trans* intelligibility in stating, "There is no such thing as someone whose sex or gender diverges from their birth-assigned sex, which means trans folk cannot exist" (p. 95). Going further, Gilbert described the social pervasiveness of trans* oppression, explaining it is pervasive through all aspects of our daily lives (e.g., government, education, health care, psychiatry, law, family, media). Furthermore, based on the created hierarchy in which trans* people are less valued than cisgender people, trans* students are forced to navigate the individual and institutional instances that create structural oppression. Examples of these forms of oppression include intercollegiate athletics that are set up along the false dichotomy of men's and women's teams, reinforcing the cultural unintelligibility of trans* people (structural); an institution's internal forms and documents with two check boxes for gender (man and woman), giving the impression there are only these two discrete options (institutional); and a student being harassed for hir gender identity by another student or a group of students (individual).

Studies (Grant et al., 2011; Rankin, Weber, Blumenfeld, & Frazer 2010) and personal narratives (Serano, 2007) have shown that not all trans* people have the same experiences with oppression. In elucidating this point in relation to Black women, Crenshaw (1989) cited intersectionality as a model to expose how developing a "single-axis framework erases Black women in the conceptualization, identification and remediation of race and sex discrimination by limiting inquiry to the experience of otherwise-privileged members of the group" (p. 140). Similarly, any analysis of trans* oppression that does not take into account the various intersecting identities of those who identify as trans* runs the same risk. Therefore, it is imperative to explore how an intersectional approach to trans* oppression can enhance one's understanding of the diversity of these experiences and, thus, the trans* community itself.

## Intersectionality and Its Relationship to Trans* Oppression

Crenshaw (1989, 1995) provided an important framework for understanding how multiple subordinated identities intersect. Discussing how antiracist and antisexist articulations of sexual violence overlook the unique experiences of women of color, Crenshaw (1995) claimed,

> When identity politics fail us, as they frequently do, it is not primarily because those politics take as natural certain categories that are socially constructed—instead, it is because the descriptive content of those categories and the narratives on which they are based have privileged some experiences and excluded others. (p. 376)

What is needed, then, is a more inclusive epistemological framework for understanding and expressing the oppression faced by trans* people who inhabit other subordinated identities, such as race (e.g., trans* people of color), social class (e.g., trans* people who live below the poverty line or have less access to adequate education, health care, and other social institutions), and gender (e.g., trans* women and trans* feminine individuals), to name but a few.

Grant and colleagues (2011) wrote that although "discrimination was pervasive throughout the entire sample," the confluence of transphobia and racism meant trans* people of color, specifically Black and African American trans* respondents, "fare[d] worse than [W]hite participants across the board" (p. 2). Situating these findings on college and university campuses, researchers reported trans* respondents of color felt less comfortable in their department or work units as well as in the classroom than White trans* respondents did (Rankin et al., 2010). Additionally, trans* people of color perceived harassment at significantly higher rates than cisgender men and women of color, substantiating the notion that the convergence of subordinated identities created additional challenges in navigating an environment tinged by trans* oppression and racism (Rankin et al., 2010).

The convergence of gender identity and class is yet another important intersection demanding attention. Grant and colleagues (2011) pointed out that trans* respondents reported higher levels of extreme poverty than their cisgender counterparts did. In fact, the results of their national study revealed that trans* individuals were "nearly four times more likely to have a household income of less than $10,000/year compared to the general population" (p. 2) as reported by the U.S. census. Coupled with this, various scholars have connected these higher rates of poverty for trans* people with such social realities as "employment discrimination, family rejection, and difficulty accessing school, medical care, and social services" (Spade, 2015, p. 46). The intersection of systemic classism and trans* oppression also affects trans* people asymmetrically, with trans* people of color experiencing heightened vulnerability as a result (Grant et al., 2011). The concomitant effects of poverty for trans* people can result in their need to participate in sex work and other illegal methods of making money (Baker et al., 2015; Mock, 2014; Spade, 2015; Valentine, 2007), which increased their likelihood of becoming enmeshed in a prison industrial complex that drastically limits their life chances (A. Y. Davis, 2016; Spade, 2015).

Trans* college students, who may have unsupportive families or may be otherwise dependent on federal financial aid to attend and persist in higher education, also face significant barriers to accessing necessary funding. The difficulty of trans* students accessing federal funding to support college could be because many of them are still dependents and thus need to report family income, which unsupportive or hostile family members may be unwilling to provide. Additionally, Burns (2011) stated,

> Transgender applicants can encounter roadblocks with the [Free Application for Federal Student Aid] due to selective service issues, and possibly with data mismatch with their name and gender markers. Both of these issues can result in the delay or the rejection of their application. (para. 3)

For trans* youths who are emancipated minors, barriers to accessing college still exist based on the rising costs associated with college. Herein one can see the need to understand not just the significant social barriers facing trans* and poor people but people for whom these two identities intersect.

Still another example where intersectionality proves to be an important lens for developing a more complex, and thereby complete, understanding of trans* people is the intersection of trans* oppression and sexism. Serano

(2007) coined the term *trans-misogyny* to describe structural intersections of how trans* oppression and sexism interlock, imposing particular challenges onto trans* women and trans* feminine people. In doing so, Serano created a situation where both identities—one's trans* and feminine identities—are recognized as adding to this unique form of oppression. Therefore, the experiences of trans* women and trans* feminine individuals are not overshadowed or covered up under the aggregating guise of either form of oppression (i.e., trans* oppression or sexism). Although there are innumerable other examples where an intersectional analysis would more accurately depict the experiences of subcultures of trans* individuals (e.g., trans* people with disabilities [Clare, 2015], Jewish trans* people [Dzmura, 2010]), the examples of the intersection of being trans* with race, social class, and femininity should be understood as a marker for the importance of not "think[ing] about subordination as disadvantage occurring along a single categorical axis" (Crenshaw, 1989, p. 140).

## *Covering*

Yoshino (2006) suggested that covering, or actively hiding aspects of one's identity that are stigmatized, is something everyone participates in, as "being deemed mainstream is still often a necessity of social life" (p. ix). One can understand covering as related to—although not completely synonymous with—the notion of passing, which other trans* and gender scholars and I have used (e.g., Garfinkel, 2006; Lie, 2002; Mattilda, 2006a; Montgomery, 2002; Namaste, 2000). Furthermore, it is important to highlight that covering or passing is something trans* people may feel compelled to do out of a perceived or real threat or fear of safety in a given environment. In this sense, one can understand covering and passing as an effect of trans* oppression, as socially dominant discourses of gender as static, immutable, and natural dictate when (and to what extent) trans* people must cover—pass as a given—their gender.

The manifestations of covering and passing can vary by individual. For example, some may cover out of a fear of violence or social reprisal, whereas others may be struggling with internalized oppression (L. A. Bell, 2007) and, therefore, are unable or unwilling to admit their subordinated identity. Snorton (2009) even suggested that "focusing on its psychic components may help to reform our understanding of passing such that we value it as the function by which one distinguishes oneself as a human subject (Jackson and Jones 2005, 11)" (p. 80). This gives rise to thinking through "the political possibilities for trans people when passing is no longer primarily defined as a deceitful practice" (Snorton, 2009, p. 80). Following these analyses, it is clear that trans* people's need to consistently decide whether to cover or pass is predicated on the social privileging of some identities (e.g., being cisgender) over others (e.g., being trans*). Who covers, when to do so, and because of what perceived or real threats are questions that remain unanswered for trans* people who choose to cover; but the cultural foundation and reality of covering, and its connection to trans* oppression, are unmistakable.

The pressures facing trans* students to cover on college and university campuses are discussed in the literature (Fried, 2000; Gray, 2000; Quart, 2008; Rabodeau, 2000). There are also various examples of trans* college students who have felt unsafe after disclosing their gender identity (e.g., Greenaway, 2001). In addition, the trans* oppression present on college and university campuses suggests trans* students must cover their gender, rendering them invisible in the process (e.g., K. Taylor, 2012). Because of transphobic individuals, policies, practices, and cultural norms across campuses, trans* students often feel they need to be careful with whom, when, and how they disclose their trans* identity. Even once a trans* student has disclosed hir gender, fellow students, faculty, and staff may still negate it (Conrad, 2012; K. Taylor, 2012). This negation means trans* students must either cover their identity or pass as either masculine or feminine to not be seen by others as trans*. If they do not, trans* students run the risk of cisgender students, faculty, or staff seeing them as illegible, impossible, deviant, or social pariahs.

Exploring the concepts of oppression, intersectionality, and covering elucidates a series of complex negotiations trans* students must navigate in their daily lives, raising the question, How might trans* college students remain resilient in their gender identity and expression in the face of such social stigma and erasure? However, before getting to issues of resilience, it is imperative to situate trans* students on college and university campuses.

## Situating Trans* Students on College and University Campuses

There is a sizable (and still growing) amount of research and literature on lesbian, gay, and, to some extent, bisexual students (Abes, 2011; Abes & Jones, 2004; Abes & Kasch, 2007; Cass, 1979, 1984; D'Augelli, 1994; Dilley, 2005; Evans & Wall, 1991; Fassinger, 1998; Patton & Simmons, 2008; Renn, 2007; Ridner, Frost, & LaJoie, 2006; Wall & Evans, 1999). Renn (2010) noted there is often conflation between "categories of sexual orientation (lesbian, gay, bisexual) and transgender (gender identity), [which] is common among activists on and off campus, [but] it is contested in theory and in practice" (p. 132). This conflation of sexuality and gender by those on and off college campuses not only is highly reductive but also threatens to overlook the distinct experiences of trans* students. This is best articulated by those who argue the lesbian and gay movement has lost sight of the trans*—and to some extent the bisexual—community in an attempt to push for certain rights (e.g., gay marriage) that would benefit the White, middle- to upper-class, able-bodied, cisgender, and gay and lesbian communities (Califia, 2003; Halberstam, 2012; Spade, 2015; Warner, 1999). Although these advancements are arguably important, advocacy groups such as the Human Rights Campaign have put most of their time, energy, money, and focus behind these efforts while other pressing issues (e.g., trans* legal advocacy, homelessness, and poverty among the trans* population) remain unaddressed (Spade, 2015). This has led to the oversight of trans* lives, narratives, and issues throughout much of what Spade (2008) has termed the *LGBfakeT movement*.

Despite this, awareness of the presence of trans* students on college and university campuses has been growing (Bilodeau, 2005, 2009; Bilodeau & Renn, 2005; Catalano, 2015b; Marine, 2011a; Nicolazzo, 2015; Nicolazzo & Marine, 2015). There is also some nonempirical literature on trans* college students, particularly regarding educational programming, trans* awareness training, and offering trans* support groups (e.g., Beemyn, 2003, 2005; Beemyn, Curtis, Davis, & Tubbs, 2005; Beemyn, Domingue, Pettitt, & Smith, 2005; Henning-Stout, James, & Macintosh, 2000; Nakamura, 1998). A prevalent theme in the small body of research on trans* college students is the violence, isolation, fear, and hatred they face individually and as a community (e.g., Beemyn & Rankin, 2011; Pusch, 2005; Rankin et al., 2010). Underscoring the social embeddedness of LGBT violence, a Human Rights Watch (2001) report stated LGBT-related prejudice "is based on rigidly enforced rules dictating how girls and boys should look, walk, talk, dress, act, think, and feel. The social regime in most schools is unforgiving: Youth who break these rules will be punished" (p. 262). Although the report specifically centered on the environment of primary and secondary schools, similar patterns of hatred, prejudice, and violence against the trans* student population persist on college and university campuses.

For example, in the *2010 State of Higher Education for Lesbian, Gay, Bisexual and Transgender People*, a significantly higher percentage of gender nonconforming students (31%) reported personally experiencing harassment than cisgender men (20%) and women (19%) (Rankin et al., 2010). Furthermore, those who identified as gender nonconforming also reported having more negative perceptions of campus climate (Rankin et al., 2010). In one of the many chilling results uncovered by the study, trans* students not only were more likely to fear for their physical safety but also reported a greater likelihood of avoiding queer areas of campus and avoiding disclosing their gender identity (Rankin et al., 2010). The amalgam of these findings means trans* students are highly isolated on college and university campuses, even within what some may perceive outwardly to be supportive communities (e.g., lesbian, gay, bisexual, trans*, and queer [LGBTQ] student centers). Trans* students' avoidance of queer areas on campus is exacerbated by the fact that cisgender and heteronormative spaces, which take up the majority of campuses, provide minimal safety and comfort for trans* students. The continued lack of comfort and safety for trans* college students is predicated on—and perpetuated by—trans* oppression. On the individual, institutional, and sociocultural levels, trans* oppression forms a matrix of oppression trans* students must wade through. Despite this, trans* college students remain resilient in aspiring toward success.

Research has also revealed that trans* people face a heightened prevalence of sexual violence (Lombardi, Wilchins, Priesing, & Malouf, 2001; Stotzer, 2009). As Marine (in press-b) clearly stated,

> While data continue to emerge, it is becoming clear that sexual violence rates among trans* individuals are as high or higher than that of cisgender populations, and yet the media continues to tell us that rape is something that (only) cisgender men do to (only) cisgender women.

In fact, studies now indicate that 50% or more of trans* people will experience intimate partner or sexual violence in their lifetimes (Calton, Cattaneo, & Gebhard, 2015; Marine, in press-b) and that trans* college students at the undergraduate and graduate levels face more sexual victimization than cisgender men or women (Cantor et al., 2015; New, 2015). These alarming statistics belie what Marine (in press-b) described as the unimaginability of sexual violence for trans* people in the social imaginary:

> In the nearly five decades since the anti-rape activist movement was born, activist educators have come to better understand a different cultural imaginary, one where a college-age woman is lured into a dangerously constructed social setting, incapacitated (either willfully or accidentally) by alcohol or other drugs, taken back to the assailant's dorm room or fraternity house, and raped. While this progression has given voice and visibility to millions of survivors, the near-ubiquity of these scenarios leaves little room for considering the experiences of survivors who are not cisgender women, assaulted by those who may or may not be cisgender men. Similarly, the system designed to serve survivors of sexual violence is not equipped to take gender diversity into full account, and as a result, responses to campus rape have been unfailingly genderist in their incarnations.

In other words, the hyperfocus on cisgender women as the only group of students who are sexually victimized continues to push trans* experiences with sexual violence to the margins, which feeds the further centering on cisgender women's experiences with sexual violence. Compounding this pernicious cycle, or perhaps because of it, Cantor and colleagues (2015) found that trans* students "were least optimistic" that a report of sexual violence would be taken seriously by campus officials "by a large margin, with 41.5% of undergraduates and 38.6% of graduate/professional students thinking it was at least very likely the report would be taken seriously" (pp. 38–39). In other words, almost 60% of trans* undergraduates, and a little more than 60% of trans* graduate students, felt a report of sexual violence would not be taken seriously by campus administrators. This finding means that trans* students are less likely to report instances of sexual violence—further occluding the prevalence of these atrocious crimes from view. When added to the increased threat many trans* people, especially trans* women of color, feel from law enforcement, and when taken in conjunction with Marine's (in press-b) previous comment, it is clear that the extreme risk trans* people face and the previous lack of comprehension of the scope of trans*-related sexual violence feed the continued lack of support for this student population and vice versa. Even now that statistics are beginning to surface regarding the overwhelming presence of sexual violence perpetrated against trans* people, Marine's words serve as a reminder of how college administrators may engage in an epistemology of ignorance, or an orientation toward knowing that represents "no mere lack of knowledge but rather is actively produced and maintained" (Gilson, 2011, p. 309), to not have to reorient the way they have previously approached sexual violence.

There is, however, a distinct and pressing need for more empirical research regarding trans* people, especially trans* collegians (Bilodeau, 2005; Marine, 2011b). I now discuss what is known about trans* collegians, including current empirical research as well as research being developed. Before turning my attention to resilience and resiliency theory, I detail scholarship that has been produced since the end of data collection for the study that grounds this book as well as research that is currently being developed.

## *Recent Scholarship on Trans* Collegians*

Between ending data collection in the spring of 2014 and my writing this book, a growing body of literature, empirical and nonempirical, has been published regarding the experiences of trans* collegians. In fact, because of the dedication of a small group of scholars, many of whom are trans*, the production of trans*-related research in the field of higher education and student affairs is experiencing a relative bump in recognition. Some of this research has sought to map trans* students' experiences in various collegiate contexts, such as my work with Susan Marine (Marine & Nicolazzo,

2014) that discusses trans* students in residence halls. Other scholars have developed nuanced understandings of particular trans* experiences, such as Catalano's (2014, 2015a, 2015b) work regarding trans* men. Even a special issue of *TSQ: Transgender Studies Quarterly* (Nicolazzo, Marine, & Galarte, 2015) focused on trans* people in education and included several articles regarding trans* collegians. Moreover, Jourian (2014, 2015b) has developed multiple trans*-centered frameworks educators can use to (re)think leadership capacities and student development. Jourian's (2016) dissertation, focused on trans* masculinities, and Simmons's (2016) dissertation, focused on trans* educators in postsecondary education and included several trans* graduate students in the sample, are also rich empirical resources.

### Forthcoming Scholarship on Trans* Collegians

Partially because of the realities of publishing, a substantial body of trans*-related scholarship is currently in press. For example, a special issue of the *International Journal of Qualitative Studies in Education* will feature the dissertations of T.J. Jourian and S Simmons, two trans* scholars. The issue will include pieces focused on organizational policy making and the college admissions process for trans* students (Marine, in press-a); trans* kinship networks (Nicolazzo, Pitcher, Renn, & Woodford, in press); an autoethnographic account of a Black, masculine-of-center, trans* person (Stewart, in press); and the potential pitfalls of using certain methodological approaches to working alongside trans* college students (Catalano, in press). Work is also being developed regarding how sexual violence prevention educators on college campuses conceptualize and talk about gender in (non)expansive ways throughout their work (Marine & Nicolazzo, in press), how trans* students develop relationships (Duran & Nicolazzo, in press), and the liberatory possibilities of collaborative methodological approaches to working alongside trans* students (Jourian & Nicolazzo, 2016). Marine (in press-b) has also written about the experiences of trans* college students who are survivors of sexual violence, as I discussed previously.

To be clear, the volume of scholarship regarding trans* college students pales in comparison to many other research topics in higher education and student affairs. Although some of this may be because of how trans* oppression operates as a gatekeeper through the research and publication process (Nicolazzo, 2014b), it is also because of the relative lack of knowledge regarding trans* people—itself a manifestation of trans* oppression—and the aforementioned conflation of sexuality and gender (Renn, 2010). Trans* people have always existed and have always gone to college, whether or not the higher education community has recognized them as doing so. In this sense, the research being produced at the present moment can be understood as a way not only to liberate the field of higher education and student affairs from binary discourses regarding gender (a phenomenon I call the *gender binary discourse*, which I discuss in Chapter 3) but also to redress the way trans* oppression has occluded trans* people's existence until now.

## Resilience and Resiliency Theory

With roots in psychopathology and psychology, resiliency theory emerged from the study of children who overcame the undesirable conditions of their specific environments (Greene, Galambos, & Lee, 2003; Van Breda, 2001). Resiliency theory focuses on risk factors, or those conditions that pose a threat to an individual or a community in succeeding, and protective factors, or those conditions that protect an individual or a community from risks. As previously discussed, the concept of trans* oppression (Catalano & Griffin, 2016) identifies many risk factors of trans* college students, which include but are not limited to gender dichotomous spaces (e.g., residence halls, restrooms, locker and changing rooms), activities (e.g., fraternities and sororities), and policies (e.g., dress codes). Although the web of trans* oppression on college campuses poses serious risks and challenges, there is reason to believe trans* college students have been able to develop and maintain self-efficacy and resiliency in achieving success throughout their collegiate experience. This belief stems from anecdotal experience (e.g., my own ability to navigate educational systems in pursuit of a terminal degree) as well as firsthand accounts of trans* college students (e.g., Rabodeau, 2000; Rogers, 2000; Quart, 2008).

Researchers have written about resiliency theory as being based on individual and community strengths rather than deficiencies (Fergus & Zimmerman, 2005; Greene et al., 2003). Therefore, resiliency theory provides an opportunity to view trans* individuals as capable of navigating the adversity they face without suggesting that they are somehow lacking in skills or abilities, or that they need to capitulate to societal expectations to thrive. Furthermore, research indicates community is an essential component of resiliency theory (Krovetz, 1999; Van Breda, 2001), including research on resiliency among trans* individuals (Singh, Hays, & Watson, 2011). When understood with the potentially tumultuous relationship of trans* individuals with others in the LGBT community (Singh et al., 2011; Spade, 2008) as well as the intragroup diversity within the trans* community itself (Califia, 2003; E.C. Davis, 2008; Sedgwick, 2008; Valentine, 2007), what exactly is meant by community and how it is formed, maintained, and navigated becomes of primary importance.

Researchers have used resiliency theory in studying underrepresented populations, such as members of subordinated racial and ethnic identities (e.g., Villenas & Deyhle, 1999). Others have also used the theoretical construct to address educational research, including in secondary schools (e.g., Krovetz, 1999). Singh and colleagues (2011) studied the resilience of trans* individuals; however, the study came out of counseling psychology and did not mention having college students in the participant pool. Therefore, a gap exists in higher education and student affairs literature when theorizing on trans* student resiliency, a gap this book addresses.

Additionally, when researchers use the term *resilience* in relation to marginalized populations in higher education, they often link it to the notion of retention (e.g., Sanlo, 2004). However, it is important to develop a fuller understanding of what resiliency means. For example, Stieglitz (2010) stated, "In adolescence and young adulthood, resilience may be reflected by achievement in career development, happiness, relationships, and physical well-being in the presence of risk factors. Therefore, resilience is complex and dynamic rather than static" (p. 202). It is clear resiliency theory and the concept of resilience itself have more to offer higher education research than a narrow focus on retention.

Understanding trans* student resilience in terms other than persistence and retention is important for several reasons. First, trans* students remain invisible throughout college records, as no data are collected on this subgroup of students. This mirrors the invisibility gay, lesbian, and bisexual students face (Sanlo, 2004) and makes tracking resilience because of persistence hard, if not impossible. Furthermore, focusing solely on retention as a measure of resilience overshadows the complex negotiations trans* students need to make on a daily basis in a college environment that continues to negate their existence (Nicolazzo, 2016). In other words, the microaggressions (Sue, 2010a, 2010b), trans* oppression, and minority stress (Haper & Schneider, 2003; Hayes, Chun-Kennedy, Edens, & Locke, 2011) trans* students regularly face are negated, denied, and overlooked when resiliency is understood as simply relating to retention and persistence.

## Conclusion

Multiple things become clear when reviewing the literature on trans* people, trans* and gender theory, and trans* college students. First, although trans* and gender-based literature has proliferated in a variety of academic fields (Whittle, 2006), trans* collegians have yet to become a serious population of inquiry beyond a small group of trans* and (a few) cisgender scholars. Thus, although trans* people have become increasingly socially visible, we remain highly invisible throughout educational research. This represents what I have come to refer to as *the trans* paradox*.

Second, of the available literature regarding trans* collegians, much of it discusses trans* people by using deficient language and perspectives. These deficit-based studies point to the heightened need not only for scholarship regarding trans* students but also for that scholarship to take an affirmative, resilience-based approach. Moreover, it is important to recognize that although the body of research regarding trans* college students is growing, some of which is unfolding concurrently with the writing and publication of this book, much of the data from which this literature comes has been taken from larger studies involving LGBTQ populations and, therefore, has not been collected with the express intent of studying trans* students' lives. Therefore, this book serves as an important contribution in stemming these grievous gaps in higher education literature by offering data from an affirmative-based study conducted alongside an exclusively trans* participant pool (for more information on the study design, please refer to the appendix). In the following five chapters, I detail data collected alongside these participants and conclude with Chapter 8, in which I discuss the implications of these data.

## Note

1. The term *trans/butch border wars* refers to the ongoing theoretical contestation between trans* people, specifically those who identify as female-to-male (FTM) transsexuals and transfeminine individuals, and butch lesbians about what it means to be female, feminine, or gender transgressive. Questions regarding when, if ever, one stops being a woman or lesbian and starts being a man, what these terms even signify, why some FTM transsexuals were ostracized from the butch community they identify or identified with, and the overarching effects of these identity and body politics serve as primary flash points in these conversations.

# INTERLUDE
## Bruised by Data

Over the two and a half years since I finished data collection for this book, I have never been able to leave the experience. Of course, I have left in the sense that I have moved to new projects and a new job. However, regardless of where my body is, or the new research I am doing, I am still with the participants who worked with me to complete the study for this book. We remain connected; have continued to be in the community; and, at my lowest moments, I still channel their brilliance, confidence, love, and perspectives. When I experience happiness, I most want to share it with the participants, staff members, and faculty at CU with whom I developed deep kinship. Although my body is no longer in Stockdale, a large piece of my heart remains there, just as I have carried the participants with me in my new adventures.

More than a few times, my mind has wandered back to Stockdale, to CU, and to the nine individuals with whom I spent so much time while researching for this book. As I sip my morning coffee, I wonder what Adem is reading. When I walk to my new campus, I think back to the walks Micah and I would take around CU's campus. When I am having an evening cup of tea, I think about joking with Silvia. When I open Instagram, Twitter, and Facebook on my phone, I pause to witness the unfolding lives of Derek, Micah, Adem, Silvia, Raegan, and Jackson. When I have gone back to CU, I have loved spending time with BC and Kade. And when I watch YouTube videos I wonder where Megan may be and what she may be doing at that very moment. These people have forever imprinted themselves on my very being, just as some have said that I have done for them. Despite our work being bound by time and space, captured in a historical moment like a bug in sap, our present and future lives will always be intertwined. Moreover, far from forgetting or having that moment fade into the past, the participants have remained so intense, so vibrant, and so very current in my life.

As Lisa Mazzei (2013) stated,

> Data is vibrant. It is, whether we acknowledge it or not. It pricks, taunts, and talks back. When I am immersed in a project, the data won't let me go, no matter how hard I resist (even when I'm reading a novel at 11:00 at night!). It is data that St. Pierre (1997) described as "overwhelming and out-of-control."

It's the vibrancy of the data participants and I developed together that keeps me up. It's the relationships we formed, the conversations we had, and the bonds of kinship we continue to carry with us that won't let me sleep. Even when my body is tired, my mind races, and I feel the pricks, taunts, and ways the data talk back. Just as the relationships the participants and I created and the ways we experienced CU, the data defy easy categorization and understanding. They resist codification and simple thematic organization. The data demand to be expressed in full rather than aggregated and ordered. Similarly, participants' identities, although they share some similarities, were far from uniform, either from participant to participant or for each participant across the duration of our working together for the study. Just as the data bruised me, leaving a noticeable mark on who I am and how I think, participation in the study pricked the participants, motivating some to make new meanings of who they were and how they navigated CU.

These complex interactions between the participants and me, the study and the participants, and for the participants themselves throughout the span of their involvement in the study created an intricate web of meanings through which data could be (re)articulated in multiple ways. Sometimes, one chunk of data could be read in various and sometimes conflicting ways. These collisions of meanings, how data came together and diverged, were a reflection of the unruliness of the category of trans* in the first place, a category that, taken at its most basic etymological understanding, is Latin for "across." So how can one capture such acrossness? How can one contain something that transgresses boundaries and categories? And if one attempted to do so, would it not be antithetical to what it means to be and do trans* identities?

For these reasons, the data (re)presented in the following chapters are not categorized into tidy themes. Readers may very well feel unsettled by the use of shifting pronouns, or the ways I (re)present specific chunks of data to articulate multiple, competing ways of making meaning of the same experience. Far from being a theoretical game, these uneasy, contested meanings and (re)presentations of data convey the very unsettledness of what it means to be, do, and practice trans* identities in a culture that does not easily recognize transgressive gender identities, expressions, and embodiments. Just as how I continue to wander back to the participants, my intention in (re)presenting the data in this fashion is to convey its vibrancy to you, the reader. I want you to feel the vibrancy, to be pricked and taunted by the data, to be kept awake, even when reading a novel at 11:00 at night. Because then, perhaps, we will be able to move forward together in creating campus environments where gender is addressed in a manner that increases the life chances of the trans* students who worked alongside me to coconstruct these data that guide this book.

# 3

## GENDER BINARY DISCOURSE

Throughout the next five chapters, I present the findings from the research that guides this book. In developing findings, I analyzed the data to understand the experiences of the participants with whom I was working. I framed my analysis by using Jackson and Mazzei's (2012) notion of "thinking with theory" as an analytical tool. I used my research questions as a way to organize my analysis of the data, consciously constructing the findings to be reflective of the research questions that framed the overall study (for more information on the research questions, please see the appendix). Rather than suggesting I had a priori assumptions about what I would find, this choice reflected my desire to provide clear answers to the very questions participants and I set out to address in this book.

The analytical process participants and I used to coconstruct these findings highlights polyvocality and, thus, encourages one to recognize the ways data come together as well as diverge. For these reasons, I conceptualize the findings of the present study as a series of *arrivals* and *departures*. By arrivals, I mean the ways data share commonalities, and by departures, I mean how data diverge from one another. The metaphor of arrivals and departures is similar to how travelers gather at an airport, itself a similar point of arrival, but then depart in several different directions. Moreover, even though some travelers may come to the same airport for the same flight, thus arriving at the same point seemingly for the same departure, the specific reasons, purposes, and meanings they make of their similar arrivals and departures may have commonalities and differences (Nicolazzo, 2016). I wrote the following chapters in this way not to be confusing or unique. Much to the contrary, what has become clear to me throughout the research participants and I did for this book is that just as others, we as trans* people have complex lives. It is my earnest belief, then, that any discussion of our shared complex lives demands complex thinking and solutions. Therefore, my using the metaphor of arrivals and departures is a strategy to mirror the complexity of our various lived realities as trans* people in a manner that is approachable and does justice to the participants' narratives.

In this and the next four chapters, I elucidate each of the following five sets of arrivals and departures generated from the data participants and I collected:

> Chapter 3: Arrival: Gender binary discourse (Departures: race, sexuality, and gender expression/embodiment)
> Chapter 4: Arrival: Compulsory heterogenderism (Departures: gender expression/embodiment, race)
> Chapter 5: Arrival: Resilience as a verb (Departures: disability, academic departments, living on campus)
> Chapter 6: Arrival: The (tiring) labor of practicing trans* genders (Departures: education, [in]visibility, multiple forms of exhaustion)
> Chapter 7: Arrival: A constellation of kinship networks (Departures: virtual kinship networks, leaving campus for kinship networks, academic kinship networks)

Each set of arrivals and departures is explored in these chapters, complete with how participants' experiences converge and diverge. Before beginning, however, I offer a detailed description of CU, the setting where the study took place. I also introduce the nine participants I worked with to collect data for this book and highlight several aspects of CU that, although common among colleges and universities, help frame the context in which participants and I experienced the five sets of arrivals and departures. In other words, although what I describe may not be peculiar to CU, understanding those things described as phenomena rooted in and influenced by trans* oppression allows a more nuanced understanding of the sets of arrivals and departures.

## The Setting

Perched on a large hill in an urban neighborhood of Stockdale (a pseudonym), CU's buildings can be seen from some distance. The red-brick construction of many of the buildings reminded me of the college architecture I saw growing up in the Northeast, although there was a distinct lack of white columns at CU. The center of campus looked and felt qualitatively different from the outlying areas of CU. Whereas most of the outer buildings were noticeably older and uniform in their construction, the inner portion of campus, which the tour guide who led me and others around in my first week at CU referred to as "the heart" and "the hub" of campus, was full of buildings with hard, metal corners and smooth, sleek facades. The change of building material and design gave a decidedly modern edge to the heart of campus and made it feel distinctly different from the brick buildings stretched throughout the remainder of campus.

This main area of campus, also known as Central Square, was a busy thoroughfare for students, faculty, and staff alike. Inactivity in Central Square was rare, and it was flooded with students between classes. The line for the coffee shop adjacent to Central Avenue, the bricked pedestrian roadway that cuts lengthwise across Central Square, often tailed out the front doors and around the building with students eager for their caffeine fix. Moving farther along Central Avenue, one passed the Campus Recreation Center on the left, which also had a dining hall called Full Press on its bottom floor. The walkway, replete with blue and gold pavers signifying CU's school colors, led to the student life building and, at the far edge of Central Square, the student union. At the union, students often gathered at outdoor metal tables with built-in chairs that, despite their intention, were anything but comfortable. However, the tables were often crowded with people when the weather was good enough to sit outside and even some days when it was not.

However, these were not the most noticeable features of Central Square. That distinction belonged to the large football stadium around which much of CU's campus was built and that abutted Central Square and Central Avenue. Like a crater, the stadium was carved into the ground, creating a bowl-like effect where one could look down onto the playing surface from Central Avenue. A scoreboard towered over the north end of the football field, which was made of artificial turf and had a 10-yard-wide likeness of CU's emblem emblazoned in its center. The first time I went to CU, the placement of the stadium as a central element of campus struck me immediately as odd. More than the hills or the architecture, the location of the football stadium illustrated the centrality of sports and sporting culture at CU. As I walked around learning more about CU, I found an area known as Athletic Valley, with practice fields and facilities, that lay beyond the south end of the stadium. The campus tour also featured a walk through the building that contained all the athletic coaches' offices, including that of the athletic director. Feeling uncomfortable, but trying to remain present, I listened as the tour guide drew the attendees' attention to the wall of trophies and the low hum of a 1980s power ballad being piped in through speakers on the wall. The tour guide told us that music was always playing to "pump up" the students to cheer their teams to victory at the games, which, aside from football and men's basketball, were free of charge for students.

Although I had been an athlete in my youth and still follow multiple professional sporting events, there was something unsettling about the pervasiveness of sports at CU. Reflecting on my experiences at CU, I think my discomfort likely came from the sheer proximity and overpowering role athletics played on campus. I also connected it to my gender nonconforming identity and, as a result, my discomfort in spaces on campus that were heavily structured by trans* oppression. On the tour, I could not help but recall what Bilodeau (2005) wrote:

> This study illustrates the need for scholarship on the ways in which higher education colludes with binary gender systems to reinforce gender oppression. For example, how are transgender students affected by college environments that cluster educational experiences around "male" and "female" identities, such as men's and women's residence halls, fraternities and sororities, *gender-segregated athletic programs* [emphasis added], gender-specific anti-discrimination policies, gendered restrooms, and even curricular offerings like women's studies? (pp. 42–43)

Despite not having met any of the students who would become participants in our study at the time I took my campus tour, I remember wondering what they thought about the heavy influence of sports at CU.

## The (D)evolution of Trans* Awareness at CU

Although trans* students had likely been attending CU for some time, when I began this book the campus LGBTQ center had been in operation for just seven years. Affectionately referred to as The Center by the staff and students who frequented it, the office was an outgrowth of the Women's Center on campus. Once it became its own space, the office moved, quite literally and much to the ironic delight of queer students on campus, to a closet space. After two years, the office, as the staff joked, came out of the closet and was given a proper office space, housed alongside several other identity-based centers. Throughout the time of research for this book, the office was staffed by two professionals and one graduate student staff member. It was a vibrant and inviting space, the front of which was all glass with full-length venetian blinds that were always slightly drawn. Two cubicles were on the left side of the office; the one farthest back was for the program coordinator, Tristan. Ornacia, the director, had an actual office to the right of Tristan's cubicle. The front half of The Center was dedicated to student space, and there was a workstation for the graduate student staff member.

Three student organizations at CU were related to LGBTQ populations, but Ornacia was quick to point out that not all the groups had a
direct connection with The Center. For example, the adviser for Pride, the
overarching LGBTQ social group on campus, was a member of the wom-
en's studies department, and the leadership of Pride rarely came in to The
Center or worked alongside staff and fellow students. The two other groups
were TransActions, a self-described activist student organization focusing on
trans*-related issues on campus, advised by Tristan, and QPOC Unite!, a
group focused on the experiences of LGBTQ people of color, advised by
Ornacia. Both groups had close working relationships with each other and
The Center. In fact, there was significant overlap in membership between the
two groups, whose memberships were often small and varied greatly during
the data collection period for this study.

Of significance for this book, Tristan identified as genderqueer, which
research indicates may not be as common as one might expect for an LGBTQ
Center staff member (Marine & Nicolazzo, 2014). Ornacia, who identified
as a Black lesbian, often made comments about her self-improvement on
trans* issues throughout the four years of her tenure as director of The
Center. However, Tristan often felt marginalized as a trans* employee, once
sharing with me that the only time he felt comfortable was when he left for
a week to attend Creating Change, a national conference coordinated by
the Consortium of Higher Education LGBT Resource Professionals. Additionally, it became clear that although Ornacia had a good rapport with
some trans* students, her interactions with them were minimal, and most
of her time was spent in her office attending to administrative responsibilities.

## The Student Body

The focus on the student body at CU was of particular interest. Similar to
other campuses, uniformity was a high priority. The same signs, fonts, bricks,
and overall look largely pervaded the campus. Even in Central Square, where
several buildings broke from the traditional red brick used for most of the
campus, there was a coherency to their metallic edges and lines. This uniformity was replicated by many on campus who talked about having "tiger
pride" (CU's mascot) or being part of the "tiger family." Before the campus
tour, for example, a representative from the admissions office talked to prospective students about how they would become a "tiger for life," which
was a bond that united all alumni. Moreover, it became clear that most CU
students adopted a specific look that was based on binary gendered logic.

The "City Look," as I came to know it, was best summed up by Micah, a participant, who stated,

> Since [CU] is as diverse as it is, there are certain standards for certain groups of people. I would say, for the most part, the standard look for CU, probably CU females, would be leggings and a shirt, and hair usually up . . . and then maybe high-tops or flats give off the feminine look. And then for the gentlemen, I haven't really noticed with them. It's more typical to see jeans and a T-shirt, and every now and then you see [a] sweatshirt. . . . I would say there's more of a look for females than for males.

Micah's observations signal two important insights. First, he highlighted the ubiquity of the City look, as a gendered—and, more to the point, a gender-dichotomous—phenomenon. This persisted even across the various diverse groups Micah mentioned at the beginning of her comment. Second, Micah quite astutely pointed to the heightened regulation of feminine gender performance and femininities at CU. As Micah mentioned, ze did not really notice the men on campus. Rather than this being a reflection of Micah's observational skills, the ability for men to go unnoticed at CU while women and femininities were highly scrutinized mirrors the way trans* oppression—and specifically trans-misogyny—operates culturally. In other words, in a society framed by trans* oppression and trans-misogyny, normative constructions of masculinity go unnoticed specifically because they are prized above all other gender presentations and, as such, become so naturalized they fade from consciousness. Serano (2007) extended this thought beyond cisgender men and women, suggesting that most people who express some level of femininity, and specifically trans* people who identify as somehow being feminine-of-center, face even further scrutiny. Serano (2007) called this phenomenon trans-misogyny, detailing how it imposed further restrictive and regulatory regimes these trans* women and trans* feminine individuals must wade through.

Thus, the City look not only had a negative impact on those who were assigned female at birth but also affected all people who in some way expressed some level of femininity, including trans* women and trans* feminine people. For example, toward the end of my fieldwork, a student approached me on campus and said, "I have to ask you a question. What's up with your shoes? Because I have never seen *that* on campus," motioning to my shoes. At the time, I was wearing heels, and, although I had a hard time fathoming the student had never seen someone wearing heels on campus, I knew this was not what he was attempting to say. What he really was doing was pointing out that he had never seen someone who looked like me, with specific features that have been socially constructed as masculine such as a beard, wearing shoes that he identified as overtly—and perhaps exclusively—feminine. Furthermore, the student felt the need to point out my feminine gender transgressions, even going so far as to suggest I did not belong on campus because he had "never seen *that* on campus," while simultaneously overlooking the masculine presentations of several women standing there with me. About a month later, a student who was not a participant in the study let me know about a similar incident. As the student explained to me via text, "Some stupid girl in here [a classroom] ran into the 'creepiest thing ever' on the way to class. A large Black man in a skirt . . . who she took a picture of and gawked at and laughed at" (J. Jackson, personal communication, April 8, 2014). These two examples not only reinforce the presence of the "City Look" but also denote the asymmetrical nature of how it negatively affected those who practice feminine gender expressions.

## Study Participants

It would be odd for me to begin writing the following chapters without first giving some context and background about the participants with whom I worked. However, I am also conscious of the fact that this study represented a specific moment in time for these participants. Any individual participant descriptions I could offer will inevitably fail to represent them fully. Particularly in relation to their trans* identities, many participants practiced their genders in ways that reflected the suggestion by several scholars that such identities are always under construction (Cooper, 2012; Stryker, 2008). In other words, although all participants had a clear sense of who they were, their identities, expressions, and embodiments were rarely, if ever, static. For example, Adem, who identified as being "in a gray space" and used they/them/their pronouns during the time of data collection, has since come to identify as a trans* man and uses he/him/his pronouns to reflect his evolving sense of his masculinity. Therefore, to write individual descriptions related to participants' trans* identities would be not only disingenuous in regard to the literature on these identities but also a misrepresentation of the ways participants queered notions of fixed, stable, and constant practices of gender.

And yet, it feels important for me to provide some sense of who participants were, however temporal and incomplete the snapshot of who they were may be. A sketch of these nine individuals will not only provide some context for the data and data analysis that follows but also allow readers to begin to develop connections to the participants as people rather than viewing them as merely providers of data. As a result of the tensions regarding representation, stasis, and emphasizing the complexity of practicing genders, I have decided to provide two types of participant descriptions. First, I describe how participants practiced their genders as a collective to recognize and honor the many ways their genders were largely influenced by others, cisgender and trans* people. In other words, rather than trans* identities just being understood as an individual identity, participants underscored a relational aspect of how they practiced their gender that a collective description will allow me to elucidate. Second, I provide brief individual participant descriptions that do not focus squarely on participants' trans* identities but are intended to fill in some of the gaps of who they were. Although gender sometimes leaks into the descriptions, they should allow readers to gain a context to understand more fully the data analysis that follows.

## Collective Description: Participants' Trans* Identities as Relational

Echoing scholarship on trans* identities, participants often described the way they practiced their trans* identities as relational (Catalano, 2015b; Jourian, 2016). Put another way, the way participants came to understand, and ultimately practice, their genders often involved some recognition of other people in their lives as well as the social contexts in which they found themselves. Thus, participants described coming to know and practice their genders in a manner consistent with Tatum's (2013) suggestion that identity is shaped by one's personal desires and the social contexts of one's life.

The relational aspect of participants' trans* identities became highly visible in conversations about their personal pronouns. For example, Micah discussed her decision to use all pronouns by saying,

> I know there's instances where people are stuck in the mind-set that, "Okay, when I was growing up, I was taught boys look like this, girls look like this," and some people make accidents, you know what I mean? They make mistakes.

Here, Micah described his choice to use all pronouns as partially a decision based on those around her. Similarly, Jackson, who often expressed their gender in androgynous ways, stated that they sometimes would just define themselves as a lesbian rather than telling people they were agender. I analyze this particular comment in more depth in the next chapter, but it is noteworthy that Jackson discussed their gender so that it would be more understandable to others. Although Micah and Jackson practiced their genders in a manner that was comfortable for them—in fact, Micah defined hir gender identity as "comfortable"—how their genders showed up in public, or came to be known by others through markers such as pronoun preferences or words used to identify themselves, was mediated by others in their environments.

Many participants talked about the notion of passing, or being read by others as the gender they identified with. For Kade, who passed as a cisgender man, he often wondered how other trans* people may see him. He expressed a sense of loss because of the invisibility of his trans* identity, while in the same breath recognizing the privilege he had in being able to navigate CU as someone who passed as cisgender. Megan talked about wanting to pass as a woman and about what she would do when she did. She told me she wanted to lie out on a grassy common area of CU. This was something Megan had never done before, but as she stated, "I just have this image in my head of my female self just relaxing in the sun, bathing in the sun."

Raegan had an altogether different perspective on what passing meant to them. Rather than passing as a man or a woman, Raegan said, "My ideal setting for passing is people not knowing my gender." Thus, Raegan's definition of *passing* was achieving a level of cultural unintelligibility that Megan was attempting to eschew. In the same vein, BC desired to create a sense of confusion for others about her gender identity. Although she said she wanted to be read as feminine, she also stated, "Ideally in the future I [would] probably change my appearance daily. Real butch to real femme and then androgynous, and always make people question." Raegan and BC both understood their gender identities and expressions as always already in relation to how others read them. Even though they desired to create similar states of confusion, their ability to achieve these goals was dependent on others, thus underscoring the relational aspect of their trans* identities.

This does not mean Raegan, BC, or any other participant could only be trans* if others saw them as such. Instead, it provides a more complex understanding of an individual's gender identity—trans* or otherwise—as being simultaneously an identity on a personal level as well as an identity that is heavily influenced by the people surrounding that individual. In other words, one's gender is a product of one's own personal identity as well as a reaction or reflection of how one is identified by others. Exemplifying how others play a role in shaping a person's gender identity, Silvia expressed confusion when she was told that other people's interpretations of her gender expression led them to assume she was a woman.

> When someone pointed out to me that how you are perceived is what people associate your gender to I was like, "Wait, really?" 'Cause it was a bizarre concept to me, and I was just like, "So people see me wear a dress and think that I'm a woman; that's weird." I don't know [but] that's weird to me.

Thus, although Silvia knew herself to be agender, her comment exposed the reality that how others read her, itself a product of restrictive cultural understandings of what constitutes appropriate women's clothing, also influenced her gender. In other words, others' (mis)understanding of her gender expression influenced the (un)intelligibility of her agender identity. These (mis) understandings changed depending on the various contexts in which Silvia found herself, but the relational aspect of her and other participants' gender identities remained constant.

Sometimes, the relational nature of gender resulted in additional possibilities for participants. For example, Adem said,

> I have found that since kind of reaching out, and since meeting you, and starting to talk to you more frequently, and being more involved on campus, it's a lot easier for me to kind of self-identify [as trans\*] if I see other concepts out there.

Adem explained this way of learning about their gender was like "stealing parts of other people's identity." The notion of stealing identities suggests that Adem's seeing various other people's gender expressions provided a wealth of possible options for thinking through what resonated most with their own identity. However, sometimes the relational aspect of gender foreclosed possibilities too. This was the case for several participants, including Raegan. When discussing how they identify their gender, Raegan discussed the frustration associated with using language others did not know.

> All the other words, like genderqueer, agender, gender fluid, gender variant—nobody knows what that means. Or even nonbinary, which is the word that I would probably use the most to describe myself . . . it's like, if I say I'm not a man or a woman, even explaining that, it's just like, they don't get it.

The words Raegan felt they could use to describe their identity were severely limited by others' (lack of) understanding. Although this did not change how Raegan expressed their gender, it did rule out the ways they felt they could identify as trans\*.

The relational aspects of trans\* identities were perhaps best summed up by Megan's use of the metaphors of *being inside* and *outside*. Megan described being inside for most of her childhood, denoting her not being out as trans\* as well as staying in her room and remaining isolated from others. However, she also recognized that she would have to start going outside as she grew up. She would need to come out as trans\*, and her coming out would be precipitated by how her gender identity showed up in public spaces. In other words, Megan's gender identity was a private, individual identity as well as a public one. By going outside, Megan knew she would encounter other people, which was something she had not had to do when she was inside. Thus, Megan's going outside symbolized her interacting with others and, as a result, the myriad ways that other people influenced how she made sense of, expressed, and discussed her gender.

### Individual Participant Descriptions

In the following section, I present a brief description of each of the nine participants I worked alongside for this study (see Table 3.1). Although the descriptions sometimes highlight nuances related to how participants practiced their genders, the intent is to focus less on their being trans* and more on the various other identities and experiences they shared as being important. I provide these participant descriptions in alphabetical order according to the pseudonyms they chose for the study.

*Adem.* A slightly built student with gauged ears and neatly styled chestnut hair, Adem had just begun identifying as trans* when we started working together. During our first semester, Adem was a main fixture in The Center, attending a variety of programs and being actively involved in TransActions. However, this participation waned over time, to the point that Adem only stopped by The Center to use the office's free printing services. Formerly an art student, they had stopped out from CU for a short period of time before returning and becoming a women's and gender studies major. After not having much of a connection to their faith, Adem had begun to explore their Jewish heritage. Adem was also a deeply committed feminist, which often caused tension for them, as they worried how being trans* while also being a feminist may be in conflict. Adem had an acerbic wit that belied the devotion they had to their pets and their partner, whom Adem dated during our second semester of working alongside each other. Adem also regularly wrestled with complex theoretical ideas regarding gender, often spurred by their coursework. For example, during the second semester of our relationship, Adem was taking four women's and gender studies courses, making them contemplate gender from multiple theoretical frameworks in conjunction with their attempting to understand their lived experience as a trans* person. After a year of working together, Adem stopped out from CU, abruptly breaking contact with me, staff members, and their partner. After a period of little to no contact, Adem reached out to me, and we remain in contact. Adem now identifies as a trans* man, uses he/him/his pronouns, and has begun to biomedically transition. Adem had also talked to me about the

## TABLE 3.1
### Participants and Select Demographic Information

| Name | Gender Identity | Proper Gender Pronouns | Salient Social Identities | Duration of Participation |
|---|---|---|---|---|
| Adem | In between, in a gray space[a] | They/them/theirs[b] | Jewish, feminist | 2 semesters |
| Brody Comeau (BC) | Trans* woman | She/her/hers | White, activist | 1 semester |
| Derek | Trans* | He/him/his | White, sex worker, sexual violence survivor | 1 semester |
| Jackson | Agender | They/them/theirs | White, psychological disability | 2 semesters |
| Kade | Trans* man, transmasculine | He/him/his | White, socially and biomedically transitioning | 2 semesters |
| Megan | Trans* woman, woman | She/her/hers | White, biomedically transitioning | 2 semesters |
| Micah | Comfortable, genderqueer | All pronouns | Black, queer | 3 semesters |
| Raegan Darling (Raegan) | Transmasculine, nonbinary | They/them/theirs | White, queer | 1 semester |
| Silvia | Agender | She/her/hers | Black, queer, multiple disabilities, adopted | 2 semesters |

[a]After the conclusion of the study, Adem began identifying as a trans* man. [b]After the conclusion of the study, Adem began using he/him/his as his proper pronouns.

possibility of transferring to another local college to complete their bachelor's degree, but at the time of writing this book, they had not done so.

*Brody Comeau "BC."* When BC and I first met, she was the president of TransActions. She had thick, shoulder-length hair, and her typical attire included skinny jeans, a black zip-up sweatshirt, and a black leather purse. She always reminded me of having a punk look, and although I never asked, I imagined she listened to the likes of the Ramones, Black Flag, and The Clash. BC was a self-identified activist who participated in CU's Race and Racism Dialogue Program as well as TransActions. Her younger brother was one of her best friends, and although she had previously come out to her mother, she came out to her father while we were working together. BC was deeply sarcastic, but it was clear that her sarcasm was a signal that she liked you. She was also incredibly soft-spoken and tended to keep a select few close friends. BC smoked marijuana frequently, citing it as a way to escape frustrations, and had moved off campus by the time we began working together. She left CU after one semester of our study, telling me she needed to make and save money. At the time, it was unclear what instigated her becoming financially independent, but she had told me her parents were not wholly supportive of her being trans*, leading me to wonder if her stopping out had something to do with her financial independence. After exchanging some texts in the fall of 2013, we lost touch for a year, after which she came back to CU and we reconnected. Of the four participants who stopped attending CU during the study, BC was the only one who returned to resume coursework (Jackson returned to school, but transferred to Stockdale State, a local community college). BC was not fully out as trans* on campus during our time working together and had two separate Facebook accounts—one using her legal name and the other with her chosen name. She said that, ideally, she hoped to be able to switch back and forth between different gender presentations on a daily basis in the future.

*Derek.* Derek was the first participant I began working with. I met him the semester before I began collecting data while getting to know Stockdale and CU. He was boisterous, and even though he was the vice president of TransActions, his talkative nature often made it seem as though he were leading the group. Derek was a mixture of intelligent, inquisitive, and brash. During our first meeting, he peppered me with questions about the study while other members of the TransActions Executive Board sat around listening. After he had gotten all the information he wanted, he nodded and told me he was really excited to be a participant. He went to The Center regularly, despite having open confrontations with staff and fellow students. Derek was a sex worker, a survivor of sexual assault, and had a polarizing personality, which was made evident by the strong feelings others had about him, whether affirmative or negative. Shortly after beginning our work together, Derek abruptly stopped out from CU, citing mental health reasons for stepping away from school. We have kept in touch irregularly, and largely through social media. Although Derek discussed transferring to Stockdale State, he was clear he would not be going back to CU. The decision not to go back to CU was in part because of what Derek cited as a hostile climate for trans* students. As of the writing of this book, he had not reenrolled in college.

*Jackson.* With light brown, short-cropped hair they eventually shaved off, Jackson and I began working together in the fall of 2013. I met Jackson at a TransActions meeting, which they rarely got to attend because of some intense work responsibilities at The Loft, a local independent theater in Stockdale. Jackson told me early in our relationship they were particularly proud of having become sober, something Jackson had tried multiple times in the past but with little success. Jackson thought they may have abused alcohol partially as an escape from confronting their gender identity but was enjoying being sober. Having stopped out from CU for a period, Jackson had come back to campus to pursue a degree in secondary education. They had attended Montessori schools throughout their childhood, where they developed a love for schooling, and had hopes of becoming an educational reformer by eventually becoming a policy maker. Jackson was from Stockdale and had a close relationship with their nuclear family. Jackson identified as having a psychological disability, and, after a year of working together, they stopped out from CU. After two years of spotty connection with Jackson, they contacted me via social media in the fall of 2015 to let me know they had begun coursework at Stockdale State and had aspirations to become a substance abuse counselor for LGBTQ youths.

*Kade.* Kade had small-gauged ears, piercing blue eyes, and a coy smile. A senior when we started working together, Kade began socially and biomedically transitioning when he was in high school. He had bounced around to a couple of high schools when he began socially transitioning, often because of prejudicial treatment and harassment he experienced in his educational contexts. A couple of weeks after starting at CU, he moved out of his residence hall room, largely because of the discomfort he felt as a trans* masculine person placed on a women's floor. A psychology major, Kade was a native of Stockdale, and was deeply connected to trans* and queer groups in the local community. He spent a majority of his time off campus, had finished up all course requirements for his major, and was spending his last year taking as many queer-friendly electives as he could. Kade had been involved with TransActions in previous years but only stopped by once or twice in the year we worked together. Kade was passionate about living a healthy lifestyle and often cycled to campus when the weather was good.

Although Kade recognized the privilege he had because of his being White and his ability to pass as a cisgender man, he also talked about the sense of loss this caused him. Specifically, he talked about feeling disconnected to trans* and queer communities, once questioning how people whose gender transgression was more visible read him and understood him. Halfway through our time together, Kade began a serious relationship with Brin, whom he remained with for a year after graduating from CU. After Kade graduated from CU in 2014, we remained in touch, participating together in a queer reading club he organized. We also spent time together when I returned to Stockdale for a weekend visit after moving to begin my faculty position at Northern Illinois University. As I was writing this book, Kade was thinking about applying for graduate programs in either psychology or gender studies.

*Megan.* Quiet, shy, and enigmatic, Megan and I first met in the fall of 2013 after she attended her first TransActions meeting. Megan shared stories of being bullied during her early childhood, forcing her to contemplate suicide and live a rather isolated life. Megan was a computer science major, which may have been a result of her interest in gaming that she developed as a child. Although she was not overtly bullied in college, she continued to be teased by her friends and peers in the residence halls, which precipitated her move off campus after her first year. She had come out to her parents and sister when we began getting to know each other and was planning on coming out to her brother shortly thereafter. She also had been going to counseling and halfway through our working together began hormone replacement therapy (HRT) and electrolysis. Megan had largely lived an insular life, spending a lot of time in her room online and playing video games. However, when we began working together, she mentioned a desire to "get outside," by which she meant she was intentionally trying to meet other people. She was not publically out as trans* but began taking steps to meet other trans* people throughout our time together as well as thinking about how she would come out to her friends at CU. After graduating, Megan hoped to move to California to pursue a career in computer program development and design. Megan and I have lost touch since the end of data collection.

*Micah.* Behind his quiet demeanor, Micah had a sense of loyalty and love that was unmatched by the many people I met throughout my time at City. A self-described introvert, Micah often could be found in Tristan's office in The Center, watching a show on her computer with earbuds in their ears. Micah was from Deerfield, a metropolitan area two and a half hours away from Stockdale. He was majoring in the sciences, and during the eighteen months of our working together, she was heavily involved in student organizations, particularly those that revolved around issues of race and gender identity. Micah was intensely committed to their nuclear family, even despite what she defined as her "love/hate relationship" with one of her siblings. Micah was dedicated to raising awareness about gender identity and sexuality on campus but also recognized he needed to see some level of others' investment in the topics for him to want to become involved in education. Micah felt things very deeply, especially things that affected them as a Black queer youth. Over the course of our time together, Micah and I became very close and remain so to this day. We would often stroll around Central Square, talking about family, our work together, classes, relationships, and the days' events. They have talked about pursuing a teaching career after graduating from CU, and although ze had lived in the same state all hir life, she had a desire to eventually land in California.

*Raegan Darling "Raegan."* Although I met Raegan in the spring of 2013 when I began collecting data, it was not until the following spring they asked to participate in the study. With a shaved head, a smile that could light up a room, an incredible sense of humor, and an effusive personality, Raegan was often in the middle of any social group in which they found themselves. They had been an emcee for one of the campus drag shows during the course of data collection, a resident assistant, and was also involved in CU's Race and Racism Dialogue Program. Prior to our working together, Raegan began dating Ginnie, a cisgender woman whom Raegan described as their best friend. Although Raegan suffered from depression, they had weaned themselves off their medication the summer before our working together, a decision they were glad they made. Raegan was out as trans* on campus as well as with their nuclear family and asked to join the study as a way to develop a friendship with me as another trans* person. Raegan and I continue to keep in regular contact. For example, during the year after data collection, it was not unusual for me to wake up to texts Raegan had sent me the previous night, checking in and wondering when we could get together. During the writing of this book, Raegan graduated from CU.

*Silvia.* With a flair for the dramatic and an effusive personality, Silvia was hard to miss. She was funny, had a bright smile, and regularly had a full schedule of meetings with her multiple student leadership roles. She also was a main fixture as the emcee for the drag shows TransActions hosted every semester, a role that well suited her sharp sarcastic wit. However, under the veneer of extroversion, Silvia kept a small, tight-knit group of close friends and was a very private person. When she was with her close friends, Silvia tended to get into philosophical conversations, especially on issues of gender and race. A native of Stockdale, Silvia was adopted and grew up with foster siblings. She developed a passion for art, especially visual and video art, and strongly identified as an artist. Silvia was neurodiverse and had several chronic illnesses, one of which she was diagnosed with during the last semester of our work together. This diagnosis was illuminating and frustrating for Silvia. Although she was glad to know what was making her feel the way she was, she worried about her own resilience, saying she did not know if she would be able to bounce back from the diagnosis. Toward the end of our work together, Silvia made the decision to study abroad for her final year at CU, finding a program in Sweden that would allow her to focus on her art. Silvia and I remain in good contact, even seeing each other when she returned from Sweden on holiday. She planned to graduate from CU upon returning from Sweden after the spring 2015 semester, but after returning, she worked hard to finish her degree through online courses so she did not have to spend time on campus.

The remainder of this chapter is devoted to elucidating the first of five sets of arrivals and departures developed from the data I collected alongside the study participants. It is worth stating again that one should recognize these arrivals and departures as places where data come together and fall apart, thereby highlighting polyvocality and the various ways to understand participants' experiences. As a result, this chapter and the four chapters that follow provide educators with a sense of how to use this complex analysis to effect cultural change on college campuses.

## Arrival: Gender Binary Discourse

This set of arrivals and departures relates to the presence of a gender binary discourse at CU. Similar to Pascoe's (2007) *fag discourse*, the gender binary discourse at CU was a constellation of words, phrases, actions, rules (written and unwritten), and social realities that regulated "appropriate" gender identities, expressions, and embodiments on campus. Participants in the study clearly described the rules about gender that existed on campus as well as how these rules were enforced. Often, individuals on campus exemplified the gender binary discourse overtly, such as through direct conversation. For example, during The Center's fall welcome event my second semester on campus, CU's chief diversity officer (CDO), who was cisgender and heterosexual, spoke about what she saw as the importance of having LGBTQ students on campus. Detailing her address in my field notes, I wrote,

> During her [the CDO's] speech, she thanked "us" (presumably LGBTQ folks) for helping "other people" (presumably hetero/cis folks) confront and learn about difference. The CDO seemed to say this without a hint of irony, as if "our" sole purpose was to enhance the education of hetero/cis folks (September 6, 2013).

In her short speech, which the CDO had intended to be welcoming and inclusive, she had effectively reinforced the notion that the people on whose behalf The Center was maintained were not like the other people on campus. In fact, she not only implied that LGBTQ students were different from the cisgender/heterosexual majority on campus—a fairly innocuous statement in itself—but also insinuated that LGBTQ students were so different that education was needed to highlight their differences and that it was the responsibility of the LGBTQ population at CU to do that. The resulting message was that having a diverse sexuality or gender was so different and so contrary to the normative manner in which gender and sexuality operated on campus, it required a level of education that only those who embodied these nonnormative positionalities could provide.

Similarly, Raegan discussed an experience several participants had of how the gender binary discourse on campus leaked into spaces that one might assume would be gender-free. Particularly, Raegan discussed going to Full Press:

> One of the women at Full Press, when I would swipe my card, she would always refer to me and Ginnie [Raegan's partner] as ladies, and it was just like every time I came in there was a microaggression. She also had a habit of—she'd look at your card and be like, "Oh," like, "Sarah [a pseudonym for Raegan's birth name]," like, "How are you today?" It wasn't until literally a couple weeks ago [that] I finally corrected her. Like, "Oh, I actually go by Raegan Darling."

Raegan's comment was striking for two reasons. First, it highlighted the administratively enforced trans* oppression whereby Raegan could not get a new college identification card with their correct name, which at the time was different from their name on their official identification documentation on file at CU. Second, and perhaps more insidiously, Raegan's comment pointed to the ways that well-intentioned interactions in supposedly gender-free spaces such as dining halls could have an overall negative effect on trans* students. When faced with a task as universal and necessary as eating on campus, Raegan's choices were regulated by the gender binary discourse at CU. Furthermore, although Raegan was talking about one specific dining hall on campus and one specific employee in that specific dining hall, it was not difficult to envision this happening in other dining facilities on campus (or even on other campuses).

The gender binary discourse extended beyond overt, spoken messages, including tacit and covert messages such as looks, attitudes, and moments of discomfort. For example, Adem stated, "There are definitely gendered expectations [for students at CU]. I feel entirely out of place in a non-women's-studies class, or anytime I am outside The Center." The feeling Adem had of not belonging, or of being out of place because of their gender identity, was the internalized manifestation of comments such as those expressed by CU's CDO and the comments made by the Full Press employee. Such overt messages took on an additional edge, as Adem began to internalize the messages to mean they did not belong at CU, save for certain specific areas perceived to be safe for Adem as a trans* student (or for certain purposes, such as the CDO suggesting that LGBTQ students needed to teach cisgender/heterosexual others at CU). Adem went on to describe the experience of being *mean-mugged* on campus (fellow students giving them mean looks on campus). Adem understood these looks, which they received frequently, to be in some way shaped by their peers' dismay, confusion, and abhorrence of their nonnormative gender expression. Sharing a similar sentiment, Megan discussed feeling uncomfortable when walking on campus between classes: "I guess definitely walking in between classes I feel really uncomfortable, which I guess is all of campus. . . . Even though I know this is definitely not true, I sometimes feel like all eyes are on me." Even though Megan clearly said that she knew not everyone was looking at her, she felt as though they were, and that everyone's looking at her was directly related to her gender transgressions. Her feeling is similar to the experience Adem shared of being mean-mugged on campus, with both experiences illustrating the pernicious effects of the gender binary discourse on an affective level.

The reach of the gender binary discourse at CU even stretched into classroom spaces. BC in particular discussed changing her major because of her faculty member's reliance on a binary (il)logic of gender:

> I am good at Econ. I understand it, but it's not what I want to do. [But] the College of Business is dumb. . . . [In] business, you had a class—it was the dumbest thing—where you had to dress up in formal wear and give these presentations. I wanted to go get a blouse and get a mixture of feminine and masculine formal wear. But that took—that would take time, money, and preparation. So I ended up throwing on a pair of pants and a dress shirt.

Although BC knew she was good at economics, she felt forced to change because of the lack of room—material and metaphorical—for trans* people in her chosen major field. Restrictive notions of what constituted appropriate formal wear for presentations pressed so heavily on BC that, regardless of how good she was at her major, or how well she understood the concepts, she did not feel comfortable remaining in the field. Thus, one can interpret the effects of gender binary discourse as having far-reaching impacts that stretch well beyond students' time in college.

Moving from the ways gender binary discourse operated in hetero- and cisnormative spaces at CU to thinking through how they operated in queer and trans*-specific settings, Derek shared a detailed list he had sent to The Center staff addressing the things he felt they needed to become more trans* inclusive. Derek's list included things such as posting ground rules for The Center; supporting a university-wide policy that allowed students, faculty, and staff to change their names in the university's database systems without first doing so legally; and hosting trans*-specific events on campus. By way of addressing Derek's concerns, staff members at The Center said they thought TransActions as a student group should be responsible for promoting cultural change at CU (e.g., for leading the charge to implement a university-wide preferred name policy). Although this could be understood as promoting student agency and voice, it could also be read as an approach that placed a heavy burden for broad-sweeping cultural change on a group that had a small and inconsistent membership and lacked intentional and developmental adviser support. Furthermore, because of their status as a student group, TransActions members may not have been able to garner the same level of respect and cultural capital to compel broad, sweeping administrative changes that The Center staff may have been able to access.

Looking specifically at how the gender binary discourse operated within the LGBTQ student organizations themselves, BC recalled, "There are safe spaces more in the queer spheres. But even at CU Pride [the main overarching LGBTQ student group on campus] and with certain LGBT people on campus, they'll say stupid shit about trans* [people] and stuff." Here, BC's comments demonstrate that aside from the gender binary discourse being just a phenomenon reinforced by cisgender and heterosexual students on campus, it occurs within LGBTQ affinity spaces and groups. Although the student leadership of CU Pride framed the group as being inclusive of people with diverse genders, gender binary discourse still operated in a restrictive way to marginalize BC and other participants in that space.

The critique of student organizations went beyond just CU Pride, however, and included TransActions itself. BC and Silvia each shared stories of feeling marginalized in the group, whose mission was explicitly trans*-inclusive. As BC recounted, "Someone in TransActions last year, [whom] I consider really queer-friendly, but wasn't trans*, they—like, I spit on occasion when I'm walking. And then she's like, 'You've gotta stop spitting—that's not very lady-like.'" The level of gender policing and overt scrutiny of BC's behavior by her peer, a fellow member of TransActions and someone BC took to be "really queer-friendly," is a prime example of how the gender binary discourse seeped into not just hetero- and cisnormative spaces on campus (e.g., dining halls) but also was present in trans*-specific spaces. Moreover, the gender binary discourse was not only present but also had the effect of alienating some students from one of the few spaces on campus constructed specifically with the intent of fostering trans* inclusion. Speaking about this paradox, Silvia said,

> I used to be pretty active in TransActions my first year here, [but was] not so much last year, and there was definitely a reason for that. There was a person [Derek]—they don't go here anymore, but they were here. They were pretty radical, like, really really radical. Like, to the point where people were pretty uncomfortable, and there was a lot of conflict, a lot of drama, and [they] were always sort of—I don't want to say dictating the meetings, but that's basically what they were doing. So they would always be like, "We're gonna talk about this," and like, "These are the only people who can talk." And then it just got to the point where I didn't want to go to the meeting. So, like, I'm there, and that's supposed to be a place where I feel supported, and it's my first time really being away from home and really feelin' like I have time to talk about these things or even think about them. . . . There's . . . a whole basket of gender expressions, and not all cis people look the same, just like not all trans* people look the same. And not all trans* people are gonna look like you and just giving the talking stick to the trans* people in the room who look like you [isn't right]. So I just eventually left the group. And then last year—back when Derek was still here—Janelle and I were just sorta having a conversation. So I was going to go to a meeting that week, and we were talking about a date I had gone on, and then they [Derek] were sitting at the table, and they were like, "Wow, this conversation really proves that I'm not a woman." And I was like . . . [pause] . . . I'm just never going back to a TransActions meeting . . . because that had been my experience of . . . not being accepted.

Many, if not all, participants shared the sentiment of not feeling comfortable in CU Pride. However, the notion that even TransActions, a space solely dedicated to trans* activism and awareness, was regarded at times as being a marginalizing space illustrates the divergences among ways participants experienced gender binary discourse on campus. I now turn my attention to exploring three such dissonances, or departures. Specifically, I address departures related to participants' racial identities, their sexualities, and their gender expressions or embodiments.

## *Departure: Race*

Gender binary discourse took on a particularly racialized feature for Micah and Silvia as Black trans* collegians that was not present for the other participants, all of whom were White. In fact, the intersection of Micah's and Silvia's racial and gender identities resulted in their experiencing trans* oppression differently from that experienced by the White participants. Thus, one must be careful not to see this departure as constituting the same sort of gender binary discourse previously discussed but with examples from Black communities and spaces on campus. Instead, Silvia and Micah's Black and trans* identities intersected to create a new set of effects that influenced how Micah and Silvia navigated the entire campus. So although Micah and Silvia discussed straying from Black communities and spaces on campus because of the lack of safety or comfort in transgressing binary norms of gender, their race also mediated their experiences in largely White spaces.

Micah was quick to point out how The Center operated largely as a White space, even in spite of Ornacia's identifying as a Black lesbian. For example, although Micah said becoming involved in The Center was an important step in learning about and reflecting on his gender identity, she also noted that The Center operated largely as a space for White queer students.

> Being involved in The Center, it's helped me a lot actually. . . . I went to a program last year that brought together The Center and the Black Cultural Center [BCC]. And during that program, we were talking and I was like, "Oh, I didn't know there was people of color in The Center." And that's what kinda turned me off in the first place. So, I started to come, I got involved, and, . . . learning about the different terms and different people, and meeting new people that were not inside the binaries when it comes to sex and gender identity and all those things; it opened my eyes and made me explore more about how I feel about myself. So, that was—it was a learning experience.

Here, Micah expressed viewing The Center as a White space with the statement, "Oh, I didn't know there was people of color in The Center." Moreover, The Center was the only space where Micah could learn about and interact with people who transgressed "sex and gender identity and all those things." In fact, Micah explicitly stated that conversations about gender identity were not happening in other places where Micah spent time on campus, not even in the BCC, which was a consistent cosponsor for events The Center staff organized. When Micah realized this, it caused her to stop going to the BCC as often and curtail their engagement with BCC events.

> I felt accepted for who I was, but I felt that it was almost one of those "don't ask, don't tell things." . . . And it didn't necessarily make me feel uncomfortable, but it made me shy away from a lot of things. . . . I feel like that made me shy away from being as involved as I could have been in the [BCC].

Thus, the Center was coded as a White space and the only space to talk about trans* identities, and the identities themselves were also coded as White.

It is worth noting there is nothing innately negative or impossible about being Black and trans*. In fact, participants and I undertook this study at a moment when some trans* women of color were experiencing heightened positive media attention. For example, Janet Mock published her memoir, leading to a subsequent book tour (which included CU as a stop) and national media attention. The popular rise of Laverne Cox as a celebrity and trans* activist in her own right led to her being the first openly trans* woman of color to be featured on the cover of *Time* magazine. Considering the many trans* women of color activists (e.g., Reina Gossett, CeCe McDonald, Monica Roberts), blogs, and news sources focused on issues of trans* people of color (e.g., the TransGriot blog), one might assume that the notion of these two categories of identity (i.e., being trans* and Black) being mutually exclusive would be irrelevant. However, this would be an oversimplified interpretation. Instead, Micah elucidated a far more nuanced relationship between his Black and trans* identities. Recognizing that The Center was the sole place on campus to learn about and meet trans* people— a result of the gender binary discourse at CU—coupled with the coding of The Center as a White space resulted in the feeling that trans* identity must also be a specifically White positionality. Thus, to be Black and trans*, while not materially impossible, was constructed as an impossibility in the sociocultural imaginary of CU. The construction of this seemingly impossible positionality was a direct outgrowth of the production of a different set of effects for the gender binary discourse because of the complex intersections of race and gender identity.

Micah and Silvia also expressed reticence in being heavily invested in maintaining strong connections to spaces coded as Black at CU, such as the BCC. For example, I recall one evening I met Silvia on campus for an event cosponsored by The Center and the BCC. The event was located in the BCC, and despite her being the emcee, Silvia did everything she could to stall for time. Already being an anxious person myself, I kept asking if we needed to begin walking over to the BCC, to which she groaned, slumped down in her chair, and said flatly that she really did not want to go but knew she had to show up. She said she did not want to go because of the event taking place in the BCC and the overwhelming nature of the gender binary discourse there. When we finally made it to the BCC, the event had already begun (a new emcee had been found at the last minute) and Silvia slipped into the back row of seats alongside Janelle, one of her closest friends at CU.

When asking Micah about his experience as a Black queer person on campus, he expressed a sense of loneliness and difficulty.

> I'm very attached to both of my identities. I can't leave one without the other, and especially my race, that's something that I can never give up. And being Black and queer on this campus has been an interesting experience for me. I'm not gonna say all bad, because it hasn't. But it's been kind of a lonely journey, because most of the Black queers that I know, they're strictly identi-fied, they don't cross those lines, they're not stuck in the middle, they're usu-ally feminine or very masculine, and especially with the females. Even with the males, it's usually one or the other, they don't have that kinda middle of the line that I tend to tread. . . . When it comes to the African American culture here, it's more of one of those things where like, "Oh, we know you're funny, but we don't wanna have that [gender] discussion, because we can deal with you if you like women and you dress completely like a girl all the time, or you are always dressed like this [masculine presenting]." Or, "If even you just accepted the masculinity that you have and you completely dressed like this, then we could accept you because you are one extreme or the other. But the fact that you walk that middle line is kinda like we don't know [how] to deal with you, we don't know how to treat you."

Thus, Micah felt that people in the Black community on campus treated hir differently because of their queer gender presentation, which often transgressed the gender binary by rarely staying consistently masculine or feminine. Expanding on this, he said,

> I see a lot of other Black queer individuals—like, queer as an umbrella term—and they're either super masculine or super feminine, and I've noticed they've almost been more accepted. . . . But on the opposite side, because I am so attached to my race, it's kinda hard bein' just a queer indi-vidual, especially, when most things queer in the media, you mostly see White, Caucasian, European gays, and it's kinda like they're the face, so where does my face belong? And I see a lot of White people who are queer, kinda like me, like they identify like me, and they can walk that middle line and be just fine, but they don't have the same struggles as me, so it's kinda like what's important for me to discuss isn't important to them to discuss. So it's one of those things where it's like, yeah, we can hang out, but all's we can talk about is specific things to LGBTQ. We can't discuss other things. We can't discuss how I am being affected by my race while I am being LGBTQ. That's not something that often comes up; it's a hard line to walk.

Micah not only expressed loneliness when asking where she belonged amid the wealth of White gay people represented in the media but also noted that his ability to navigate space as a Black queer person was more difficult and created a more liminal existence for them than for White people who may identify and express their gender queerly. Moreover, Micah felt a deep tension because of the barriers to her being able to explore their Black queer identity with others in spaces coded as White (e.g., The Center), but there were also barriers to expressing and talking about genderqueerness in Black spaces on campus. Therefore, even though Silvia and Micah knew there were queer Black students at CU, some of whom even spent time in the BCC, they largely covered their queerness because the BCC was a space that promoted the gender binary discourse by not welcoming discussions, expressions, or embodiments of genderqueerness.

Micah's and Silvia's experiences regarding the gender binary discourse also resonated with my first interactions with Nadia, a BCC staff member, which I recorded in my field notes:

> I mentioned I was searching for participants and was wondering if she knew of any trans* students with whom she could connect me, or if there were any student organization meetings I could attend to recruit. At this moment, she took another deep breath. She explained this was a difficult topic . . . [and] Nadia mentioned the Black community on campus was just starting to come around on issues related to sexuality and gender. (March 3, 2013)

I had a similar encounter again with Nadia at the beginning of the following fall semester during a welcome event for The Center. I wrote in my field notes:

> One of the things I heard at The Center Meet and Greet came to mind again today in light of one of my interviews (with Micah). She was saying how it is hard and a bit lonely being Black and queer, which made me think of Nadia telling me at the Meet and Greet that she can't think of anyone who may be a fit for my study. Here, the confluence of race and gender identity reinforce what Micah has told me about feeling like she needs to choose (or feels forced to choose). If Nadia cannot think of anyone who is Black and trans*, I wonder if this is a symptom of (or a result of) the trans* oppression present in the BCC and/or that she has been socialized to think [that way] (September 18, 2013).

These two encounters made clear that the gender binary discourse at CU was readily present in the BCC in the way the staff structured programming and involvement opportunities as well as how staff and students were (not) allowed to discuss or make room for gender transgression. Furthermore, Micah's and Silvia's experience of the gender binary discourse on campus and its influence on how they navigated campus—finding places where they felt safe, comfortable, and willing to spend time—was further mediated by the intersection of their racial and gender identities.

## Departure: Sexuality

Sexuality was another social identity around which participants' experiences navigating the gender binary discourse at CU diverged. At times, others reinforced the gender binary discourse because of the perception of participants' sexualities. Kade offered a particularly poignant example of this, recounting an experience in which a gay couple confronted him on campus:

> I had this experience last year. . . . There was, I would assume, a queer couple. It was two men, they were holding hands, and they walked past me and I stared at them, 'cause I thought one of them was cute [laughs], and one of them . . . I think that he thought that I was straight and was offended by them, or was feeling something negative toward them because I was looking at them, and he gave me a dirty look and called me a breeder. And it was a really weird experience for me because I was like, "Whoa," [laughs], I feel like the tables have really turned from wanting to hide this othered kind of part of my identity to not wanting to be perceived as this normative straight male.

Despite Kade's not identifying as straight, the two men Kade passed on campus coded him as straight. Their doing so was rooted in a sense that all people who passed as normatively masculine—which Kade admitted was a reality for him—must be men who are then attracted to women and, thus, would be insulted by being called a *breeder*, a pejorative term for heterosexual people. The couple in Kade's story did not think that Kade may not identify as a man; in fact, similar to Micah and Silvia, his being trans* was seen as an impossibility in that moment largely because of the gender binary discourse the couple Kade passed by were steeped in.

Additionally, several participants spoke about the trickiness of dating as a trans* person. For example, Jackson talked about one person with whom they were in and out of a relationship over the year of their involvement in the study. Part of Jackson's ambivalence about being in the relationship was their partner's inability to recognize Jackson's agender identity in the way they wanted it to be recognized.

It didn't really work very well [chuckles]. I mean, it was kind of the same issues. And the issues were not necessarily understanding where I was coming from about my gender, you know? . . . We would try to talk about things, but for the most part, it had to do with her saying, "Well, I don't understand. I don't see how this is any different from how I feel just being a gay woman." And she's like, "It's the same," and I'm like, "No, it's really not the same," you know [laughs]? . . . You know, you can only really fit and go along with that for so long before it just becomes . . . too much; where you know where this person's not gonna be able to accept things about you that you've already readily accepted.

Silvia also recounted a particularly painful story about a dating experience she recently had:

It was probably one of my most uncomfortable dates, I should say. So we're walking into the Cheesecake Factory, and we just had this awkward door moment of who gets the door first, and, like [laughing], I don't even know. We are both standing there, and I reached for it, and they reached for it, and then it was like, who goes in first? So, I just went in first, like I can't see what they're assuming, but I went in first, so I don't know. . . . And then ordering. Just, like, ordering for me, or the check went to them, and I'm like, "Oh my God!" It was so awkward. I was wearing a dress; I like dresses. They weren't wearing a dress. It's just perceptions and how they were being determined in that space, and how they were treating me, and how they were treating me [was] dictating how the staff was treating us, and it was just very bizarre.

Jackson's and Silvia's narratives point to the complexities of dating as a trans* person. The prospect of dating provides challenges in any given relationship, as they both said; however, navigating social space as a couple provided additional challenges. Silvia exemplified this additional complexity when she discussed the waitstaff at the Cheesecake Factory taking gender-based cues from not only how she was dressed (i.e., in a dress) but also how her date was treating her.

Despite these complexities, participants continued to go on dates and seek romantic partnerships, finding ways to do so that aligned with their trans* identities. For example, Kade found that dating within explicitly queer and trans* circles allowed him to escape some of the negative experiences he had, particularly with some of the gay men on campus he had dated. Raegan had a long-term cisgender partner, Ginnie, and they had ongoing conversations about their trans* identity and how gender was mediating their relationship. Similarly, several other participants (e.g., Jackson, Micah, Adem,

Silvia) continued to seek partners with whom they felt comfortable being themselves.

## Departure: Gender Expression/Embodiment

Another departure in how participants experienced the gender binary discourse at CU was related to participants' gender expression/embodiment. For example, discussing the gender binary discourse on campus, Jackson said,

> I've noticed there's certain people that are definitely—not just on the CU campus—people who will expect people to be a certain way based on their biological sex. I don't see that much animosity toward people who don't adhere to that on campus, which . . . maybe I don't see it that often because I'm kind of passing as a woman, you know?

Here, Jackson gave voice to the reality that they may experience the gender binary discourse differently than others specifically because of their passing as a woman (and, thus, fitting into the logic of the gender binary because of being assigned female at birth). In other words, although Jackson's identity as agender did not adhere to the gender binary, they supposed that at times others read their gender expression as feminine or, perhaps more to the point, not masculine. Thus, Jackson thought their being coded as a cisgender woman allowed them to navigate CU differently than someone whom others coded as transgressing the gender binary.

As Jackson's previous comment suggested, other participants experienced CU differently because of their different gender expressions and embodiments. For instance, BC, who had not begun HRT and was not attempting to pass as a woman on campus during her participation in the study, stated, "I'm always a little worried about comments about when I carry a purse, now that I do." BC knew she may not pass as "woman enough" for some people at CU, and as a result she worried about receiving negative comments when she wore her purse, a feminine-coded artifact. However, right after acknowledging this, she went on to say,

> But it really helps with being gendered, ah, what do you call that? Female. It's funny, I went with Heidi to buy alcohol last night for her, and the guy called us ladies and he used feminine pronouns throughout. And I was like, "All right. Cool."

Although BC discussed not passing in most social settings, the ones in which she did pass were invariably easier and induced less panic. Thus, BC's comments are a direct indication of how others make sense of trans* students' gender expression and embodiment and how, as a result, trans* students' abilities to navigate space become more or less restrictive.

BC's remarks also made clear that whereas one's gender may be understood in a certain way in one time and place (e.g., her being read as a woman when buying alcohol), this was not always consistent across times and spaces (e.g., her fear of receiving negative comments for being read as not a woman while carrying a purse on campus). This reflects how the presence of the gender binary discourse requires trans* students to be flexible and open to adaptation when thinking about how they navigate their campus environments. It also points to the very instability of the gender binary itself, as participants like BC and Jackson could be recognized as being woman and not-woman at different times and in different spaces. If this were the case, then it would stand to reason that trans* students could leverage those spaces on their campuses where their trans*ness was recognized as a potential strategy to resist the gender binary discourse itself. In other words, if there were certain spaces on campus in which others understood and appreciated trans* students' transgressing the gender binary, then these students could potentially create ways to maximize time in these spaces, thereby subverting the overwhelming press of the gender binary discourse.

# 4

# COMPULSORY HETEROGENDERISM

Rich (1980) first coined the term *compulsory heterosexuality* to high-light the way "women's choice of women as passionate comrades, life partners, co-workers, lovers, tribe, has been crushed, invalidated, [and] forced into hiding and disguise" (p. 632). Through the exploration of the literature in which this phenomenon operated, Rich demonstrated the culturally embedded assumptions on the supposed naturalness—and thus the centrality and validity—of heterosexuality. Further, Rich demon-strated that the supposed naturalness of heterosexuality came at the cost of lesbian existence, which had been largely constructed "as a less 'natural' phenomenon, as mere 'sexual preference,' or as the mirror image of either heterosexual or male homosexual relations" (p. 632). Later, Butler (2006) discussed compulsory heterosexuality as a by-product of the ongoing cul-tural centrality of heterosexual practices, experiences, and activities. Fur-thermore, she was concerned with, among other things, exploring "to what extent . . . gender identity, constructed as a relationship among sex, gender, sexual practice, and desire, [was] the effect of a regulatory practice that can be identified as compulsory heterosexuality" (Butler, 2006, p. 24). Thus, for Butler, there was a link between the cultural notion of compulsory het-erosexuality and one's gender identity. This link, which she described as a "matrix of intelligibility" (p. 24) involved the cultural linking of binary notions of sex, gender, sexual practice, and desire in ways that deemed any transgressive practices of gender socially abhorrent, abject, deviant, and impossible.

Expanding on the work of Rich (1980) and Butler (2006), the data from the present study suggest the existence of *compulsory heterogenderism* at CU, a term I developed to explain the ways participants' gender identities and sexualities were consistently understood in and through each other. Although the study participants' sexualities (i.e., gay, lesbian, or bisexual) are distinct from their gender identities as trans*, the way other nontrans* individuals could make sense of the participants' gender was through their sexuality. These misperceptions were largely rooted in sexuality-based stereotypes that dictated one's sexuality as a direct result of gender presentation (e.g., a masculine presenting as female being understood by others as a lesbian). As a result of the linking of sexuality and gender identity that makes up heterogenderism, participants' gender identities often went unrecognized, rendering their trans* identities invisible.

Jackson spoke of the effects of compulsory heterogenderism, particularly in how it regulated how they interacted with others at CU. When explaining how they discussed their gender identity with others, Jackson stated, "For a while it was easier for me to identify as a lesbian, because people understood it, you know?" Here, Jackson reflected that their being agender was so unknown—and unknowable—at CU (itself a product of the gender binary discourse across campus) that instead they used a culturally intelligible sexuality (i.e., lesbian) as a marker of their gender identity. Thus, Jackson just identified as a lesbian, grafting gender identity and sexuality—two distinct yet often overlapping categories of difference—onto one another as a result of compulsory heterogenderism on CU's campus. The presence of compulsory heterogenderism at CU dictated that Jackson set aside their agender identity—an identity that was particularly salient for them—in favor of a more knowable, or legible, identity marker. Similar to Rich's (1980) suggestion that compulsory heterosexuality threatened one's lesbian existence, the social reality of compulsory heterogenderism stood as a deterrent to Jackson's existence as agender at CU.

Micah expressed sentiments similar to Jackson's regarding others' lack of knowledge about trans* identities and expressions. He was also able to clearly demonstrate that such a lack of knowledge—again a result of gender binary discourse at CU—affected the way she was read and understood on campus. In one of our first conversations, Micah stated,

> Gender expression—most people don't ask me about my gender expression because they just assume, "Oh, you're a girl, but you dress like a guy." They don't really know what it is, so they don't ask. They are just like, "Oh, you're a dyke," or, "You're Micah." That's how they know me.

Micah's statement highlights the prevalence of the gender binary discourse at CU in saying that most people just assume she was "a girl" but dressed "like a guy." Although he used different words, Micah's statement exposes that there were two, and only two, legible gender categories at CU: men and women. Any gender expressions that transgressed or challenged the supposed naturalness or immutability of this discourse were unintelligible. In Micah's own words, people "don't really know what it [transgressive gender expression] is, so they don't ask."

Micah went further, though, suggesting that instead of asking about his gender expression, others made assumptions and "are just like, 'Oh, you're a dyke,' or, 'You're Micah.'" Others replaced Micah's gender identity—which ze described as comfortable or genderqueer—for a derisive marker of lesbian identity (i.e., dyke).[1] Even when others did not read Micah as "a dyke," they still did not recognize her gender identity, instead opting to see him as "You're Micah." Although one may think of this as liberating in the sense that others were recognizing Micah, and as a result, his gender identity, as exactly how they were expressing themselves in these moments, there might be an alternative, more pernicious reading of this comment. Specifically, Micah's comments indicate how others read his gender identity as a singular aberration or a unique facet of her particular life rather than recognizing Micah as a part of the trans* community. Thus, even when people did not read Micah's gender expression through hir (perceived) sexuality, the resulting effect was the same as if it had been; their gender identity and expression were still deemed culturally unintelligible.

Adem highlighted the presence of compulsory heterogenderism at CU in our first interview. When I asked Adem in which spaces they felt uncomfortable on campus, we had the following exchange:

Adem:       I don't necessarily feel comfortable walking around after dark, which is not necessarily because I am female-bodied [*sic*] and I think I'm gonna get raped, but mostly, I—I have a lot of issues with this because I never know which one it is—'cause there's not only that, but also what if somebody sees me and is like, "You're queer, and I wanna teach you a lesson." And I'm kind of perpetually afraid that I'm either going to be raped or get my ass beat.

Z:       Now when you say people will mark you as queer, do you mean genderqueer? [Or] are you talking sexual orientation?

Adem:       Anything.

Z:       Okay.

Adem:       Anything. I'm leaving that one completely open.

Through this exchange, it is quite clear that Adem felt unsafe at night on campus. However, what is less clear, even to Adem, is why they felt unsafe. It could have been because Adem's sex was assigned female at birth. However, it could also have been because others were reading Adem as queer, which they left open in terms of being understood as a sexuality or gender identity. Thus, Adem stated they could never know which identity might result in physical or sexual violence: their sex, their sexuality, or their gender identity.

Adem's inability to disentangle their tightly coupled identities illustrates the reality that they may easily see one identity as overshadowing, negating, or replacing another. Such difficulty for Adem underscores how they had been socialized by their educational environment to see these identities as interchangeable, precisely because that is how sex, gender, and sexuality had been culturally (re)enforced at CU. In other words, Adem's inability—and unwillingness—to differentiate what caused their feeling unsafe was not because of a lack of insight on their part but because of their socialization in an environment steeped in compulsory heterogenderism.

Turning from the focus on how Adem was reading their identities in and through each other, it is also worth mentioning that Adem's perception of how others read their identities also highlights heterogenderism. Adem left the definition of *queer* open in our exchange, thus allowing it to be understood as a sexuality as well as a gender identity. Adem did not know whether the threat of violence may result from people's irrational fear or hatred of their sexuality or their gender identity, which reflected others not knowing, seeing, or perhaps caring about the differences between these identities. Thus, compulsory heterogenderism was an underlying logic that explained the threat of violence that existed for Adem. In other words, the threat of violence for Adem, while possibly linked to their sexuality as queer—itself an internal and thus an invisible identity—was also very likely a result of their genderqueer expression—an external manifestation of their internal gender identity. Although compulsory heterogenderism may not discriminate based on which particular identity might initially provoke others' irrational fears or hatred (i.e., sex, sexuality, or gender), the results could be equally deleterious.

The threat of violence Adem felt is reminiscent of Namaste's (2006) suggestion that what some termed *gaybashing* was ultimately a form of *genderbashing*, or violence based on one's transgressing culturally intelligible constructions of gender. In fact, based on Adem's commentary, one way to read Namaste's nuanced articulation of genderbashing might be through a lens of compulsory heterogenderism. Put another way, the rationale for why genderbashing is mistaken for gaybashing may itself be an effect of compulsory heterogenderism. Again, this underscores the cultural unintelligibility of trans* identities and expressions and the subsequent ways they are read in, through, or are replaced by culturally intelligible sexualities.

## Departure: Gender Expression/Embodiment

Revisiting the experience recounted in Chapter 3 that Kade had of the queer couple he walked past on campus calling him "a breeder" provides another salient example of the prevalence of compulsory heterogenderism. The following excerpt is the portion of Kade's interview in which he talked about this experience; the particular sections that reflect the cultural logic of compulsory heterogenderism are in italics. Although I discussed this situation previously in Chapter 3, returning to it here provides a new way of understanding Kade's experience. Moreover, doing so demonstrates the close coupling of the gender binary discourse with compulsory heterogenderism at CU. In many respects, both of these phenomena coexist as twin cultural realities, constantly reinforcing and propagating each other in deleterious ways. In his interview, Kade stated:

> My experiences [of being trans\* at CU] have really shifted. . . . My first year was spent wanting to just be average, I guess. *Now most people don't read me as anything but cisgendered and usually straight. . . . I feel this sense of loss of my identity in a way.* I had this experience last year in the College of Music, and there was . . . a queer couple. It was two men, they were holding hands, and they walked past me and I stared at them, 'cause I thought one of them was cute [laughs], and one of them . . . *I think that he thought that I was straight* and was offended by them, or was feeling something negative toward them because I was looking at them, and *he gave me a dirty look and called me a breeder.* And it was just a really weird experience for me because I was like, "Whoa," [laughs], *I feel like the tables have really turned from wanting to hide this othered kind of part of my identity to not wanting to be perceived as this normative straight male.*

As Kade articulated, most people perceived him as embodying a normative gender (i.e., cisgender) and, as a result, having a normative sexuality (i.e., straight). Thus, the way others read his perceived gender identity and sexuality had the effect of collapsing them on each other, making Kade fear others may see him as a "normative straight male." In other words, Kade worried that his passing for male meant that his trans\* identity was erased and was instead supplanted with being straight. Thus, the sexuality others perceived him to have, like the couple who called him a breeder and indicated their perception of him as straight, covered his trans\* identity.

Furthermore, Kade's commentary shows how because of compulsory heterogenderism he experienced a sense of loss regarding his identity as trans\*. When I asked him to expand on this feeling, he stated,

> It kinda hurts. It's something I'm still kinda dealing with. . . . I always thought it was silly in high school where people would wear pride bracelets and things like that. But it was to, you know, find a sense of community and to express your identity. And my identity always had pretty

much been on my sleeve in a way, and now that it's not, I feel this urge to somehow express my identity. So, for example, one of the classes I am taking, there's an individual who I sit next to who presents very androgynous. I keep wanting to ask what their preferred pronoun is, and [to] talk to them, but it's not really a class where we can talk much. And occasionally I will see people on campus who I think might be gender nonconforming in some way, and I feel this sense of community, and almost, like, familial ties with them, because we have such a small community, and I just feel like they most likely are just perceiving me as one of those normative jerks [laughs].

Kade's remark about pride bracelets and other visual queer artifacts is telling, as it uncovers one of the ways queer people have been able to signal their queerness to others. These sorts of visual signifiers have existed in multiple forms throughout history, with the neoprene bracelets Kade alluded to having become one of the more recent iterations. Now that Kade's gender expression and embodiment meant he passed as cisgender and thus straight, he understood the importance of using these visual signifiers. As he stated in the previous excerpt, he felt a sense of familial ties with other people who challenged and defied the gender binary discourse at CU. However, without having a visual signifier himself, he worried that other trans* folks were "just perceiving [him] as one of those normative jerks."

In shifting from Kade, whom others perceived as expressing and embodying his gender as a man, to Megan, who identified as a trans* woman but was not yet expressing herself as the woman she knew herself to be, a differential effect of compulsory heterogenderism emerges. Because others did not perceive Megan as a trans* woman, she was often derided as gay. This had happened throughout Megan's childhood, which was a time of intense bullying. In describing the effect this bullying had on her, she said, "I was being bullied, so I was trying to stop the bullying, so I was like, 'Well, obviously they think I am gay, so I have to play the guy role.'" Here, Megan understood that, in the minds of the people who were bullying her, to be gay was synonymous with being feminine. In other words, others substituted her being gay in place of her feminine gender expression, thereby erasing her gender identity.

Moreover, the result of the bullying Megan experienced was that she did not feel comfortable expressing her trans* identity publicly and even contemplated suicide on multiple occasions. In fact, the semester Megan and I began working alongside each other was the first time she began connecting with other trans* people beyond virtual online spaces. She had spent most of her life as a trans* woman being, as she phrased it, "inside" and was now trying to "go outside." In other words, she spent a lot of time in her room, playing video games, learning and connecting with others in online chat rooms and spaces but had yet to meet and interact with other trans* people in physical spaces. Much of her hesitancy to go outside was likely because of the effects of compulsory heterogenderism. Because others continued to perceive her as gay and continued to bully and tease her about her perceived sexuality, she felt more and more compelled to "play the guy role," as she worded it. Thus, her being bullied and called gay affected how she expressed her gender identity. She had an opposite reaction to Kade's; namely, instead of feeling a sense of loss about not being perceived as trans*, she tried to be perceived as straight and, as a result, cover her trans* identity.

Megan's experiences of being bullied throughout her life also signal the ways that compulsory heterogenderism as a cultural phenomenon is present outside higher education environments. Although Megan and I worked together to talk about her experiences as a trans* collegian, her comments expose how compulsory heterogenderism affected her life beyond CU's campus. Since concluding data collection, I have also witnessed other experiences of compulsory heterogenderism in the public sphere. For example, in a song called "Transgender Dysphoria Blues," Laura Jane Grace, the trans* woman lead singer of Against Me! sang, "You want them to see you like they see every other girl / they just see a faggot" (Grace, 2014, Track 1). In this lyric, Grace details how compulsory heterogenderism works socially to erase her trans* gender by others seeing her as "a faggot." In this sense, Megan's comments—as well as Grace's song—bridge the educational and broader social spheres and emphasize the presence of compulsory heterogenderism beyond college campuses.

It is important to point out that Megan's attempts to cover her trans* identity were not a character flaw on her behalf. In fact, Megan had very important and real reasons for covering her identity. Because of being bullied and teased throughout her youth as well as during her time at CU, she worried that her coming out would result in potential violence. She expressed this most poignantly when she was reflecting on her experience of working together on this study.

> I always knew that I was gonna get outside of my room eventually, and so I guess this whole time I've sorta been preparing myself for some things I might encounter. And so I've always been reading articles, like the bad articles, you know? The sad articles about transgender stories. . . . I guess some of them are more funny stupidity articles about Fox News not accepting trans* people. But then other stuff, you know, stories about where [*sic*] trans* people are beaten, or raped, or stuff like that.

For Megan, her experience of compulsory heterogenderism was that if she challenged the people bullying her and questioned their perceptions that she was gay—itself used as a pejorative marker of her feminine gender expression coupled with her not yet expressing her gender as a trans* woman—there might be violent repercussions. Thus, her choice to cover was a wise one for her regarding her own safety and vulnerability. Moreover, feeling the need to cover her gender identity by promoting an image of straightness illustrates the negative cultural climate that results from compulsory heterogenderism. Recalling again Rich's (1980) comments about compulsory heterosexuality threatening lesbian existence or Butler's (2006) notion that the cultural unintelligibility of diverse genders produced by compulsory heterosexuality delimited possibilities for trans* people, Megan's remarks stand as a stark reminder of the potential real-life costs of resisting such cultural expectations.

## Departure: Race

As I discussed in the previous chapter, CU has a history of deeply entrenched racism that reflects the racism and race-based divisions in Stockdale. In fact, during the fall 2013 semester, a particularly egregious racist event occurred on campus, causing the resignation of a high-profile Black administrator and instigating a series of campuswide conversations about race. Upper-level administrators also responded by bringing several nationally known antiracist educators to campus for a series of free lectures in the hope that these speakers could help contextualize the presence of racism on campus. Because of the history of strained race-based relations and events at CU, race became a significant lens for viewing the manifestations of compulsory heterogenderism as a cultural phenomenon that shaped life at CU. It was not surprising that the study participants elucidated the reality of compulsory heterogenderism, which was qualitatively different when viewed through a racial lens. Particularly, the enforcement of compulsory heterogenderism took on a decidedly community-based aspect for the participants of color rather than the individual enforcement experienced by the White participants.

One of the more significant examples of the way race mediated the effects of compulsory heterogenderism occurred during the summer of 2014. At the beginning of June, an upper-level Black administrator known affectionately as Captain (a pseudonym), for his omnipresence on campus and the high esteem the campus community had for him, posted a picture of Black National Basketball Association star Quame Smith (also a pseudonym) on Facebook. In the picture, Smith appeared to be wearing dark leggings or tight jeans and a brightly colored floral-patterned jacket. In posting the picture, Captain also added the comment, "Metro sexual or suspect? TALK TO ME." A series of Black colleagues and peers then commented on Captain's original post, suggesting that Smith was gay. These comments ranged from one by an individual who posted, "HOMO SEXUAL"; another writing, "If this isn't openly gay, what is?"; to yet another posting, "Interesting when someone says, 'Why worry about what they wear, it shouldn't matter?' But when the next hour I hear, 'Where are all the single [Black] men?' . . . their [*sic*] somewhere wearing dresses."

Far from being a private conversation among Captain's friends, the Facebook post garnered attention from many members of the faculty, staff, and student communities at CU, including Tristan; Ornacia; Silvia; Janelle, who was then president of TransActions; and Raegan's partner, Ginnie. Sharing her reactions in a blog post, Janelle wrote:

> The word "suspect" is used to convey the idea that basketball player Quame Smith may not be straight and/or a cisgender man. Captain is soliciting input about Smith's gender identity and/or sexual orientation based on a single photo of Smith dressed in a floral jacket and close-fitting pants or leggings. The implication—that gender identity or sexual orientation can be determined by what someone is wearing (or their "gender expression")—is entirely false and harmful to the LGBTQ+ community. (personal communication, June 2, 2014)

Thus, Captain's post not only attracted a number of people who supported his suggestion that Smith was *suspect*, a pejorative term for someone who is gay, but also encouraged a range of individuals to speak up in resistance of such a display of compulsory heterogenderism. Furthermore, of particular note, the individuals who spoke out against Captain's post identified as being LGBTQ themselves.

What was clear from Captain's post and the subsequent visceral response from a wide array of Black colleagues and peers was the overwhelming community support for enforcing compulsory heterogenderism. In other words, in this incident Captain did not alone question Smith's sexuality based on the athlete's attire; it was a community effort. The ability to understand how race mediates the differential effect of compulsory heterogenderism takes on an additional context when recalling Nadia's comment in Chapter 3 that the Black community at CU was just starting to become comfortable with sexuality and gender-based issues. Thus, compulsory heterogenderism was not just something that was enforced between individuals (as was the case for Kade or Megan, who are White); it took on a community aspect with many in the Black community proclaiming that transgressing gender reinforced the perception that the individual was not straight.

Silvia also spoke at length about the impact of others telling her she was a paragon of Black womanhood. As an active student leader involved in a variety of student clubs and activities, Silvia had quickly become well known among faculty and staff at CU. In speaking of her obligations, she said,

> When everything sorta starts picking up and you're doing three programs a week, and you have an awards ceremony on Saturday, and all of these things are happening, and everyone is just going, "She's an example of an excellent woman, an excellent woman," and that's what [I'm] hearing all the time.

The notion of being an "excellent Black woman" was what others often placed on Silvia, despite her not identifying as a woman, because of her leadership skills and heavy involvement in campus life. In fact, her involvement had started to snowball, leading staff to suggest she get involved in honoraries and sororities for Black women, all of which then led to her feeling the weight of others' expectations that she was a "perfect Black woman."

> Being in those spaces where I am praised for being active and involved, it's sort of assumed that I'm gonna go on to do other things. We have women's honoraries on campus, and there is one specifically for Black women, so I've been told a lot that I behave like that, or I should emulate these women. . . . So it's kinda like how I am as a student leader, the people that I associate with, and the people that I date, and all of these different tiny, tiny specks that amount to the perfect Black woman or something.

While Silvia was being complimented as an "excellent Black woman," she was also being encouraged to join Black women's sororities, honoraries, organizations, and activities, all of which would have signified her being "the perfect Black woman." Additionally, Silvia knew that who she dated was one of the "tiny specks" that amounted to being seen as the "perfect Black woman." Thus, the campus staff members who were encouraging Silvia to join Black women's organizations—many of whom were Black themselves—were perceiving Silvia's gender as an "excellent" or a "perfect" Black woman through the people she dated, which was held as a signifier of her sexuality. Moreover, when Silvia was involved in groups organized by Black staff members specifically for Black women, she said that it was assumed that she and the other

Black women involved were all heterosexual. For example, she talked about participating in one group in the following:

> My first meeting there, we were all in the room, going around saying our name. And when that was over, my mentor goes, "Okay, so who here has a boyfriend?" And I'm just like . . . you know, keep my face in passive, don't react externally. . . . I was in this tiny room with five other girls. . . . I just felt completely outcast, and I just wanted to leave immediately. So, I was sorta traumatized after that, and I sort of didn't go to any of the [future] meetings.

Thus, Silvia was caught in an endless loop in which she was expected to be heterosexual and comfortable talking about her presumed heterosexuality and to be involved in organizations for Black women, which she had been encouraged to join specifically because others perceived her as being an excellent Black woman. This was a community expectation placed on her by many Black people at CU, whether faculty, staff, or student members of the organizations, who were encouraging her to join these groups. Furthermore, she felt pressure to participate because of the assumption that she was already an excellent Black woman. Here, Silvia's status as an excellent Black woman, denoting a gendered identity as a woman, was in some part mediated through her need to maintain a heterosexual identity. Because this became a community-based expectation placed on Silvia by fellow Black colleagues, mentors, and peers, one can again see a different nuance in how race influenced the maintenance of compulsory heterogenderism.

It bears noting that although race influenced the maintenance and effects of compulsory heterogenderism, my expressing this does not suggest a normative judgment. In other words, I am not suggesting the compulsory heterogenderism manifested in Black communities and spaces is any more or less pernicious than the compulsory heterogenderism present in White communities and spaces. Instead, I am stating that race matters when it comes to understanding how trans\* collegians experience compulsory heterogenderism. To not talk about the influence of race in relation to compulsory heterogenderism may inadvertently suggest that race does not matter, thereby overlooking a particularly salient identity for the Black study participants and how they understood and responded to compulsory heterogenderism as a cultural reality. Moreover, elucidating this particular departure may help educators respond in more precise ways to this cultural phenomenon depending on the student populations they work with.

# Note

1. It is worth mentioning that some in the lesbian community have reclaimed the word *dyke*, refashioning it as not being derisive. However, in the context Micah used the word, it was clear the word was being assigned to them in a negative manner. This, then, substantiates my describing the word as derisive in the preceding analysis.

# 5

---

## RESILIENCE AS A VERB

E tymologically speaking, *resilience* is a noun, connoting the impression that it is something one either does or does not have. Framed this way, one might think that if trans* students have the ability to persist through college despite negative cultural climates (e.g., the gender binary discourse, compulsory heterogenderism), or if trans* students can respond positively to any potential negative experiences they may face, they are resilient. Viewed from such a perspective, resilience is something that one must possess. Educational scholars doing resilience-based work have yet to address adequately the question of how individuals may be able to develop their own resilience, if they can at all. However, I suggest that resilience might not necessarily be something that one has or does not have (e.g., an ability) but a practice. Thus, the notion of resilience becomes less of a noun, or a thing one possesses, and more of a verb, or an action one can practice. In this sense, even if one does not feel resilient or does not think of hirself as resilient, one may be able to practice resilience as a strategy to overcome individual enactments of trans* oppression as well as the cultural realities of the gender binary discourse and compulsory heterogenderism.

Understanding resilience as a practice also allows a more complex and nuanced understanding of the notion itself, as one may be able to practice resilience with varying degrees of success. In other words, one's practice of resilience may not hold consistently across time and space, as might be suggested from the suggestion that resilience as a noun is something one has and, thus, something one may use in all contexts. Thus, the notion of resilience is transformed into an action one develops through practice, the successful deployment of which may shift across time and space. It follows, then, that resilience as an action suggests one must repeatedly attempt to put the concept to work in various contexts and across various times in one's life.

Such a perspective of resilience suggests there may be something performative about the concept. I use the word *performative* not to suggest that practicing resilience is disingenuous or that it signals a falsity in intention or action. Instead, these data compel an understanding of performativity closely aligned with Butler's (2006) definition of the term. Specifically, as I wrote in Chapter 2, Butler coined the term to describe the ways individuals repeatedly practiced their genders in an attempt to make their genders culturally legible and, thus, their lives more livable. Butler also suggested that one's need to practice gender repeatedly was because of the consistent failure to emulate culturally intelligible expectations on gender, especially in relation to cultural expectations related to how gender should align with an individual's sex, sexual desires, and sexual practices. In other words, because we as individuals all fail consistently in our attempts at practicing an intelligible positionality in relation to gender and its entailments (e.g., sex, sexual desires, sexual practices, race, disability), we are left with no other option than to repeatedly practice, or *do*, gender. Put another way, a practice is a habitual act we all engage in and does not necessarily insinuate one gets better at what it is one is practicing (e.g., a person's gender). Recognizing practice as a habitual action rather than a process of getting better also strips away the mythical notion that there is one good or right way of practicing or doing one's gender. Therefore, I use the concept of performativity to highlight how participants repeatedly practiced resilience in various contexts and across the duration of our work together as a way of *doing resilience.*

Viewing resilience as a practice-based orientation also has the added benefit of aligning with the affirmative approach that the trans* participants and I took as we worked together. In other words, our work together was less about figuring out if they were (not) resilient and more about developing strategies they could use to practice resilience. In this sense, if participants were able to practice resilience in ways that were particularly successful for them, they could reenact those practices in other spaces or at other times. However, if their practices of resilience did not prove effective in particular environments, they could attempt different practices the next time they were confronted with a similar situation. They could also choose to practice resilience by not going back to such environments, thereby allowing them to better navigate their college environment by avoiding places and spaces where they met resistance.

Approaching resilience as doing, then, is not about getting better at the practice but figuring out where and with whom one can best be successful and, thus, best navigate the collegiate environment. In this way, the notion of viewing resilience as a practice challenges the staid preconceptions that trans* people must always already face victimization by recognizing the alternative possibility that trans* people have agency, which we are able to use to navigate the gender-dichotomous collegiate environments in which we inevitably find ourselves. Extending this even further, recognizing resilience as a verb for trans* people also depathologizes those of us who feel unable to practice resilience in various contexts. So reorienting one's perspective of resilience allows one to recognize how particular environments might limit practicing resiliency because of cultural manifestations of transgender oppression (i.e., the gender binary discourse and compulsory heterogenderism). One's environment is interrogated as the source of such an inability to practice resilience rather than suggesting a character flaw or a problem that reflects negatively on any particular individual.

Recognizing resilience as a verb, or an action one can repeatedly practice, is less about affirming or negating the ability to be resilient. Instead, it suggests an ongoing practice that can be developed over time and that may be more successful at certain times and in certain spaces than others. In this sense, individuals can *question* their own resilience while still *practicing* resilience, which is something a number of participants did. For example, during our second interview, Silvia stated, "I don't really feel resilient at all." Similarly, thinking about the seeming incompatibility of his genderqueerness and Black racial identity I discussed in the previous chapter, Micah mused,

> Before I got the idea of, like, "You know, I'm just gonna be me," I would sit and think, like, "Maybe I'm not supposed to be a part of this community. Maybe I am not supposed to function inside of this community. Maybe it's not something that I'm supposed to do. Maybe it's something I'm gonna have to let go."

Adding to Silvia's and Micah's internal doubts, Jackson also questioned their resilience in our first formal interview, saying they had not faced overt, extreme hardship (e.g., gender-based violence) and because of that was wondering if they even had anything to overcome. However, at the same time, participants discussed how they practiced resilience, often doing so in close succession to questioning their own resilience.

Although the specific practices of resilience varied widely, there were two overarching similarities across participants' experiences. First, how they practiced resilience changed based on the particular environments in which they found themselves. For example, when I mentioned to Adem that I often listened to music on campus as a way to tune out other people's reactions to my gender presentation, they stated, "I won't put earphones in if I am walking around campus, because I want to know what the hell is going on behind me. . . . I'll text, but I am not going to be that distracted." For Adem, texting someone while walking across campus was a practice of resilience that reflected their environment, specifically wanting to know what was happening around them in large public spaces. Another way Adem practiced resilience as a result of their discomfort with the large public nature of CU, and particularly Central Square, was to know about, and remain as close as possible to, queer-friendly areas of campus.

> Usually, if I am within a certain radius to the Student Life building, I'm okay, because I'm like, "Oh, well The Center is right there, and the Women's Center is right there, and Coffee Express is right there, and Coffee Express is always safe for queer people, and . . . this is good, this is like my area."

Adem's practice of resilience, then, was about developing a sense of their area on campus. Although Adem traversed spaces beyond that area, they knew it was always a space they could return to. Furthermore, developing a sense of their area of campus increased Adem's feelings of safety and comfort as well as their ability to navigate less welcoming spaces.

Raegan Darling also based their decisions on how to practice resilience according to their environment. Raegan would often rely on Ginnie's support to navigate resisting gendered norms and expectations. For example, Raegan talked about having Ginnie help in confronting staff members in Full Press when they were misgendered. As Raegan said,

> Ginnie actually helps me a lot with it. Because sometimes I'm so emotionally exhausted from all of this . . . I don't want to say anything. It's like, literally, if I say something, I'm gonna burst into tears. . . . So Ginnie's like, "Well, would you like me to, like, correct them? Would you like me to say something?" And usually I'm okay with it. 'Cause someone will be like, "Oh, hey ladies," and she'll be like, "Oh, just one lady."

In this case, Raegan and Ginnie were able to work together to find ways for Raegan to practice resilience in a way that resisted the emotional exhaustion of continually confronting the gender binary discourse on campus (I write more about the emotional labor associated with gender nonnormativity in the next chapter).

Moreover, Raegan's partnership with Ginnie to practice resilience relates to Adem's resilience-based practice of texting people when they were walking around campus. These practices demonstrate that practicing resilience is not solely an individual or solitary process (Gupton, 2015) or what Wolff (1995) referred to as being "an enduring aspect of the person" (p. 568). Much to the contrary, I contend there may be an interactional or relational component to practicing resilience. In other words, participants often practiced resilience *alongside and with other people.* This nuanced perspective of resilience, namely, that it can be viewed as a group and individual practice, is significant in expanding conceptualizations of resilience. If one can practice resilience alongside other people, then it may open up resilience as a concept to populations that may place more value on community rather than individuality. Recognizing the group aspect of practicing resilience also serves to dissolve the individualistic, colonial logics that have pathologized populations that operate from communal values (e.g., indigenous peoples) and, as a result, may previously have not been thought to be resilient through such oppressive frameworks.

The second similarity of how participants practiced resilience related to their level of outness. Kade spoke about this in the context of classroom spaces when he said,

> I think that for me, coming out in most classes, like a lecture hall, there is no point, you're not even talking to anyone else. And even in smaller classes if I don't feel like it's relevant to what we're discussing, to me there is no point in coming out. Um . . . but if it's a, you know, what I would consider a safe space [I will come out].

For Kade, sharing his trans* identity was an important act of resilience, especially because of his passing as a cisgender man and feeling a loss of his trans* identity as a result. However, he did not come out in all situations. Instead, he gauged his level of safety and comfort in particular contexts, thus allowing him to make good choices about where and when he would disclose his trans* identity. For example, Kade suggested that his coming out as a practice of resilience in classes had to be relevant to the course. In the previous comment, Kade linked his comfort with the notion of relevance, giving them equal weight in determining how, when, or if he practiced resilience in the classroom by coming out. He started by saying that if coming out was not relevant, he would not do it, but if he considered the class a safe space, he would. Thus, he connected the two concepts, needing both of them for him to come out.

Kade further expressed this linkage by talking about one particular class in which his trans* identity was relevant but coming out would not have felt safe for him. The course had been challenging for Kade because of what he described as the anachronistic way the professor framed trans* identities. He said, "Just the title of that class [session] being 'sex changes' [*sic*] . . . already I'm like, 'Uh, I don't know how this is gonna be.' So those are maybe, like, risky spaces." Although the particular class session Kade mentioned was discussing gender confirmation surgery for trans* people, thereby making his trans* identity relevant, the space still felt risky. Thus, rather than coming out, Kade practiced resilience in other ways in that class, such as addressing the professor individually and, eventually, asking Tristan to intervene on his behalf.

Megan's and Silvia's level of outness on campus also mediated how they practiced resilience. Because they were not out publicly as trans*, they had to find other ways to practice resilience. For Megan, who was a computer science major, this came in the form of gaming. For example, when Megan played single-user role-playing games, she would often play as women characters. She explained:

> There's [*sic*] games out there that basically you play as a fantasy character, like a Madge [from *The Hunger Games* series] or warrior or stuff like that. Nowadays, most of the games like that you can choose your gender as well. And I used to only play guys whenever I was in high school. But now, I have switched over to playing females. . . . For me really, I [am] trying to play myself.

Although Megan had begun HRT midway through our working together, she had yet to come out as trans* to her peers, faculty, and staff on campus. She also had not come out at the company where she was doing an internship. Far from seeing Megan's choice not to come out as a negative reflection of herself, her choice was rooted in her feeling unsafe. This lack of safety was largely because of her previous experiences of being bullied and teased as well as reading articles and seeing news stories about trans*-based violence. Therefore, instead of coming out, Megan used her passion for gaming to practice resilience by playing herself or playing characters that resembled who she was: a woman.

Silvia explained her choice not to be out by simply stating, "That's not really a thing for me. It's very much centered to TransActions stuff and people who go to TransActions." Partially, Silvia's choice not to be out revolved around issues of safety, especially when thinking about being Black and agender. Additionally, Silvia had learned that the gender binary discourse on campus did not allow others to see her not having a gender as a legible or possible choice to make, thus reinforcing her choice not to be out. Because she was not out, however, Silvia needed to find other ways to practice resilience. These strategies largely revolved around creating spaces in which her agender identity almost ceased to matter or be relevant. One particularly salient way she was able to practice resilience was through making art. In fact, she spoke about one art course specifically, stating:

> Last semester . . . I was enrolled in my first video arts studio class, and I know that it's really dramatic to say that a class saved your life, but I sort

of feel like that without that class, I would not have made it through the semester. I sort of found the outlet to put everything into and get to work on an independent project, and direct it, and produce it, and edit it, and go through the process of getting it critiqued. So, it really helped me.

In contrast to Kade's looking for spaces where his trans* identity was relevant for him to practice resilience, Silvia practiced resilience by finding spaces where gender was not primary. A main difference between how Silvia and Kade practiced resilience revolved around their varying levels of outness at CU, particularly in terms of their safety and comfort being out. Although Kade did not feel safe in all settings, he did feel comfortable in several spaces, thereby allowing him to use coming out as a way to practice resilience. Because Silvia did not feel safe, and because she had ascertained the campus community's overall lack of awareness and comfort with nonbinary gender identities, she practiced resilience by not coming out and, in fact, existing in spaces where gender faded into the background. Of course, it is important to point out how Kade's being White and his ability to pass as a cisgender man mediated his comfort and ability to leverage coming out as a practice of resilience. However, Kade's ability to pass made him feel as though he lost a part of his trans* identity, suggesting that even his passing as a man—something he actively worked to do as a result of his biomedically and socially transitioning—was implicated in how he was able to practice resilience.

## Departure: Disability

One particularly salient departure from the practice of doing resilience is related to disability. Silvia shared having several disabilities, including post-traumatic stress disorder, temporomandibular joint dysfunction (TMJ), and identifying as neurodiverse. Additionally, Silvia was diagnosed with fibromyalgia during our last semester of work together. The TMJ and fibromyalgia made navigating the hilly terrain of City's campus increasingly difficult for Silvia during the winter months, often causing her to miss whole days. Her diagnosis of fibromyalgia in particular seemed to affect Silvia on a deeply personal level, shaking her own belief that she could practice resilience. Prior to being diagnosed, Silvia had likened resilience to a fabric that after being stretched out can return to its original shape. In reflecting on her own experiences as a Black agender student, she said,

I feel very stretched out when I'm at campus. And I'm okay living this life that other people have sort of assigned to me. Do I [then] retreat home and go back to how I naturally feel? I think that some days I do more than others. I certainly hope that those moments increase for me, because I think I'm healthiest when that happens.

Silvia's feeling "very stretched out" while on campus was emblematic of the effects of gender binary discourse and compulsory heterogenderism. The overwhelming presence of these twin cultural realities for Silvia as well as how her being a Black agender student mediated her experiences of these phenomena stretched her out of shape and made her feel discord and discomfort. However, by going home, she was often able to shrink back to how she naturally felt. Thus, one way Silvia practiced resilience was by leaving CU, which is important as it suggests there is not any preferred outcome of resilience, such as students' staying on campus. In fact, remaining on campus had various negative implications for the participants, as was often the case for Silvia. Her practice of leaving campus as a strategy of resilience expands possibilities for what resilience could look like for other students as well as how educators could best work with students to promote the practice of resilience. This finding also corresponds to Jourian's (2016) work, specifically that trans* students must often leave campus to cultivate community and that their leaving is a signal of self-care. Furthermore, as I discuss in Chapter 8, student affairs educators must think about reorienting their practice in ways that encourage and promote trans* students to seek community beyond what has traditionally been thought of as the campus grounds. Specifically, educators need to think about how they use virtual landscapes and local communities in their work, as both are generative locations for the creation of trans* community and kinship (I discuss trans* kinship in more detail in Chapter 7).

Silvia also associated practicing resilience with the notion of health. At the end of the preceding comment, she stated she hoped the moments of her being able to practice resilience and, as a result, shrink back to her natural state, would increase in frequency. She then stated, "I think I'm healthiest when that happens." Thus, for Silvia, practicing resilience was linked with health and remaining healthy. Resilience as a practice, then, was more than a way to navigate campus successfully for Silvia; it was a way of maintaining her physical and emotional health.

However, her own self-reported ability to practice resilience shifted significantly after her doctor diagnosed her with fibromyalgia. During our last formal interview, Silvia described feeling a lack of resilience:

Well, I was thinking about the word *resilient*. And I was sort of doubting my own resiliency. . . . Coming out of [the] fall semester with sort of, like, hit after hit after hit, like, never in my entire life . . . has so much happened all at the same time. And I sort of came to a moment with myself where I was like, "I don't really feel resilient at all." . . . I feel like I have not gotten up yet. I feel like I am still just dealing with those hits. . . . I don't feel like I'm over it. I don't feel stronger. I don't feel put back together.

Silvia went on to compare her current feelings with those of the previous semester, saying,

I do things that I did last semester, and they don't feel the same. And I don't think I do them as well, and then that leads to more guilt, or, you know, I can't make a meeting because I'm in bed cuz my legs hurt so badly. So, I don't feel physically like I'm standing again. I don't feel like I'm on the same level of productivity, but also socially or emotionally, there's just a lot that I can't deal with right now. So I feel like I may have regressed.

Again, Silvia discussed not only the physical impact of her new diagnosis but also the social and emotional impacts. Her ability to practice resilience allowed her to maintain not only her physical schedule (i.e., going to meetings) but also her emotional and social well-being. Because of her new diagnosis and the dissonance she experienced in not feeling stronger or put back together she felt unable to practice resilience. Due to this seeming lack of resilience, she felt as though she could not cope with a lot and, as a result, suggested that she had regressed in her abilities to shrink back from feeling stretched on campus.

Linking resilience and health again, Silvia further stated, "I don't know if I'm gonna bounce back. Point blank, that's it. That's all. I know that I'm never gonna bounce back from having a chronic illness. I'm never gonna be a healthy person or whatever that means." Two elements in this statement are interesting. First, Silvia continues to link the concepts of resilience and health, specifically her feeling that her lack of ability to be resilient is also reflective of her lack of being healthy. As she stated, if she would never bounce back from having a chronic illness, then it follows that she would never again be healthy. Second, and perhaps more important, it seemed as though Silvia was beginning to come to a critical consciousness over the notion of *health*, especially what it means to be healthy and who controls this definition. Her last sentence, "I'm never gonna be a healthy person *or whatever that means*" (emphasis added), suggests that Silvia might not have been completely sold on the idea that she was or necessarily would always be an unhealthy person. In this sense, Silvia's dismissive "or whatever that means" comment signaled a dormant critique of what it means to be healthy. Extending this thought, if Silvia ever were to truly challenge notions of health, particularly who controls the definitions of *health* and how such definitions may diminish possibilities for those pathologized as unhealthy, then it may stand to reason that she could either uncouple her sense of resilience from being healthy or she might reconceptualize health altogether. Both possibilities might rearrange how she could practice resilience and, as a result, feel successful as a Black agender individual with several disabilities.

In fact, since the conclusion of data collection for this book, Silvia has challenged dominant, ableist discourses of health. She has continued to embrace and affirm her neurodiversity through her art, particularly her poetry. Her resistance of normative notions of health is yet another iteration of her ongoing practice of resilience. Moreover, her practice of resilience in relation to her disabilities increases possibilities for how the notion of resilience as a verb could hold great promise for rethinking people's experiences beyond their genders. In other words, although Silvia is trans*, practicing resilience in relation to her disabilities connotes how understanding resilience as a verb, and as an ongoing practice, could push back against various systems of oppression beyond just trans* oppression, such as *compulsory able-bodiedness* (McRuer, 2006).

This extended analysis of Silvia's practicing resilience is striking for two additional reasons. First, several participants shared they had disabilities, including Jackson, Raegan, and Derek. Although none of these participants said their disability had an effect on their ability to be resilient, their identifying as trans* and having disabilities suggests future research should look at this particular convergence of identities. Second, although there is no way to quantifiably measure an increase in trans* students pursuing postsecondary education, evidence suggests trans* students "are growing in visibility and voice" (Marine, 2011b, p. 59). Similarly, evidence also suggests that students with disabilities are increasing in number on college and university campuses (Haller, 2006; National Center for Education Statistics, 1999). Taken together, these facts indicate that far from being an aberration, trans* students with disabilities may be more numerous on a national scale than these four participants from one university suggests. Indeed, these four participants made up almost half of the participants in the overall study, and while I am not suggesting that almost half of all trans* college students might identify as having a disability, it stands to reason that perhaps the phenomenon is more pervasive than one may think. Therefore, Silvia's experiences may suggest a call for further research into the lives of trans* college students with disabilities. Although previous scholarship has focused on the convergence of these two identities, most notably the work of Eli Clare (2001, 2003, 2015), it has yet to focus on college students and higher education.

Thus, the departure related to Silvia's disabilities and how they mediated her (in)ability to practice resilience yields an important call for future research.


## Departure: Academic Departments

Another departure for participants in how they practiced resilience related to their academic departments. Although some departments allowed trans* collegians to thrive in practicing resilience, others delimited possibilities of how they felt they could talk, act, and express themselves. In the spaces where students did not feel comfortable practicing resilience, they had to make choices about whether they would stay in their major field of study. Thus, some trans* students' inability to practice resilience had long-lasting effects that extended beyond their college experience, as changing majors could result in their changing career paths.

BC is one example of a student who was in the process of changing majors because of a negative academic department. As discussed in Chapter 3, BC told me she had planned to stop majoring in economics because she felt unable to practice resilience in classroom spaces. She shared a particularly frustrating story describing how she had to "dress up in formal wear" for a class presentation (see p. 65). Although she had wanted to mix women's and men's professional attire for her presentation, she ended up not doing so. Instead, she said she "ended up throwing on a pair of pants and a dress shirt," further explaining that to queer notions of professional attire "would take time, money, and preparation." A couple of salient points are worth elucidating in BC's comments in relation to her inability to practice resilience as an economics major. First, she linked the ability to practice certain forms of resilience to money. For her, she needed some money to be able to blend women's and men's attire for required class presentations, which would have allowed her to practice resilience in the classroom. However, because of her lack of money, her ability to practice resilience in the classroom was ruled out.

Second, and perhaps less clear, is the connection between the practice of resilience and preparation. It is possible that what BC meant when using the word *preparation* is that she would have had to think ahead about what she wanted to do. Perhaps this was difficult for her as a student who usually worked on deadlines because she did not have the foresight to prepare an outfit with mixed articles of clothing. However, there is another way to understand her need for preparation. As I stated in Chapter 3, BC had disdain for her academic field of study, particularly in relation to the lack of space for and recognition of gender diversity. Thus, BC knew if she were going to transgress the gender binary discourse that regulated her classroom environment, she would need to be ready for some pushing back on the part of the other students and her faculty. Therefore, perhaps her suggestion that she would need to prepare was a reflection of the need to prepare for the microaggressions she would likely face from her peers. Rather than have to face these, BC made the choice to wear a pair of pants and a shirt. In this sense, then, BC was practicing a form of resilience in not choosing to transgress the gender binary discourse in her economics classrooms. Because BC knew she would confront hostility, not transgressing gender norms—and ultimately deciding to leave her major—was a way for her to practice self-care and persist as a student. BC's experiences in the College of Business and her subsequent choice to switch majors are understandable as a practice of resilience and a reflection that she was prevented from practicing resilience in certain academic spaces (e.g., the College of Business). Thus, she decided to change majors in favor of finding an academic department where she could be more comfortable and safe practicing resilience on a consistent basis (e.g., by talking about her queerness in academic papers, which she said was something she liked to do).

Contrary to BC's experiences as an economics major, Jackson discussed their field of education as liberating. In our first interview, Jackson had worried about what it would mean for them to transgress gender as a teacher in classroom spaces. However, four months later in our second interview, they had become far more resolved about their gender expression. In part, this was a reflection of the education curriculum at City and, specifically, the faculty's explicit approach to gender diversity, which Jackson described as follows:

> I can remember when we had the syllabus up in one of my [education] classes on the first day and [the professor] was talking about how we need to be respectful of race, gender, sexual orientation, and gender variance is what [the syllabus] said. That was great.

The simple act of including the term *gender variance* in a syllabus and then demonstrating it by respecting and honoring gender diversity in the classroom made Jackson feel much more capable of practicing resilience in education classrooms. In fact, Jackson felt comfortable enough to raise issues related to gender identity during class presentations and discussions, saying,

> A lot of my projects that I do, or presentations, I try to gear them toward trans* issues just because I think it's important for people to hear about [them] to get more exposure to that and see that it's normal.

Focusing projects and presentations on trans* issues was not only a reflection of Jackson's comfort in the classroom, which in large part was because of the acceptance of inclusive values, but also a way for Jackson to practice resilience. By sharing information and reflecting their life through presentations and projects, Jackson felt as though they belonged in their education classes and, thus, could have a future as a teacher.

Similar to Jackson's experiences in the education department, Adem and Silvia felt that the College of Art was a comfortable department to practice resilience openly. Most poignantly, Silvia said,

> I love [the College of Art]. It's sorta like the quirky cousin [at CU], and it's sorta like, "You're kinda weird, but I like you." And every time I'm there [at CU], I just walk into [the College of Art] and I feel home or something. I feel like it's okay to be a little weird because there is someone else in [the College of Art] who is weirder than you. So it just feels okay.

Silvia's use of the word *weird* in this statement is far from pejorative. In fact, she was providing a queered definition that signals something to be desired and embraced. Thus, from Silvia's perspective, being weird by transgressing the gendered cultural expectations at CU was openly embraced in the College of Art. This space became a haven for her and Adem to do gender as they wished and on their own terms. Therefore, the College of Art provided an environment where they could practice resilience in ways that were not open to students in different settings, such as BC's experiences in the College of Business.

Adem thought that this ability to practice resilience in the College of Art was because of the perception that many students in the college were queer. In our first interview, Adem stated,

> I know [it] is not statistically true, but at least when I think of the stereotypes in my head, most of the people that would have need of an LGBTQ Center would be in [the College of Music] or [the College of Art].

Although Adem admitted this was not statistically accurate based on the students who frequented The Center, there is something powerful about the perception of certain academic spaces on campus being open to queerness and transgressing gender. The perception that the College of Art and the College of Music were more welcoming of gender transgressions than other academic departments offered Adem the ability to practice resilience in different, and perhaps more comfortable, ways than they were able to do in other academic spaces and settings. So, although it may not have been true that more queer and trans* students gravitated toward the colleges of art and music at CU, the perception signaled how these academic spaces promoted liberatory practices of resilience on campus.

It is also worth pointing out that Adem had stopped being a College of Art student after their first year at CU. However, when we were first getting to know each other, they took me to the College of Art, which they said was a significant area to them on campus. Adem described the space as still being comfortable and where they felt they could return and be themselves. Thus, the ability to practice resilience in certain academic spaces on campus, such as the College of Art, was not dependent on students currently being enrolled in these colleges' academic programs. In this sense, there was something about the College of Art and the College of Music that superseded the need to enroll in these academic programs. Furthermore, instead of students having to enroll in certain academic programs to practice resilience in the classroom, this demonstrates a particular ethos regarding gender identity and expression in the College of Art and the College of Music that potentially could be adapted by other academic departments on campus. In other words, rather than suggesting that all trans* students study in particular academic programs, there are ways the programs could change to embrace gender diversity. I discuss educators' need to create a new ethos regarding gender diversity in Chapter 8.

Perhaps unsurprisingly, participants' perceptions of certain departments as being spaces where they could practice resilience conflicted with one another. For example, although Adem described the Department of Women and Gender Studies as being a welcome space for them to practice resilience, Silvia and Kade said it was not always a place they felt comfortable doing so. Additionally, Kade spoke about his confusion regarding the psychology department at CU, particularly the failure of some psychology faculty to create their classrooms as spaces where he could practice resilience.

> The psych department, which is my department, I always expect them to be better. The teachers in general are really good, but most of the student population is not. They're super binary and a lot of them have proven to be really homophobic and transphobic. And I think that I just expect people in that field to be more progressive.

Kade shared stories not only of the students holding regressive ideas regarding gender identity but also faculty expressing negative views toward trans* identities in the classroom. In one class, a faculty member neglected to correct a student's pejorative commentary regarding gender diversity. This experience signaled to Kade that he could not be out as trans* in the classroom, as he did not feel protected in that setting.

In his final semester at CU, Kade had a class with a psychology faculty member who continually expressed marginalizing views of trans* people. The instructor used the pronouns she/her/hers when discussing trans* men, discussed trans* people as feeling "trapped in the wrong body," and suggested that all trans* people were in need of "correction" (e.g., gender confirmation surgery, HRT) to be recognized by their cisgender peers as being "in the right body." This viewpoint linked being trans* to a purely embodied identity, and particularly requiring trans* people to change their bodies to gain cisgender people's recognition and approval. Although Kade was biomedically transitioning, he knew this view was extremely limiting for other trans* people who chose not to do so and was appalled that his teacher promoted these limiting—and damaging—ideas. Thus, despite Kade's statement that "the teachers in general [were] really good" in the psychology department, there were still several faculty members in the department with whom he had negative experiences. Furthermore, the lack of progressive students in the major, and the neglect by some faculty to correct negative views of trans* people and identities, underscored Kade's conflicted relationship with his academic department. Even in areas that some had hoped would be or viewed as supportive (e.g., psychology, women's and gender studies), it was unlikely that these departments were wholly supportive or that these classroom spaces were always places where participants felt comfortable practicing resilience.

## Departure: Living on Campus

Although many of the study participants had experienced living on campus, only Raegan lived on campus throughout the duration of our working together. In fact, many participants said the reason they did not live on campus was because of repeated run-ins with gender binary discourse in the residence halls. For example, the following is Kade's description of his short time of living on campus:

> I lived on campus for a week. . . . I wanted to dorm on campus my freshman year because I think it's really good experience and an easy way to meet other people and get involved in college life and I wanted the full college experience, but none of my gender markers were changed, so I had to dorm in the female dorms. [Because I started at CU] in the middle of the [academic] year [my roommates] had already been there for half the year and I introduced myself and . . . one of my roommates, she freaked out, and she was like—'cause I supposed [I] passed to her as male—"Well there was definitely a mistake; we'll get this fixed out" [*sic*]. She was really sweet about it, but she was convinced [the residence life staff] accidentally put a boy in the girl's dorm. And so I had to explain to her that I was trans*, and she was pretty nice about it. I had three roommates, and the other two—one was

kind of ambivalent about it, and then the third one, I think I met her once, because she refused to come back to the dorm because she was afraid that I was going to sexually violate her in some way, just because of my identity. [So] obviously that's not a good living situation. And I made friends in the dorm from other floors and stuff like that, and there was this constant fear that I would be outed [as trans*] just by where I live[d]. So I just decided not to do it anymore.

Kade's experience living in a sex-segregated residence hall designated for cisgender women posed several challenges for him. First, his roommates were less than accommodating, showing a distinct lack of awareness and understanding about his trans* identity. Although Kade said that one of his roommates "was really sweet about it," his suggestion that she was "convinced [the residence life staff] accidentally put a boy in the girl's dorm" belies her being really sweet about living with someone who transgressed binary conceptions of gender. Second, the experience of having a roommate who would not even come back to their room for fear of Kade sexually violating her is consistent with the pejorative assumption that all trans* people are perverse or sexual predators (e.g., Nicolazzo & Marine, 2015; Serano, 2007). Because of Kade's history of bouncing around between primary and secondary schools due to transphobic school climates, it makes sense that he would not want to deal with the living situation he was confronted with upon arriving at CU.

Similarly, Megan shared negative experiences living in the residence halls, which she did for her first year at CU. As she told:

> Everybody on my floor were [*sic*] the best of friends. We were the [Foley] Nine—we lived on the ninth floor. . . . We were just this big group of buds, just doin' whatever. But there were a lot of times where they would go out and play Frisbee, or they would go out and play soccer and I would play with them, too, just to get outside and do stuff, but at the same time, I felt like, I don't want to do this. . . . Or there would be some times where I would want to watch a movie or something, but they wouldn't, cuz it would be too girly, or they would want to get outside and do stuff.

Although Megan began describing her floor mates as being "the best of friends," she went on to express feeling unable to express her femininity around the men with whom she lived. She also said that the men often teased her when they saw her doing something that could be construed as, to use her word, *girly*. Returning to her practicing resilience by playing female video game characters, Megan said the cisgender men she lived with often teased her about it:

I do remember that some of my dorm friends would occasionally catch me [and would say], "What? [Sue, a pseudonym for Megan's legal name], you're a girl character?!" I would get really embarrassed for a second; then I would use the excuse, "What? Girls are cute. Would you rather play someone that looks nice or would you rather play someone that's a guy?" So, I guess I would try to play the gay card on them.

Although Megan's strategy for combating the teasing she faced was problematic, it underscores the incredible reach of gender policing—via gender binary discourse—that she encountered in the residence halls. She also said her roommate would tease her, stating, "There would be the occasional joke, like, 'Oh [Sue], you're so girly.'" These instances of teasing mirrored the teasing and bullying Megan experienced as a youth, which did little to encourage her to come out and were part of her move off campus after her first year at CU.

Kade's and Megan's experiences were far from the only negative ones shared by participants about living on campus. The sum of these experiences might seem to suggest that to practice resilience meant living off campus. However, living off campus for most participants had another negative implication, namely, that studies have shown that living on campus positively influences student persistence (e.g., Jacoby, 2015). Although these studies do not indicate a causal relationship between living off campus and the lack of persistence, it is worth noting that four of the nine participants involved in the study (i.e., Derek, BC, Jackson, and Adem) stopped out from CU. Of these four students, only one (BC) returned to CU after a year, with another (Jackson) enrolling at Stockdale State after two years, and a third (Adem) exploring transferring after two years and after beginning HRT (although, as of the writing of this book, Adem had not started coursework again). This means that of the eight participants who lived off campus, half of them stopped attending, and three of them did not return to CU to complete their degrees. Furthermore, although Adem was exploring the possibility of transferring after two years, Adem's change in gender identity means that Adem would have a qualitatively different experience of the gender binary discourse (see Chapter 3) and compulsory heterogenderism (see Chapter 4) at Adem's new institution. Regardless of the reasons for their leaving, which were varied, it stands to reason that living on campus might have helped them remain enrolled, if only doing so had not been such an alienating or frustrating experience for them.

It is also important to point out that although the participants were all practicing resilience, sometimes doing so was not enough to allow them to navigate campus successfully. In other words, the significance of participants leaving CU and never coming back cannot be overlooked. In fact, it suggests that despite these students' efforts to practice resilience—and perhaps despite their leaving campus *as an act of resilience itself*—they still did not earn a degree, potentially decreasing their future possibilities and opportunities. In other words, regardless of participants' abilities to practice resilience, the twin cultural realities of gender binary discourse and compulsory heterogenderism were so large and so pervasive and overwhelming that they could not successfully navigate CU's campus no matter how hard they may have tried. Rather than indicating that something was lacking for those participants who left CU and chose not to return, these data suggest the omnipresence of systemic trans* oppression and the suffocating effect it had on participants' ability to be successful in college.

And yet, one participant, Raegan, lived on campus during their involvement in the study. Moreover, Raegan was a resident assistant (RA), which illustrated their taking a leadership role in the residence halls. During our time working together, Raegan had been an RA for a year, and they were intending on returning for a second year in the position. Although Raegan shared experiences in which their gender identity was not recognized by fellow staff members, their desire to return to the position and thereby extend their time living in the residence halls at CU suggests this was a comfortable environment where they could practice resilience. In fact, it suggests that being in a leadership role gave Raegan the ability to practice resilience in a manner that other participants might not have been able to do while living in the halls. However, because becoming an RA would involve committing to living in the residence halls beyond just one week (in Kade's case) and one year (in Megan's case), and there would be no guarantee of an improvement in climate or experiences, the possibility of attempting to be an RA may be too much of a chance for some trans* students to take.

Moreover, as I have written elsewhere (Nicolazzo & Marine, 2015), the RA application and selection process can be a marginalizing space for trans* applicants. Several CU staff members mentioned to me throughout my time on campus that a number of upper-level staff members in the Office of Residence Life (ORL) were not receptive to efforts to increase trans* inclusion in the residence halls. In fact, the perceived lack of interest in trans* inclusion on the part of several staff members, including some new staff who had been hired toward the end of my time working with the study participants at CU, led one genderqueer ORL staff member to leave the college. It's also worth mentioning that Raegan came out as trans* masculine after becoming an RA. They discussed the experience of coming out as trans* to the ORL and their RA staffs:

I had training for my RA job, and . . . during the diversity training . . . I was like, "I would like to be called Raegan Darling now. I'm not really sure about . . . ah, what pronouns yet. But, I'll tell you if they change, and also, like, don't call me 'girl.' Don't be like, 'Hey, girl.' Don't refer to me and another woman as 'ladies,' and the closest word I can find that describes my gender is genderqueer." But I [didn't] know if I want[ed] to identify as that, so it was kind of like a—like a precautionary little spiel I did. And then . . . a month later, I was like, "Okay, I'm trans*."

It is impossible to say what effect Raegan's gender identity might have had on their application process if Raegan had been out beforehand. However, given the perceptions of a noninclusive ORL staff, and the negative experiences many participants had while living in the residence halls, it is reasonable to suggest that trans* students may not be interested in living in the halls longer than they need to, let alone apply for, be selected, or serve in leadership roles in the ORL. This reality, then, has drastic and powerful implications for residence life staff, which I have written about elsewhere (Nicolazzo & Marine, 2015) and discuss further in Chapter 8.

# 6

# THE (TIRING) LABOR OF PRACTICING
# TRANS* GENDERS

*Diversity work can involve an experience of hesitation, of not knowing what to do in these situations. There is a labor in having to respond to a situation that others are protected from, a situation that does not come up for those whose residence is assumed.*

(Ahmed, 2012, pp. 176–177)

Although Ahmed (2012) was writing specifically about diversity practitioners in higher education, there is precedence for thinking about trans* students needing to take on the work of educating others about gender identity. For example, during the welcome speech made by CU's chief diversity officer (CDO) at The Center's fall welcome event, I made the following reflections in my field notes:

> In talking with Tristan, I mentioned to him that at The Center Meet and Greet, the Interim Chief Diversity Officer on campus thanked the queer students for being on campus, because we "teach people about difference," and "help other people learn," and "educate students" (*as if that is our job*) [emphasis added] (September 18, 2013).

Here, the CDO linked students' trans* and queer identities with a form of labor, namely, educating the heterosexual and cisgender campus population on issues related to gender and sexuality. Referring to Ahmed's words, the CDO was suggesting that we, as trans* and queer people, were needed to undertake the labor of responding to a situation (e.g., education on diverse genders and sexualities) that others (i.e., heterosexual and cisgender people) were protected from. Furthermore, the protection heterosexual and cisgender people enjoyed was based on the false assumption that gender was so normalized and so institutionalized that it ceased to exist to them. In other

107

words, the cultural embeddedness of the gender binary discourse, along with the reality of compulsory heterogenderism, had so cemented normalized binary understandings of gender that to practice gender differently was itself a form of labor. As Ahmed (2012) stated, "When things become institutionalized, they recede. To institutionalize *x* is for *x* to become routine or ordinary such that *x* becomes part of the background for those who are part of an institution" (p. 21). Therefore, if one understands *x* to signify gender, then the institutionalization of gender—via the cultural realities of the gender binary discourse and compulsory heterogenderism—means that gender itself recedes into the background and, as a result, is unimportant or irrelevant. This seeming unimportance, however, is incongruent with the effects of the gender binary discourse and compulsory heterogenderism. Moreover, it has been up to trans* people to do the work of dragging gender out from the background, pulling it out from the shadows and back into the light.

The presumption that trans* people must teach others about gender connects to the current wave of neoliberalism coursing through U.S. educational contexts (e.g., Giroux, 2015). According to neoliberal logic, education, which was once viewed as a public good, is turned into a private and individual commodity (Giroux & Searls Giroux, 2004; Harvey, 2007a, 2007b). The fact that neoliberalism has become an underlying logic that postsecondary education operates from is widely known and discussed by various scholars (e.g., Giroux, 2015; Giroux & Searls Giroux, 2004; Tuchman, 2009). However, the connection between neoliberalism as an ideology and its press on those with diverse sexualities and genders is less discussed (Elia & Yep, 2012). Discussing this very connection, Elia and Yep wrote, "Identity-based production, distribution, and consumption—as products of consumer culture—have increased exponentially in an ever-expanding neoliberal economy" (p. 882). Thus, the commodification of diverse genders and sexualities as something to be discussed, dissected, distributed, and understood suggests that one's very identity is imbued with the potential to be traded, sold, or purchased like any other good. In other words, the CDO's suggestion that trans* people should teach others about gender was based on the commodification of diverse genders as something one could acquire through participating in a training, educational session, in-service, or class experience. In this case, one's own identity (a some*one*) is turned into a some*thing* that others can gain, pass along, or overlook. In other words, trans* genders are turned into objects of curiosity (Pusch, 2005) and educational sessions that offices, departments, and organizations could contract out to educate their staffs about diverse genders. Furthermore, the onus of doing such gender-based work, of pulling gender out from the shadows either by practicing or by educating others about trans* genders, was squarely placed on trans* members of the CU campus community. This burden, itself connected to the omnipresence of neoliberalism in education, was often overwhelming for participants, many of whom expressed feeling tired, worn out, or exhausted from practicing or educating others about trans* genders.

Raegan provided an example of the exhaustion brought about by constantly having to confront the gender binary discourse on campus. When they talked about being misgendered, they stated, "Sometimes, I'm so emotionally exhausted from all of this, I just don't want to say anything. It's like, literally, if I say something, I'm gonna burst into tears." For Raegan, it was the consistent and constant misgendering they faced that wore them down emotionally. Although these incidents were not always malicious in intent, the impact was overwhelmingly negative for Raegan. BC shared similar feelings of fatigue from confronting the gender binary discourse and compulsory heterogenderism on campus, suggesting that one of the ways she dealt with these cultural realities was by detaching and "reading, playing video games, [and smoking] pot a little bit."

Whereas Raegan and BC mentioned feeling exhausted by confronting external trans* oppression at CU, Adem felt a different type of exhaustion connected to their own intrapersonal process of coming to understand their trans* identity. In particular, Adem talked about not knowing how to consolidate their feminist identity with their emerging trans* identity. In trying to work through the complexity they felt, Adem stated,

> I know there is a lot of tension between feminism and the transgender community, especially with the Michigan Womyn's Festival and all that. . . . [pause] . . . And I don't know how well I would be able to straddle that tension. And I wouldn't want to have to sacrifice one part of myself for another, so . . . I think it's definitely all intertwined, and it's weird to say that, "Okay, well, feminism and transgender issues are totally connected," because at the most obvious surface level, there is a disconnect. Especially if you are female-to-male transgender, because you are like, "Well, this is a feminist movement, this is for women and females," and you are not [a woman]. Even if you were at one point, you are not anymore. And I think a lot of people forget that, yes, maybe, and I didn't feel comfortable identifying as [a woman], but at the same time, I understand what it's like, I've been through it, I've dealt with it, I've seen the things that you're talking about and I can give evidence of them existing even in today's society. And so, I think it's kind of encouraged me to stay in an in-between space.

This statement came at the end of a long conversation in which Adem shared deep anxieties about what it may mean if they identified openly as trans* and how they felt that some would question their identity as a feminist, which was also a salient identity for them. After Adem finished, there was a pause, and I reflected, "That's a lot." "Yeah," Adem said, "it's been a very exhausting semester so far." Thus, Adem's exhaustion was less about confronting trans\* oppression on campus and more about trying to articulate their own sense of self as a trans\* person.

The tiredness participants experienced from the labor of addressing gender, which Henderson (2014) termed *bringing up gender*, made some participants state they did not want to do any education about gender on campus. Moreover, when participants did decide to educate others by bringing up gender, they did so only under certain conditions or with certain people. These choices about whether, when, how, and with whom to bring up gender were a mode of self-care and self-protection. In other words, participants brought up gender in situations that allowed them to practice resilience. Conversely, participants often chose not to bring up gender in situations where they were likely to be dismissed or overlooked, or with people who did not have a vested interest in them as individuals. By not bringing up gender, they were able to save their energy for people and situations that helped them feel refreshed, rejuvenated, and able to cope with the cultural realities of gender binary discourse and compulsory heterogenderism they experienced at CU. Therefore, participants' choices on whether to bring up gender were often a reflection of how best they could practice resilience in that situation and remain successful at CU.

The aforementioned sanguine reading of participants' decisions to bring up gender or not belies another more insidious reading. Specifically, the overwhelming cultural press of gender binary discourse and compulsory heterogenderism turned some participants into "docile bodies" (Foucault, 1975/1995, p. 138) who, by not bringing up gender, allowed the status quo to be maintained. As Foucault wrote, "Discipline produces subjected and practised [*sic*] bodies, 'docile bodies.' Discipline increases the forces of the body (in economic terms of utility) and diminishes these same forces (in political terms of obedience)" (p. 138). In other words, participants were disciplined via the cultural realities of gender binary discourse and compulsory heterogenderism to obey and comply with the norms of gender rather than resist and push back. Additionally, trans\* people were trained to be docile for the utilitarian service of others, reinforcing how neoliberalism functioned as a way to commodify trans\* identities as something to be bought, sold, and traded. By not bringing up gender, the study participants became complicit in furthering gender binary discourse and compulsory heterogenderism.

This, however, is not to say the participants are to blame for their docility. Indeed, Foucault (1975/1995) suggested that a number of social institutions—and he specifically named education—encouraged all community members to be docile in the face of cultural norms and expectations. Thus, participants' lack of bringing up gender is one way of how cultural norms and privileges (e.g., trans* oppression) are maintained through a variety of modes (e.g., gender binary discourse, compulsory heterogenderism) that evoke a sense of tiredness and, thus, promote inaction. Although such inaction could very well be a practice of resilience, it is also undoubtedly a practice of compliance with overarching systems of privilege and power, thereby reinscribing the norm and allowing trans* oppression to persist.

For example, Kade talked about times when he would cycle in and out of openly resisting the gender binary discourse on campus. He talked about doing this by being out as trans* and suggested that at times being out was a tiring experience. During our second interview, he said,

> I cycle through periods in my life where I change the level of outness I have. Sometimes I'm like, "Yeah, I want to be super out, and be a voice for the [trans*] community or a part of the community [at CU]," and I think that's really important. And then I have some bad experiences, or it just gets to be too much, [and I get] tired of being a spokesperson.

Kade made choices about when to bring up gender, which he did by disclosing his trans* identity in public settings on campus such as classrooms. His decision-making was largely influenced by what would allow him to practice resilience; if he felt he could be out in a given situation, and that by being out he would be able to successfully resist gender binary discourse or compulsory heterogenderism, he would disclose his trans* identity. However, being out and, in his words, "being a spokesperson" for the trans* community got to be tiring. At these times, Kade retreated and did not come out as trans*. Not bringing up gender in these situations was itself a practice of resilience for Kade, allowing him to navigate campus successfully. However, it also meant that Kade was complicit in the persistence of gender binary discourse and compulsory heterogenderism.

Some might say that my implying that the study participants were complicit in the discourses and overarching systems of inequity that allowed trans* oppression to persist at CU is unfair, that suggesting that trans* participants helped to further the systemic oppression that harmed them is somehow saying they are the makers of their own negative destiny. However, it bears repeating that Foucault (1976/1990, 1975/1995) discussed one's inescapability from the institutions that turned all citizens into docile bodies. Therefore, it is less a matter of fairness and more a matter of reality that everyone complies with and resists the cultural norms that regulate life chances (Spade, 2015). These participants were no different, and we all—myself included—resist and comply with gender binary discourse and compulsory heterogenderism present in educational contexts.

An individual's compliance or resistance is mediated by various factors. For example, at one point, I was misgendered by a Black undergraduate student in a group setting. Although she knew my pronouns, I paused in correcting her. I worried that our different educational backgrounds (i.e., I was pursuing an advanced degree, and she was pursuing her bachelor's degree), racial identities (i.e., my Whiteness and her Blackness), and gender identities (i.e., my gender nonconformity and her cisgender identity) may have a negative impact if I were to correct her on my pronouns. Put another way, I was worried what it may look and feel like to her as a Black cisgender woman to be corrected by a White gender-nonconforming person, whom she has positioned as a man because of her misuse of pronouns when referring to me. I worried that my correcting her would position me as angry, which for me was reminiscent of how many Black women and women of color are continually positioned when they stand up for themselves (e.g., Ahmed, 2010; Patton & Catching, 2009). I worried that my educational level might suggest that correcting her incorrect use of pronouns when referring to me was theoretical in nature rather than something I experienced as a microaggression. I was also worried that because she saw me as a man—no matter how incorrect this was—my correcting her would be seen as a form of "mansplaining" (Rothman, 2012). For these reasons, I chose not to correct her, nor did anyone else in the group. Although I had reasons for not bringing up gender in that situation, I myself was complicit in allowing the gender binary discourse to persist by allowing the student to believe (and promote) the notion that there were two distinct gender categories that people must fit into. Therefore, even though it is difficult to uncover the ways that we as trans* people are complicit in furthering trans* oppression, it is an important reminder of the reality that we have agency in making choices on whether to resist gender norms and that our (in)actions come with consequences.

## Departure: Education

As discussed previously, participants felt compelled to educate others at CU about gender. However, participants' doing the educating rarely came without conditions. For example, Micah and Jackson talked about the importance of engaging in educational conversations with cisgender peers only if those individuals showed an investment in them as trans* people. In holding to this condition, Micah and Jackson were resisting the pejorative notion that trans* people are strange, exotic, abnormal, or objects of curiosity (Nicolazzo, 2014a; Serano, 2007, 2013). For example, Micah stated emphatically, "I'm not a teacher; I'm not gonna educate [people] about everything." When asked if there were times at which she would engage in educating others, Micah said,

> I will educate you if you are genuinely open-minded about it. . . . I'm okay with stepping out of my bounds and educating that way. But, if you're just blissfully ignorant, I could care less about educating you, because I don't want [it] to be a waste of breath. That's just what it is.

For Micah to engage in conversations about trans* identities, others needed to show an investment beyond mere curiosity. The development of this condition for engaging in education was likely informed by the many instances of cisgender individuals objectifying hir and other trans* students. For example, on numerous occasions during our 18 months together, cisgender students would visit the TransActions meetings in which Micah was a regular participant. The cisgender individuals would say they were visiting because they needed to do a class project focused on a marginalized student population and they wanted to learn about trans* people. Without exception, these people would never come back to any other meetings, and conversation when they were there was stifled, as if the trans* members of the group, including Micah, were wary of the new cisgender participant.

Jackson talked about one of the conditions for participating in education about gender identities:

> In terms of explaining myself I just don't [laughs]. I don't really feel the need, [especially when] it's just like, "Oh, I want to find out if that's a dude or not," you know? If they are coming at me from a different way than that, then I would definitely be really accommodating. But aside from that, I don't really feel the need.

Jackson puts into words the phenomenon of cisgender people trying to figure them out. This sort of experience is certainly not new, as the trope of trans* people being deceptive or trying to fool people about our genders has a long and unfortunate tradition (e.g., Halberstam, 2005; Nicolazzo, 2014a; Serano, 2007, 2013). In fact, this is the same illogical thinking cisgender individuals use with the notion of *trans*panic* to defend the murder of trans* individuals (e.g., Between the Lines Staff, 2014).

Raegan discussed their being more comfortable addressing and correcting individuals rather than groups. Raegan also mentioned they had ceased
talking with people as much over the past year, saying, "I get really overwhelmed with just so many thoughts and so many things that I have to do
on a daily basis," including the constant need to educate people on their
trans* identity. Raegan further explained their hesitancy to educate others,
stating,

> When it's just me and another person, I'm more comfortable being like,
> "No, not she, they." But when [I'm] in a group of people . . . it's like we're
> all laughing about something, having a good time, everybody's laughing,
> and [when] somebody [refers] to me as she, I'm like, "God." . . . And I'm
> like, I want to correct this person, but if I really corrected people as often
> as I would like, it would be, like, every five minutes. So, and I wouldn't
> mind doing it, [but] I guess my fear [is] sounding repetitive and sounding
> particular, you know what I mean? Like sounding petty and nitpicky.

Raegan felt more comfortable addressing microaggressions as learning opportunities when they were in one-on-one situations. Raegan's comment aligns
with those of others who have written about the complexity of addressing
gender misidentification in group settings (Spade, 2010). It also provides
further context for why Raegan had withdrawn from much social interac-
tion throughout the past year and asked Ginnie to assist with correcting
others when they were misgendered in public venues. Adem, Micah, and
Silvia also discussed being burned out from doing trans*-related education
at CU, which shows that being asked to educate others was not an isolated
experience. Furthermore, the year after our study concluded, two of the three
(Adem and Silvia) ceased all leadership positions; Adem stopped attending
CU the last semester of the study, and Silvia traveled abroad to focus on
coursework. Although Micah remained involved in educational organizations, they did so reluctantly and as a general member rather than a main
leader. Thus, Raegan's comment also stands as a potential sign of danger,
as student involvement and community building—the very opportunities
Raegan, Adem, Silvia, and Micah had withdrawn from over our last year
working together—have consistently been shown to increase student success
in college (e.g., Astin, 1993; Kuh, Hu, & Vesper, 2000; Renn, 2007).

However, Raegan's comment also reveals something that is perhaps more
frustrating. Raegan mentioned not wanting to correct people because of
potentially being perceived as "nitpicky," "repetitive," or "particular," all of
which were conveyed as being pejorative. Although Raegan was quick to
identify that their feelings were likely a result of their gender socialization,
they also reflect neoliberalism in that Raegan was made to feel as though they

should be able to get over or rise above such incidents without the need for supposed special treatment. In particular, Raegan's experiences reflect their neoliberal context by suggesting everyone was on equal footing and, as a result, Raegan's inability to get over such incidents indicated that something in them was lacking. In other words, Raegan was made to feel as if they were asking for special attention and as if they were a nuisance for asking for their human dignity as trans* to be recognized by others by using their proper pronouns. Under neoliberal logic, Raegan should not have needed such supposed special treatment as they should have been able to push through on their own. In light of the illogical assumptions of neoliberalism and the burden such a perspective placed on Raegan and other trans* participants, having to confront these experiences on a regular basis was exhausting for Raegan. In addition, this exhaustion also led Raegan to not address microaggressions in certain contexts and to recede from public settings, both of which could have a negative impact on trans* students' ability to remain resilient.

## Departure: (In)visibility

Although some participants wanted to see more trans* representation at CU on the student, faculty, and staff levels, the sentiment was far from universal. Furthermore, participants had different views of what trans* representation may look like, mentioning the diversity of trans* communities, and for some, the desire to resist trans* normativity or the notion of a unified and stable understanding of who is trans* (Boldly Go, 2013; Jourian, Simmons, & Devaney, 2015). For example, Raegan said,

> If I'm at The Sandwich Depot, or places like that [on campus], it matters to me [to see other nonbinary people]. I may never meet this person in real life, I may not ever interact with them, but if I know that they're there, it makes me feel better. . . . I'm kinda biased [chuckles].

Raegan's supposed "bias" toward seeing other nonbinary people on campus makes sense given their own identity as nonbinary. It makes further sense given Raegan's desire to reclaim the notion of passing as a process of being read by others as being neither a man nor woman. In fact, Raegan stated, "My ideal setting for passing is people not knowing my gender." Thus, it makes good sense that seeing other people who are similarly playful with their gender expression would increase their comfort. This was much the same for BC, who said her ultimate desire was to "change [her] appearance daily; real butch to real femme, and then androgynous, and always make people question."

However, as previously suggested, the politics of trans\* visibility were far from settled. Recalling Kade's profound feeling of loss of community because of his passing as a man, it is hard to know just what heightened trans\* visibility would look like. Kade discussed being trans\* but not being perceived as trans\* because of his socially intelligible masculine gender expression. In this sense, one might understand Kade as being trans\* but not feeling trans\* enough because of not being read as trans\* by other students, faculty, and staff at CU. I recorded something similar in my field notes at the start of my second semester at CU:

> I am intrigued by the fact that I have no clue who may be a potential participant in my study! . . . There are not obvious physical indicators (or not necessarily anyway) that "mark" trans\* students. Even those markers that may exist (e.g., "boys" wearing nail polish, "women" dressed in a butch way) does [sic] not always translate to someone's identifying as trans\*. This *invisibility* could be both challenging *and* wonderful. . . . This also makes me think about all the assumptions *I make* about bodies, expressions, and identities. For example, I see many bodies around me, all of which I immediately ascribe particular sex and gender designations. . . . Maybe this means sex/gender designations say as much (or more) about the one designating them as about those on whom they are being designated (August 28, 2013).

Although Kade and I would have preferred to know there were more trans\* people at CU—Kade spoke at length about the importance of trans\* community, which I discuss in the next chapter—the contestation was over what *(in)visibility* meant. In other words, the questions Kade and I were asking related to assumptions we were making when we said there was a lack of trans\* visibility on campus. Were we privileging nonbinary and openly disruptive expressions of gender? How might this privileging dismiss those who did not feel safe, comfortable, or interested in expressing their trans\*ness in this way?

Recalling Micah and Silvia's comments about the community effects of compulsory heterogenderism in Black groups and spaces on campus provides yet another way to think through the implications of trans\* (in)visibility. Reflecting on the departure of race discussed in Chapter 4, trans\* (in)visibility for Micah and Silvia was influenced by community-sustained compulsory heterogenderism. Simply put, Micah and Silvia were not recognized as trans\* not because of White supremacy but because of the conflation of gender and sexuality that make up compulsory heterogenderism. In this sense, although I as a White researcher could understand the desire for increased trans\* visibility as furthering White supremacy, my suggesting this also serves to recenter Whiteness when discussing trans* visibility in ways that are incongruent with the data, particularly for the Black participants of the study.

Adem pointed out yet another nuance in the ideal of having increased trans* visibility. In our second interview, they stated,

> I would definitely like to see more [of a trans*] presence. I would like to see that in the hiring practices. That would give me hope for the future, but at the same time, I feel like that automatically pigeonholes [me]. . . . Like, if there's a trans*-identified professor in computer sciences and there's me, and someone happens to know both of us, or somehow we end up connect[ing]—like, it's because of that [their shared trans* identity]. I don't know, I feel like it narrows my scope of possibilities [for meeting people].

Although Adem recognized their desire for trans* inclusion to be embedded in institutional practices like the hiring process, at the same time they also suggested it may serve to limit them and, by extension, other trans* students. Specifically, Adem felt that increased visibility for trans* people may mean their cisgender peers would only encourage them to interact with fellow trans* people. Again, this is a form of identity commodification reflective of the neoliberal context in which Adem and all the study participants, including myself, found ourselves. By turning our identities into something to be seen, which could be a potential by-product of increased trans* visibility, Adem worried their lives would be limited by others regulating whom they could befriend and with whom they could associate. In this sense, Adem's comment reflects my field notes in which I suggested trans* invisibility could prove to be challenging and liberating.

It is worth further emphasis that neither the participants nor I suggested that an increase of trans* students, faculty, or staff would be a de facto bad phenomenon. In fact, as Adem's previous extended comment suggests, participants had an acute awareness that in terms of structural diversity alone, increased representation and visibility for trans* people at CU was incredibly important. Participants and I were steadfastly in agreement on this particular point. However, at stake for us was what such representation and visibility meant in relation to the wide diversity among trans* communities. Thus, it was not a matter of our wanting there to be more trans* people at CU but of the assumptions we made about who counted as trans*. In other words, when we admitted we desired increased trans* visibility, we were suggesting there was a lack of people we would identify as trans*. Thus, we all had a vision of what trans* people looked like and, by extension, did not look like.

This complexity is particularly painful to discuss, as it underscores the ways the participants and I have been socialized to buy into the very concept that continues to harm us as trans* people, namely, notions of not being trans* enough. For example, when participants and I shared our desires for increased trans* visibility, we were implicitly suggesting there was a particular way to embody trans*ness. This, however, defies the liberatory values of proliferating possibilities for how trans* people always already resist normative assumptions about what it means to look, be, or practice trans* genders. Going back to the various ways systemic oppression encourages docility, it is clear that the participants and I were complicit with furthering trans* normativity at the very same time that we sought to disrupt and resist its deleterious assumptions.

Therefore, although structural diversity—and thus an increase of visible trans* bodies—continues to be necessary, it is by no means sufficient to recognize the multiplicity of trans* lives. In fact, stopping at mere structural diversity may reify various other forms of systemic oppression (e.g., racism, classism, ableism) by suggesting there is a particular way trans* people should show up on campus to be counted as visibly trans*. Applying this concept to educational praxis, one can see how initiatives like capturing aspiring students' gender identities via formal measures such as questions on college applications (Jaschik, 2014) could unwittingly further specific visions of who is seen as trans* and, thus, reify various intersecting systems of oppression. I write about this further in Chapter 8 when I discuss the need for educators to move beyond best practices.

## Departure: Multiple Forms of Exhaustion

Although multiple participants talked about the tiring aspect of bringing up gender (Henderson, 2014), the form that tiredness took was not uniform. Some participants (e.g., Kade, Micah, Raegan, and BC) discussed a mental fatigue with educating others about gender. This mental fatigue then caused different effects for each participant. For example, during our last formal interview, Micah described himself as being "a lot more snappy" than usual, explaining that she thought it was "specifically being fed up with certain situations," such as bringing up gender. Micah then went on to discuss her brother, who had particularly frustrated her regarding issues related to gender identity and expression. Although they loved each other, Micah felt his brother did not allow her to identify and express their gender how ze wanted.

He's very stuck on gender roles and things like that . . . and I'm just like, "That's not me." Personally, I don't identify with either . . . and sometimes I don't think he gets that. . . . He's very binary. . . . I feel like he thinks of gender as just . . . the sex you're assigned at birth. . . . And I'm just like, "It's a lot more mental to me than physical."

Micah's feeling snappy with her brother had spilled into other areas of her life. Although she originally suggested the feeling she had was "just senioritis," as he began talking, Micah began to express that hir tiredness was a direct result of the constant need to bring up gender with people and in situations where his trans* identity was not being recognized or respected.

Raegan also felt a similar mental exhaustion when they had to educate others constantly about gender. They described the frustration of having to correct people on their incorrect use of pronouns. Going back to a previously quoted comment from Raegan, they said, "Sometimes I'm so emotionally exhausted from all of this . . . I don't want to say anything. It's like, literally, if I say something, I'm gonna burst into tears." Although Raegan had particular strategies for counteracting the exhaustion of having to bring up gender, most notably working with Ginnie to have her confront issues when they were together, the frustration and exhaustion was still palpable for Raegan. Moreover, because Ginnie and Raegan were not always together, it was highly likely that Raegan often encountered situations in which they were alone and needed to make a choice about whether to bring up gender.

Kade and BC also discussed the emotionally exhaustive element of constantly having to bring up gender, particularly in the classroom. They both encountered multiple situations in which incorrect or negative representations of trans* people were discussed in class. BC described one particularly terrible incident, telling me, "I've heard death threats or similar things like that [in classroom spaces, which] made me feel shitty." Similarly, Kade shared stories of teachers laughing at jokes students had made during classes about intersex individuals and one particular professor who continued to convey incorrect and negative information about trans* people to Kade's entire class. When Kade attempted to bring this up with the instructor, he was dismissed by the professor, and the incorrect information was not addressed adequately with the rest of the class. Kade described his experiences in these classroom spaces as conflicted, stating, "I'm not really feeling this external threat anymore now that I'm read as male. But internally, it's still not great knowing people think these negative things about your identity."

The exhaustion BC and Kade felt from the microaggressions, threats of violence, and the persistent sharing of inaccurate information regarding trans* individuals in classrooms was made all the more difficult given the imbalance of power between instructors and students. Kade described this in stating, "They [students] can say anything. But the teacher has the ultimate power to step in and say, 'No, actually . . . [trails off].'" Although Kade mentioned having several faculty members who would correct inaccuracies about trans* people, BC's experience was far different, leading her to change majors entirely. Thus, the exhaustion felt by BC was more than a particular annoyance in that it reoriented her future career possibilities and aspirations. Furthermore, it is important to remember that BC decided to leave CU after our first semester working together. It would be misleading to say that leaving CU was a direct result of her negative classroom experiences. However, given their persistence and gravity, it is hard to deny that these experiences had an impact on BC's decision. At the very least, BC's negative classroom experiences did little to encourage her to stay enrolled. In fact, when BC came back to CU, she had switched her major to political science, thus adding more weight to the claim that her negative classroom experiences as an economics major contributed to reorienting her future academic and career aspirations.

Conversely, Silvia described her tiredness as physical. In our last formal interview, Silvia linked her fatigue regarding gender to the tiredness she felt in her body because of fibromyalgia: "This semester already dealing with fatigue physically, I just can't fight two fatigue battles right now, you know? I have to focus on not feeling tired all the time. Like, just in my body." Here again, one can see a link between Silvia's gender identity and her experiences as a student with disabilities. In particular, the emotional fatigue of bringing up gender that Kade, BC, Micah, and Raegan discussed was transformed into an embodied exhaustion for Silvia. Moreover, Silvia noted that she was unable to "fight two fatigue battles" at the same time and that she had "to focus on not feeling tired all the time . . . in [her] body." This statement reveals how Silvia did not have the energy (physical and otherwise) to bring up gender because of the already present fatigue from her multiple disabilities. Additionally, Silvia's description of the confluence of multiple forms of exhaustion illustrates the importance of addressing the intersections of gender and disability identities. In particular, because there were no spaces at CU that accommodated this specific intersection of identities, Silvia felt she had nowhere she could go and no one to whom she could turn to help her make sense of her identities as an agender student with disabilities. Thus, Silvia's remark not only stands as an important reminder of the embodied nature of the exhaustion that bringing up gender induces but also shows the importance of addressing multiple intersections of identities throughout educational praxis. Had this been the case at CU, Silvia would likely still have felt exhausted, but she may also have had an outlet for her exhaustion, allowing her to begin to process and make meaning of her experiences as an agender student with disabilities rather than feeling the need to choose which form of fatigue she had to focus on. In other words, having this outlet at CU would have provided a venue for Silvia to practice resilience that was otherwise not possible.

# 7

# A CONSTELLATION OF KINSHIP NETWORKS

The last set of arrival and departures revolves around notions of kinship networks. Although the phrase itself may evoke images of blood relatives or family of origin, many scholars have extended notions of kinship beyond this limited understanding. In particular, Rubin (2011) noted that anthropologists have long been exploring kinship as a phenomenon that transcends one's bloodline: "A kinship system is not a list of biological relatives. It is a system of categories and statuses which often contradict actual genetic relationships. There are dozens of examples in which socially defined kinship statuses take precedence over biology" (p. 41). Weston (1991) put this nonbiological notion of kinship to work in gay and lesbian populations, suggesting that "gone are the days when embracing a lesbian or gay identity seemed to require a renunciation of kinship" (pp. 40–41). Weston's ethnographic study stands as one of the first empirical analyses of the creation and maintenance of kinship networks among queer populations, specifically the gay and lesbian communities in San Francisco during the late 1980s. Although Weston's study did not explicitly include trans* people, my study participants and I found that the notion of kinship, and the development and maintenance of kinship networks, was an important factor for successfully navigating the gender-dichotomous college environment. This development is unique in its own right as it is the first study in the field of higher education to specifically explore notions of community, coalition, and kinship-building exclusively with trans* students. To date, only one other article has been written that focuses on notions of trans* kinship as a strategy for promoting college student success (Nicolazzo, Pitcher, Renn, & Woodford, in press). Furthermore, although Carmel, Hopwood, and dickey (2014) wrote, "Those of us [trans* people] who build connections to supportive community do better" (p. 325), they neither cited literature to support this claim nor explained what they meant by the phrase "do better." Therefore, this chapter regarding trans* kinship-building could be foundational when thinking about how trans* students build, maintain, and leverage kinship networks to navigate campuses that remain far-from-welcoming spaces for them.

For the purposes of this book, a kinship network is a close group of peers who

- recognized and honored participants' gender identities, expressions, or embodiments;
- provided a refuge from the cultural realities of gender binary discourse and compulsory heterogenderism on campus; and
- acted as a potential site for participants to use to resist or push back against systemic trans* oppression if they chose.

Additionally, participants' kinship networks were not exclusively trans*. Although some participants talked about the importance of engaging in trans*-only spaces, this was not a prerequisite for the development and maintenance of a kinship network. Participants also spoke about interacting with multiple kinship networks. Therefore, this book expands on Weston's (1991) discussion of kinship from a singular perspective, or of gay and lesbian people developing one unified family of choice rather than multiple kinship networks.

The kinship networks of the trans* participants did not always overlap with each other. Some networks were mutually exclusive, meaning there was no overlap of individuals or goals from one group to the next. For example, Adem spoke about creating a kinship network in the women's and gender studies department, specifically among graduate students. This group operated separately from TransActions, which Adem was also a member of for the first semester of our work together. The two networks had completely different purposes and goals; the departmental group was academic and social in nature, whereas TransActions was activist-focused and aimed at developing campuswide educational programming. Many of these kinship networks were also associated with particular locations on and off campus. Therefore, one might imagine these networks as sites on a map with participants' movement in and among these networks creating a constellation of relational spaces where they could retreat for temporary respite from the cultural regulation of gender.

Participants often spoke of the kinship networks they created as "queer bubbles." For example, Jackson stated, "There's a queer bubble, and I'm all up [in it]." Similarly, BC spoke about several "queer spheres" where she felt comfortable and safe, naming "TransActions, Pride to a certain extent, and The Center" as three of those spheres. During our second interview, Adem provided perhaps the most cogent statement on their need for, and subsequent development of, multiple kinship networks:

> I joke around a lot about being in a queer community and, like, my little bubble. But at the same time, I think I need to expand that. And I am not necessarily [suggesting] expanding it beyond a queer bubble, because I am definitely still in a queer bubble, but it's just not the rainbow room.

Adem is suggesting the need to expand their queer bubble beyond the *rainbow room*, a term they used to refer to The Center. Adem was careful to point out that although they still wanted to create queer-only spaces, they needed more spaces than The Center, where they had been spending the bulk of their time. Therefore, one can see that queer-only groups were important spaces where Adem could retreat and avoid the effects of gender binary discourse on campus while also demonstrating the need for more than one space where Adem could go to find solace and comfort.

Participants varied in how they made sense of and used their kinship networks. For example, some participants used them as social sites where they found a safe haven from the cultural regulation of gender via gender binary discourse and compulsory heterogenderism. For example, Megan discussed her decision to seek out a trans* community group in Stockdale: "The main reason why I went was to . . . meet other transgendered [*sic*] people and make friends." Megan also explained wanting social spaces as a reason for curtailing her involvement with TransActions, stating, "They do have social meetings every now and then, but at the same time, it feels like it's more about activism than socialization." For Megan, who had spent most of her youth in isolation, an important aspect of developing a sense of who she was as a trans* woman was meeting and socializing with other trans* people. She was not interested in gender-based activism but was mostly looking to create friendships and have fun with other trans* people to increase her own comfort with her trans* identity.

Conversely, Kade spoke about kinship networks as sites for developing deep and meaningful relationships, participating in activism, and even finding potential people to date. Kade talked about the strong bond he felt with other trans* people, stating, "I will see people on campus who I think might be gender nonconforming in some way, and I feel this sense of community, and almost familial ties with them, because we have such a small community." By using the word *familial*, Kade was emphasizing the importance of connecting with other people who transgressed gender. More than just wanting to develop social friendships, as Megan had sought to do, Kade felt a deep sense of connection with other trans* people, and his investment in these connections underscored his desire to participate in kinship networks alongside other trans* and queer people.

Kade also saw his kinship networks as fertile sites for activism and resisting cultural gender norms as well as developing romantic relationships. During our second interview, Kade shared several stories about going on dates with gay men the previous year. These experiences all turned negative when he disclosed his trans* identity, making him wonder if he should be thinking differently about where to find people to date. Since those negative experiences, however, Kade had begun dating Brin, who identified as genderqueer and whom he met through one of the off-campus kinship networks he was a part of. Speaking about the dynamics of dating within his kinship networks, Kade stated,

> It's always more comfortable dating someone in the community. I definitely don't even feel like I have to behave in any specific way. . . . I would say it's more likely that I'm gonna be happier with someone in the community and so I tend to date them more often, cuz I don't have to deal with all this other stuff. You know, I spent a good bit of time going on dates with a lot of cis gay men on campus. . . . But I really just got really sick of the transphobia and having to come out and having to explain.

Thus, by seeking potential romantic partners from within his kinship networks, Kade was able to avoid the transphobia that had marred some of his earlier dating experiences. He was also able to connect with people he did not have to educate or worry about negotiating their feelings or reactions to his trans* masculine identity. In this sense, Kade's shift to dating within his kinship networks also highlights a practice of resilience for him, as it allowed him to navigate finding partners successfully rather than deal with the triggering and frustrating incidents that occurred when he dated outside his kinship networks.

It is also worth noting that kinship networks were neither equally comfortable for participants nor consistently comfortable across each particular participant's time at CU. Returning to Adem's earlier comments about expanding their queer bubble, I witnessed a noticeable shift in where Adem spent their time during our second semester together. Whereas Adem had spent almost all their free time on campus in The Center our first semester working alongside one another, they hardly spent any time there the following semester. Although some of this was admittedly because of a new partner Adem had begun dating, it was also a result of Adem's discomfort with being in the space as much as they had been:

Last semester I didn't really have anybody outside of The Center. So I would go in and talk to Tristan and Silvia and Janelle and that would be it. And that was fine. But I think that once I got involved in more student groups and met more people . . . I needed and I wanted a little bit more, so I went out and got it. And at the same time, I feel kind of . . . not uncomfortable being in The Center as often as I was, but weird about it. . . . Now I have people in my program that I like a lot, which I have never had before.

Whereas Adem had originally relied on The Center as a locus of support and developing friendships, they had since branched out and made kinship networks through their academic coursework. As a result, Adem became uncomfortable with how often they had been in The Center, causing a shift in their behavior. Similarly, BC's earlier comment about Pride being a comfortable space to be "to a certain extent" illustrates the inconsistency of particular kinship networks. In other words, although BC thought it was important to attend Pride meetings, and she sometimes felt comfortable doing so, she was only comfortable to a certain extent, signaling there were other times in which she was uncomfortable.

Furthermore, although some participants viewed some kinship networks as comfortable, other participants viewed these same spaces as uncomfortable and avoided them. Expanding on the example regarding Pride, although BC tried to attend meetings on a regular basis, several other participants explicitly stated they did not attend Pride meetings primarily because of what they viewed as the group's dismissive attitude toward trans* people and their issues. Participants' negative sentiments about Pride were so strong that many of them would laugh or make jokes about Pride when it came up in conversation, perhaps as a way to practice resilience in relation to the previous hurts they had experienced. Adem even went so far as to publicly mock Pride, posting a photo on one of their social media accounts of them making a face with a caption that read, "When someone says 'my friend in Pride,'" denoting Adem's disdain for Pride and those who were members of the organization (Figure 7.1).

Similarly, participants had different perceptions of spaces like The Center or groups like TransActions. For example, although The Center was an important space to cultivate kinship networks for some participants (e.g., Micah and BC), other participants distanced themselves from it. As previously discussed, Derek felt The Center was not a welcoming space for trans* people because staff members were not doing enough to promote trans* inclusion in the office. Similarly, Raegan discussed not spending much time in The Center during our interview:

My freshman year I fucked around a lot. I did a lot of just sleeping around. And it's awkward now. I'm not embarrassed by it. I'm totally okay with it . . . and I don't regret what I did. But it's really awkward for me.

Thus, contrary to many participants' experiences of The Center as a comfortable space to develop kinship networks, Raegan had a drastically different experience. Furthermore, it is worth mentioning that Raegan's lack of interest in viewing The Center as a site for developing and maintaining kinship networks is a result of previous romantic relationships with people who frequented the space. This is in contrast to Kade's comment that he preferred dating within his kinship networks. However, both Kade and Raegan were in significant committed relationships during our study, so their experiences provide multiple (conflicting) strategies of dating and finding romantic partners as a way to practice resilience.

**Figure 7.1**. Adem's face.

## Departure: Virtual Kinship Networks

Although the development of kinship networks occurred in physical places (e.g., The Center, TransActions, local Stockdale areas), a number of participants also talked about the importance of virtual spaces in cultivating and maintaining community. For example, in our first interview, Jackson stated, "I exist primarily on the Internet, you know? That's pretty much my hometown." Jackson then proceeded to tell me how they used the Internet as a venue to locate and develop a sense of community and connection with other agender people. They said they would often just type trans*-related words into Google and then peruse the search results as a way to connect to people throughout the world who identified in ways similar to them. Thus, although Jackson expressed wanting more trans* representation at CU, they used the Internet as a tool to locate and maintain the sense of kinship they lacked in physical spaces.

Other participants echoed the importance of the Internet, particularly in relation to learning about trans* identities. For example, when Kade discussed first coming out as trans*, I asked where he sought information, if he used books and other print publications as a source for knowledge. He replied, "I wouldn't know where to go in terms of print publications. I researched through the Internet." BC shared a similar perspective, stating, "I found Tumblr, and there is quite a queer community there, and that's what started it" (*it* meaning developing an understanding of her trans* identity).

Megan discussed using the Internet to learn about trans* identities in a way that was comfortable and safe for her. As previously mentioned, she experienced bullying during her youth, making her hesitant to come out as a trans* woman or talk with others in physical spaces about gender diversity. Thus, the Internet became a safe haven for Megan to learn about and connect with other trans* people. She talked about websites and chat forums like Laura's Playground, which she said allowed her to get to know other trans* people for the first time. In detailing her early experiences using the Internet to connect to other trans* people, she stated,

> I guess the biggest [site I used] would be Laura's Playground, which is a forum for transgender people of all types. They have chat sessions and everything. They even have suicide prevention rooms where you can go in and chat with moderators. . . . [We would] mostly just talk about general stuff . . . about, like, "I went out with a friend today." I guess chatting like you would with a friend.

The importance of Megan's ability to connect with other trans* people through virtual spaces cannot be overstated. As the preceding comment suggests, Megan was able not only to connect with other trans* people but also to talk with them "like you would with a friend." It is worth noting that although she was connecting with other trans* people, her conversations were not limited to gender or trans*-related topics. Instead, she was able to develop a network of relationships that allowed her to understand and appreciate that trans* people's lives were not as sensationalized as media outlets may have often suggested. In talking about how this media coverage influenced her early thinking about trans* lives, she said,

> I've always been reading articles . . . the bad articles, you know? The sad articles about transgender stories. . . . I don't know, I guess some of them are more funny stupidity articles about Fox News not accepting trans* people. But then other stuff, like stories about where [*sic*] trans* people are beaten, or raped, or stuff like that.

Megan went on to talk about representations of trans* people in film, specifically mentioning the movie *Boys Don't Cry* (Sharp & Peirce, 1999), a fictionalized account of an actual case in Nebraska in which a trans* youth was raped, beaten, and killed because of his gender identity.

> Whenever I do see those movies, after I'm done watching it, I sorta have a hatred for the world. . . . [A]t the end of the movie, there's always that climax where something really bad happens to the trans* person, and after I see that, it's like, "How am I living in this world? How is this world the way that it is?"

Thus, the ability to connect with trans* people through the Internet served as an important counterstory to the array of negative media portrayals Megan had read about and watched. In fact, being able to connect with others and see positive representations of what it meant to be trans* allowed her to realize that trans* people were, as she said, "Just normal people trying to live their lives." Indeed, just as cisgender people often lead mundane and everyday lives, so too do trans* people. Although this may seem fairly obvious, Megan's interactions with other trans* people through online chat forums allowed her to gain an appreciation for this fact, which was eschewed by the media coverage she followed.

More than just using the Internet to learn about trans* identities, the participants also talked about the Internet and virtual spaces as locations where they could spend time. For example, one evening Raegan texted me asking what I was doing. In the course of our impromptu conversation, Raegan said they were at home playing around online. They then texted, "I've found that YouTube is the most comforting place, second to meeting trans* people in person. I like watching people's transitions and hearing their advice and stories." In this comment, Raegan highlighted the importance of the Internet, and specifically YouTube, as a location where they could spend time. Furthermore, Raegan's description of getting advice and listening to life stories mirrors the way friends may talk with one another. Therefore, although Raegan had never met anyone from the YouTube videos they watched in real life, they felt a sense of kinship and connection with those people. As a result, they regarded YouTube to be "the most comforting place" to be, aside from meeting trans* people in person.

Shifting back to Megan, one can gain an appreciation for the breadth of the virtual spaces in which the participants engaged. For example, Megan spent a lot of time playing video games. As previously mentioned, Megan used this time to confirm her identity as a trans* woman by playing female characters. Thus, Megan was able to use virtual spaces as a way to reflect who she was in a way that was comfortable, safe, and accessible to her. Along with other examples of how participants used the Internet, Megan's use of gaming as a way to mirror her identity also underscores a potential implication for practice, specifically the expansion of notions of space to include more than just physical, campus-bound contexts. As I discuss in the next chapter, educators should consult the various virtual contexts in which trans* students are already engaging as a guide for how to engage others with diverse genders or people who may be exploring their genders. Although not every trans* student may benefit from or desire to connect with virtual communities, the use of virtual spaces is important for developing and maintaining kinship networks that reflect myriad ways of practicing gender that certain campus contexts may not be able to support or maintain. In other words, by using the Internet and other virtual spaces such as video games, educators may be able to help trans* students find others who reflect similar trans* identities, expressions, and embodiments. As discussed in Chapter 6 in the section on trans* (in)visibility, this was something many participants said they wanted. Although there may not always be a wide diversity of trans* identities, expressions, or embodiments on any one particular campus, leveraging virtual spaces as a way to develop and maintain kinship networks could proliferate possibilities for making these very connections.

Finally, it is important to recognize that virtual spaces, specifically social networking sites such as Facebook, were instrumental in developing and maintaining kinship networks between the participants and me. Although the Internet was not expressly a requirement of the research process, participants sought me out through virtual space, and as a result we were able to develop and maintain our own sense of kinship. In this sense, the participants and I used the research process in which we were exploring notions of community and connection to develop and maintain our own kinship networks. Reflecting on this in my field notes, I wrote,

> For Adem, it seems like they are reaching out to me and envision their participation [in the study] as a way to build relationships and develop community. Community, then, is not something [exclusively] external to the research process, but is also coming as a result of the research process. I can also see this from Adem and Derek "friending" me on Facebook (April 3, 2013).

Participants continued to develop relationships with me in virtual spaces throughout our working together and after the formal data collection process ended. Sometimes these virtual connections served as a conduit for developing deeper kinship networks in physical spaces. For example, Kade invited me to join a monthly book club by adding me to a closed Facebook group. Additionally, Raegan's participation in the study was itself a result of their desire to include me in their kinship networks. At the time, Raegan did not have a Facebook account—itself a practice of resilience for Raegan. They had deleted their account so they would not have to encounter transphobic comments from family and acquaintances online. However, Ginnie, Raegan's partner, did have an account and sent me a friend request. Raegan then approached me on campus, saying they wanted to join the study. When talking about the impetus for their desire to do so, Raegan said, "Half the reason I wanted to do this [join the study] was because I wanted to get to know you." Thus, although the relationship Raegan and I developed occurred in person, it was facilitated through virtual kinship networks.

This specific departure is an important disruption to staid notions of the loss of community in U.S. culture, which is often positioned as being because of the expansion of social media and virtual platforms. For example, Putnam (2001) suggested that the decline of community-based activities such as bowling leagues pointed to a similar decline in the notion of community itself. However, this departure proposes an alternative understanding of community and kinship, and resonates with the current literature about how various marginalized groups are using virtual spaces to create community (Miller, in press). The participants' use of the Internet and virtual spaces as a method to develop, maintain, and engage in kinship networks means it would behoove educators to reorient how notions of community are conceptualized. In other words, thinking of virtual spaces as generative sites for the development and maintenance of kinship networks may very well expand the possibilities for how educators could work alongside students with diverse genders to learn more about who they are, make connections with others with similar identities and experiences, and increase their sense of comfort and safety.

## Departure: Leaving Campus for Kinship Networks

Another divergence in the development of kinship networks was that several participants spoke about developing kinship networks by leaving campus. Kade, who was in his last year as a student during our work together, described his seeking kinship in the local Stockdale community in terms of a progression from moving on campus to off campus.

> I feel like the trans* community around here for the longest time was just through people, like, a network of people. So, you would meet one trans* person and they would have a friend who was trans* and then you would just all . . . [trails off]. So that was my initial experience. And then [in] TransActions I met a handful of people. And [now] I would say that the trans* community is developing a decent community in Stockdale right now. Um, so there's Stockdale Community Trans* Alliance, which I volunteer for. I would say that I meet the most trans* people now through there.

Kade's comments reveal multiple insights, the first of which is his explicit use of the word *network*. His comment breathes life into the arrival these data depart from, particularly in its explicit reference to kinship networks as a development of relationships in and among other trans* and queer people. In other words, trans* community did not just happen in one location but evolved for Kade over time because of the people with whom he was in contact introducing him to other trans* people. Second, Kade did not describe his seeking community as a binary between on and off campus. Instead, he talked about his off-campus kinship networks occurring as a result of his previous on-campus involvement. Therefore, Kade considered his leaving campus for developing kinship as an *extension of* rather than *as opposed to* notions of campus-based kinship. This insight is important for educators, as it signals how one could view local communities as fertile sites for extending kinship networks. Kade's comment compels educators to work with local trans* networks as a possible extension of what is occurring on campus. In doing so, educators working alongside trans* students could assist in the development of deeper kinship networks. Furthermore, extending kinship networks past the campus environment may also ease students' transition postgraduation. Although Kade did not speak about his kinship networks in this way, having such networks likely eased his transition after graduation, especially because he has remained active in local communities and now resides in Stockdale.

Jackson also strayed from campus to create and maintain kinship networks. Jackson found kinship in their workplace, where they ended up spending a lot of their time. Talking about the Loft Cinema, where they worked, Jackson said:

> I guess work is overly important to me. I know that it's not what I am going to be doing forever, but I really like my job. I spend too much time there, like whenever I am at my house and I can't do schoolwork or something, I'll just walk over to The Loft and clock in and start organizing things.

For Jackson, the Loft was a space where they felt comfortable; so comfortable, in fact, they went there to decompress when they could not focus on schoolwork. Therefore, even though Jackson said work was "overly important" to them, they kept returning to the Loft because it was a comfortable space where they had developed a meaningful kinship network.

Similar to Kade's development of kinship networks as an extension of his on-campus networks, Jackson's network at the Loft was not wholly separate from previous networks they had developed. During our first formal interview, Jackson said, "One of the other managers at work, I have known her since middle school, and we have been best friends [since then]." Furthermore, when Jackson became a general manager for the Loft, they were moved to a secondary location. In talking about the staff there, Jackson said, "I knew a few people there [already] so it's not as scary as it would be with any new job." From this, it is clear how Jackson's kinship networks transgressed work boundaries because of knowing some of the people they would work with in their new role as the general manager. This insight further emphasizes kinship networks as not just being developed or maintained in discrete spaces. Instead, Kade's and Jackson's experiences illustrate the ways in which some kinship networks led to the development of additional networks. Their comments also demonstrate how kinship networks often traversed multiple spaces and locations, meaning educators would be well advised to seek partnerships across various locations on and off campus to assist trans* students in developing and maintaining kinship networks.

## Departure: Academic Kinship Networks

Participants described academic departments and classrooms as contested spaces to develop and maintain kinship networks. Although several participants (e.g., Jackson, Adem, and Silvia) described academic spaces as fruitful environments to develop kinship networks, others' experiences (e.g., BC's and Megan's) told a more ominous story. Thus, academic departments and classrooms mediated participants' abilities to create and maintain kinship networks in various ways.

Jackson spoke positively about the education department at CU, suggesting there was wide support for gender variance there. Revisiting Jackson's comments about their coursework in education classes, they said,

> Education classes are very [welcoming] because when professors are talking about the variance in the students you are going to be teaching, they're wanting to respect the variances in everyone in a lot of ways. I can remember when we had the syllabus up in one of my classes on the first day and it was talking about how we need to be respectful of race, gender, sexual orientation, and gender variance is what it said, and I was like, oh, that's really—that was great, you know?

The open nature of Jackson's education courses encouraged them to focus their projects and presentations in these classrooms on issues related to trans* students.

> A lot of my projects that I do, or presentations, I try to gear them toward . . . trans* issues just because I think it's important for people to hear about [them] . . . if they haven't, or even to get more exposure to that and see that it's normal, you know?

In addition to education classrooms as a comfortable place to discuss diverse genders, Jackson said they had also been able to develop friendships with classmates they had originally thought may not be interested in discussing trans*-related issues. Therefore, the inclusive ethos that seemed to pervade Jackson's education courses promoted the development of kinship networks for them. Speaking about one such unexpected friendship, Jackson said,

> I had a girl in one of my classes, and we were paired up for something and I had a lot of preconceived notions about her. . . . We just got to talking, and we started talking about what we wanted to do with education, and . . . we talked about Montessori school and stuff like that, and we started talking about . . . trans* issues in the classroom and . . . gender variant students, and different variances other than that with students and she was there with me, you know? And for me it was like, "Oh, I need to stop prejudging these people."

Jackson's ability to make connections and friendships with peers, despite their seemingly different backgrounds and experiences, particularly as they related to gender identity, is highly noteworthy. Thus, for Jackson, the positive climate regarding gender variance allowed positive connections with peers.

Adem's experiences in the women's and gender studies department also convey how a positive academic climate regarding gender transgression can motivate the development of kinship networks. During our second interview, Adem began talking about the shift they were making from spending the bulk of their time in The Center to developing a peer network through their involvement in women's and gender studies classes, saying, "Now I have people in my program that I like a lot, which I have never had before; I have never had friends who are people in my classes, so that's a weird experience." The weirdness Adem mentioned was a positive sentiment, as they had not previously experienced building kinship networks through coursework. However, their ability to do so was a welcome development that allowed them to create kinship networks beyond The Center, signaling their ability to be comfortable in multiple spaces across the CU campus.

In contrast to Jackson's and Adem's experiences in classroom spaces, BC and Megan faced academic environments that were far from trans* inclusive. As previously discussed, BC was so disillusioned with her inability to transgress gender norms in the College of Business that she changed majors. Describing her decision not to come out in classroom spaces, BC told me, "Classrooms I don't come out in. Ever. . . . I don't want to deal with people being dumb and I don't think they would respect me or use my name or pronouns. I think I would just get shit for it, so it's not worth it." When I asked her to expand on what negative reactions she thought others would have if she disclosed her trans* identity, she responded, "Um, just people telling me I'm not a girl, or that I can't be a girl, or that I'm sick. All sorts of stuff." For BC, the possibilities of confronting overt hostility in the classroom influenced her decision not only to not come out but also to switch majors. Furthermore, gender identity played a major factor when she was deciding on her new major.

> It [my major] will be changing to journalism, I believe. The College of Business is dumb. I think very few queer people are there. And the English department probably won't be as good as women's studies, but even women's studies isn't that great at CU.

BC's comment not only suggests the salience of gender in her decision about which major to switch to but also points to a different understanding of the women's and gender studies department from what Adem had described. BC's and Adem's different experiences of women's and gender studies mirrors the differences participants expressed regarding the previously discussed comfort of various spaces and organizations across campus. In other words, there was rarely, if ever, one space—academic or otherwise—that was beyond contestation for participants. Thus, as discussed in more depth in the following chapter, educators would be well advised not to seek a specific list of best practices they can implement to increase trans* inclusion on campus, as such lists will undoubtedly lead to suggesting practices and policies that may have an impact on students in a variety of potentially negative ways.

# INTERLUDE
## AN ENDING FULL OF BEGINNINGS

In describing the process of thinking with theory, Jackson and Mazzei (2012) stated that the analytical approach was "a process to diffract, rather than foreclose, thought" (p. 5). They further stated that to think with theory was "meant to be irruptive in an opening of ways of thinking and meaning. . . . [A way] to shake us out of the complacency of seeing/hearing/thinking as we always have, or might have, or will have" (p. 14). Although Jackson and Mazzei focused on pushing data to their analytical limits, the process of thinking with theory has an impact in terms of how one thinks about the data that are stretched, (re)presented with multiple meanings, and (re)constituted from divergent vantage points. As they suggest, the effect of thinking with theory is to see/hear/think about data in unconventional, untraditional, and unconstrained ways.

For these reasons, readers will find that the following chapter diverges from what may be expected from a chapter focused on implications for practice. That is, rather than focusing on a series of best practices educators can implement when working alongside trans* college students, the study participants and I offer a series of problems, challenges, questions, and complications. Our purpose in doing this is to invite readers to think with us about the ways gender regulates not just the lives of trans* people but of everyone. Once this is established, it will become clear that we all have a stake in confronting the insidious nature of trans* oppression, including the many ways we are all complicit in or resist the limiting constraints of binary notions of gender. In other words, rather than providing an easy list of tasks to complete, suggesting that trans* oppression is out there to grasp and tame, we suggest trans* oppression is something that is in us and has a grasp on us all. Because of this, providing a list of best practices, despite its envious simplicity, will never adequately help us address the full complexity of the issue.

Spade (2015) wrote that critical trans politics "helps us investigate how the norms that produce conditions of disparity and violence emerge from multiple, interwoven locations, and recognize possibilities for resistance as similarly dispersed" (p. 3). Thus, for Spade, the multifaceted nature of trans* oppression requires a series of interventions and new ways of thinking about solutions that are equally disparate and various. Spade went further, advocating for a completely inverted strategy to address the pernicious effects of trans* oppression through what he calls the trickle-up approach of activism. In doing so, Spade suggested that rather than working on rights for a few and then coming back for more marginalized populations, we should work to attain rights for those who are the most marginalized and who experience extreme threat. In doing so, Spade said that these rights would invariably cover those who do not experience overt threat and hostility, thus allowing the rights won for highly marginalized populations to trickle up. In the tradition set forth by Spade, the study participants and I propose that college educators adopt this inverted model of activism and begin to ask themselves what it would mean to approach their work by thinking first about the needs, barriers, and life experiences of those highly marginalized and potentially invisible populations on college and university campuses (e.g., trans* people of color, trans* people with disabilities). Indeed, we suggest it may even behoove student affairs educators to approach their work from a perspective of how they can make campuses more equitable in an attempt to welcome those who do not even currently have broad access to higher education (e.g., homeless trans* youth, trans* people living at or below the poverty line, incarcerated trans* people).

Although this book ends with Chapter 8, in many ways it is the first chapter in the work educators can (and should) undertake alongside trans* college students. Thus, the following chapter has been written intentionally as a call to action that is full of potential beginnings educators are encouraged to take up in their daily practice. Just as the participants and I worked alongside each other for 18 months, we now invite our readers to work alongside us in making strides to promote cultural change that bends toward gender equity and trans* inclusion. Rather than handing readers a list of what to do, we extend our hand and ask you to wade through the murkiness of systemic trans* oppression with us. Just as we have done for this study, we believe the only way to proceed is with one another. Therefore, we invite you to join us so that we may go on, and we may do so together.

# 8

# IMPLICATIONS

As discussed in the previous chapters, collegiate contexts are awash in trans* oppression. The findings detailed in this book also elucidate the complex interplay of multiple identities and how these intersections mediate trans* students' experiences to varying effect. Thus, the complexities of participants' experiences demand complex solutions to promote more welcoming collegiate environments. In this chapter, I present a variety of implications based on the data presented in the previous five chapters, all of which address how educational researchers and practitioners must continually (re)think the effects of gender on college and university campuses. Similar to the work of Spade (2015), I offer suggestions as an attempt to increase life chances for trans* people in higher education. Furthermore, in a manner similar to Butler (2006), I adamantly believe such liberation is only possible if those in the fields of higher education and student affairs are willing to actively work to increase possibilities for practicing gender. This does not mean everyone needs to transgress gender expectations. However, it does suggest that everyone needs to be involved in interrogating, exposing, and resisting the insidious ways gender regulates all our lives, particularly the ways it regulates the lives of those who identify as trans*.

I offer the following as implications for practice. As educators and student affairs practitioners, we should be:

1. Moving beyond best practices;
2. Recognizing how gender mediates everyone's life;
3. Embracing a trickle-up approach to diversity and inclusion work;
4. Reconceptualizing college environments;
5. Recommitting to intersectional praxis; and
6. Developing an epistemology of love.

Each implication is framed as a call to action for educators to imagine new possibilities and ways of working in college and university settings that would expand possibilities of how to think about and practice gender. These calls for action are intended to have liberatory potential rather than indicate what postsecondary educators have been doing wrong. In other words, these implications signal a hopeful turn toward working alongside people with diverse genders to address the pernicious effects of systemic trans* oppression in higher education.

## Moving Beyond Best Practices

On the surface, best practices, or sets of recommendations that all educators should seek to emulate and reproduce on their campuses, seem like a good idea for me and others working toward gender equity and trans* inclusion on college campuses. Indeed, creating best practices seems like a best practice. However, when taking a critical trans politics approach to gender equity, the notion of best practices is increasingly reaching for a singular point of arrival, which, on further investigation, is a utopian myth.

Dean Spade (2015) wrote,

> I hope to show how critical trans politics practices resistance. Following the traditions of women of color feminism, this critical approach to resistance refuses to take for granted national stories about social change that actually operate to maintain conditions of suffering and disparity. It questions its own effectiveness, engaging in constant reflection and self-evaluation. And it is about practice and process rather than a point of arrival. (p. 1)

Thus, for Spade and others committed to practicing a critical trans politics, to suggest that one has arrived is antithetical and counterintuitive. Although it may indeed be the case that gender activists and those seeking trans* inclusion may get somewhere (and certainly this is the hope), to be content with that somewhere elides the reality that critical trans politics is a process. In fact, as Spade pointed out, critical trans politics is a practice, which mirrors the Butlerian concept of gender as a practice, or something that one continually repeats (Butler, 2006).

If critical trans politics is a practice, and if it being a practice means one must continually repeat it—or one must practice "constant reflection and self-evaluation" (Spade, 2015, p. 1)—then to provide a list of best practices becomes a gilded experiment that provides the veneer of progress regarding trans* inclusion but may in its very existence cover up practices, attitudes, and an overall ethos of trans* exclusion. For example, as I and Susan Marine

(Nicolazzo & Marine, 2015) have written previously, the emergence of trans*-inclusive housing as a best practice in student affairs works in a couple of ways. It increases some options, albeit with limitations, of where trans* students may live on campus in a comfortable environment. However, at the same time, suggesting that creating trans*-inclusive housing is a best practice overlooks the fact that not dedicating a floor, a wing, or an entire building to the practice of inclusive housing provides a rationale for trans* oppression in all other campus housing assignments. In other words, providing a space for trans* students to live comfortably on campus, although a positive step in many ways, overlooks the fact that trans* oppression continues to regulate how all other residential spaces are organized. Thus, if creating a trans*-inclusive building on campus is a best practice, then that best practice simultaneously promotes gender inclusion *and* trans* oppression (Nicolazzo, 2106; Nicolazzo & Marine, 2015).

Another example of the way best practices overlook systemic trans* oppression in the name of progress is the creation and dissemination of campus climate indexes, such as the LGBT-Friendly Campus Pride Index (Campus Pride, n.d.-b). First, many of the measures of inclusion on this (and other) indexes are policy based (e.g., a campus that has an LGBT-friendly housing policy or a campus that recognizes sexual and gender diversity in its nondiscrimination statement). As I discuss later in this chapter, such policies are symbolic and do little to improve the daily lived experiences of trans* collegians. Suggesting that inclusion comes as a result of adopting certain policies is overly optimistic. Second, the Campus Pride index does not require student input in its collection of data (Campus Pride, n.d.-a), and because of this, the determination of which campuses are LGBT friendly is based solely on administrators' impressions of support, inclusion, and comfort. In other words, campuses that may appear to be LGBT-friendly—maybe the campus has not had a reported LGBT-motivated bias incident or perhaps the campus has several gender-inclusive restrooms—may also be unfriendly places. As in the case of trans*-inclusive housing, providing several gender-inclusive restrooms reinforces the persistence of trans* oppression in all other restrooms across campus. Additionally, if a student attends a school that is found to be LGBT-friendly by these indices but then feels that the campus is unsafe or uncomfortable, the student becomes the problem rather than the campus because it has officially been marked as safe (e.g., the accommodations on campus for LGBT students may not be enough, or the violence the student may experience is considered an aberration).

Miami University, the institution where I earned my doctorate, provides an example of this logic. During the time I was a student, Miami had a rating of 4.5 out of 5 stars on the Campus Pride index (Chaffee, Davis,

Smith, & Walsh, 2013). These ratings, however, belie the fact that homophobia and transphobia were regularly experienced by queer students, faculty, and staff, and the campus only offers "gender-neutral housing on a limited basis, [which means] space is limited to two suites in two halls (four students per suite) and one apartment" (Conrad, 2012, para. 11). Given the inconsistencies between the campus ranking and student experiences, it becomes clear that suggesting that Miami University is a friendly campus is troubling, and, as a result, such a suggestion itself must be troubled.

Again, it bears repeating that by resisting the pull of best practices, I am not suggesting I and other trans* activists are directionless. Much to the contrary, moving beyond best practices means recognizing we always have more work we can (and, I would argue, should) be doing to promote gender equity and trans* inclusion. It means recognizing that although some efforts are positive steps (e.g., the creation of trans*-inclusive housing areas on campus), they must not be seen as an end goal. As Ahmed (2012) wrote, "I would argue that 'good practice' can be a showcase, a way of repackaging and rearranging the organization, so that it puts on its best display" (p. 107). In this sense, best practices do not actually redress trans* oppression but suggest institutions of higher education are doing better through the creation of their best display (Nicolazzo, 2016).

Moving beyond best practices means asking ourselves as educators hard questions about how we may still be complicit in furthering trans* oppression in our policies and practices even when we take positive steps (Nicolazzo, 2106). Moving beyond best practices wrestles educators out of the mythical notion that we can ever arrive at fully inclusive practices and demands that we see our work as being about practice, process, reflection, and self-evaluation, to use Spade's (2015) words. Such a paradigmatic shift also requires educators to reach out to trans* students, faculty, and staff so that our voices are central in the practice of a critical trans politics that seeks liberation for us as a marginalized population. This process may be messy and likely will not fit neatly into neoliberal rubrics for measuring effectiveness or campus friendliness. However, the move away from best practices and toward a critical trans politics is one that educators would be well advised to take as a way to promote gender equity and trans* inclusion on college and university campuses.

## Recognizing How Gender Mediates Everyone's Life

Although this book focuses explicitly on trans* students, it is important to stress that the cultural manifestations of trans* oppression at CU (i.e., gender binary discourse and compulsory heterogenderism) regulated everyone's life.

All students, faculty, staff, and visitors to CU were (re)oriented in overt and tacit ways regarding how they should think about, present, and do gender (Ahmed, 2006). At first blush, this realization appears innocuous; of course cultural notions of gender influence all members of that culture. However, what is more complex is the way this implication—a finding largely about cisgender people—continues to recenter trans* people and their counterstories of success. This implication suggests that if binary notions of gender influence everyone, then it would behoove cisgender students, faculty, and staff to shoulder the burden of initiating large-scale cultural change on college campuses because of the negative impact of gender binary discourse and compulsory heterogenderism on all lives, in particular those of trans* people. Furthermore, if this were to happen, and trans* students were to be released from the need to continually fight for recognition and an adequate redistribution of time, attention, energy, and resources, they would be better able to focus on developing and maintaining the kinship networks the study participants identified as being particularly important to their success at CU.

Admittedly, I feel uneasy about forwarding this implication, as it revolves largely around the notion of interest convergence (D. Bell, 1989) or the idea that progress will be made only when what is best for marginalized populations also benefits majoritarian populations. However, recognizing how gender mediated everyone's lives at CU serves the purpose of continually calling people back to the narratives, experiences, and needs of trans* students, which is a central tenet of the critical tradition this book is rooted in (Anzaldúa, 2007; Solórzano & Yosso, 2002; Spade, 2015). Moreover, as stated earlier, it would also allow trans* students to focus more time and attention on building and maintaining the kinship networks that were vital to their success.

Recognizing the myriad ways gender mediates everyone's life also resists the need to answer questions about how many trans* people there are on college and university campuses. In other words, if educators embraced the notion that everyone's life is regulated by gender, there would cease to be a need to count and categorize trans* people, a practice that several trans* scholars have viewed as a problem and that I discuss in Chapter 2. Determining how many trans* students there are relies on positive investments in, and comfort with, being publicly out in order to be counted. Also, as I discuss in previous chapters, the question of how many trans* students are present in higher education is also rooted in potentially deleterious raced, classed, and able-bodied assumptions about what it means to be trans* enough to count in the first place (Catalano, 2015b; Spade, 2010).

In realizing the ways gender influences everyday modes of being, acting, and thinking, cisgender people are forced to see themselves as benefiting from the promotion of gender as an unstable and flexible construct. As discussed in Chapter 1, there are people who do not identify as trans* but who may blur normative understandings of gender. Examples include Wilkins's (2008) discussion of Goth men who paint their nails and wear makeup and Pascoe's (2007) discussion of the "Basketball Girls" (pp. 115–155), who dressed and acted in stereotypically masculine ways despite being assigned the female sex at birth. Thus, it is clear that more than just trans* people would be well served by cracking open restrictive social understandings of gender. The expansion of gender as a category could result in the convergence of interests from multiple populations, thus benefiting trans* students without requiring them to shoulder the burden of constant education and resistance, which the participants said was often exhausting and they sometimes refused to do. Moreover, the reduced burden of expanding notions of gender according to interest convergence (D. Bell, 1989) would allow trans* students more time and energy to focus on developing and maintaining the kinship networks participants identified as essential to their success. That is, by not having to constantly address gendered microaggressions, or not having to think about if, how, or when to address problem situations caused by the twin cultural realities of gender binary discourse and compulsory heterogenderism, trans* students would have the time and space to create and be among the kinship networks the participants identified as being essential to their success on campus.

To recognize the ways gender organizes and influences daily life, educators need to be prepared to think about the multiple ways gender shows up in one's life. From the mundane and tacit to the provocative and explicit, educators must ask themselves questions about how gender influences their actions, attitudes, behaviors, dress, policies, and practices. For example, questioning why dress codes are necessary; how dress codes enforce normative gender expectations; why gender-specific language is used in policy documents; how gender structures conversations with colleagues; and what assumptions are made about others based on appearance, style, demeanor, or voice inflection are all important ways educators can uncover how gender influences an individual's life. By asking these questions and encouraging other cisgender individuals to do the same, trans* people will be released of the burden of always having to bring up gender (Henderson, 2014).

## Embracing a Trickle-Up Approach to Diversity and Inclusion Work

In Chapters 3 and 4, I discuss how the cultural realities of a gender binary discourse and compulsory heterogenderism mediate trans* students' ability to successfully navigate CU. Moreover, as I suggest in the previous section, these culturally reinforced notions of gender as an already naturalized and dichotomous set of social identities press on everyone in the college environment, not just trans* college students. In other words, gender was culturally (re)enforced at CU, and all members of the campus community, including guests and visitors, were continually (re)oriented toward binary notions of gender. Therefore, echoing the work of Ahmed (2006), the question educators should seek to answer is how they can work to reorient themselves and others toward more liberatory modes of thinking, being, and doing gender on campus.

In answering this question, it may be seductive to think of grand gestures from upper administrators regarding gender equity and trans* inclusion as providing the best way to counteract trans* oppression. However, to suggest such a facile solution to such a complex cultural phenomenon is oversimplified. For example, a wide array of social movements have demonstrated that state-based solutions are unlikely to solve adequately such systemic oppression. Additionally, historical perspectives on social action rightly point out that the state itself has often fueled the very forms of structural inequities systemic oppression is based on (e.g., Hanhardt, 2013; Orleck, 2005; Spade, 2015; Sylvia Rivera Law Project, 2007; Warner, 1999; Worley, 2011).

Translating the state's complicity in furthering systems of inequity on college campuses, it could be suggested that grand gestures from upper-level administrators to counteract gender binary discourse and compulsory heterogenderism may have little influence on improving the life chances of highly marginalized populations such as trans* students. Indeed, recalling Adem's comments in the introduction, they discussed the inclusion of the phrase "gender identity and expression" in CU's nondiscrimination policy as being akin to "caution tape." Adem meant that the policy acted as a suggestion of what community members should not do rather than provide a hard rule that all abide to. Similar to caution tape, which can be easily pushed away, torn down, or otherwise disregarded, including language about gender identity and expression in CU's nondiscrimination policy did little, if anything, other than move beyond a mere symbolic gesture, to increase life chances for trans* students on campus. In fact, as I have written with Susan Marine (Nicolazzo & Marine, 2015), relying on such policies may provide little protection. Such was the case for Kaeden Kass, a trans* man who filed a discrimination lawsuit against Miami University. Despite the inclusion of gender identity and expression in the university's nondiscrimination policy, Kass's case was ultimately dismissed in 2012 because of a supposed lack of evidence (K. Taylor, 2012).

Although symbolic inclusions such as the phrase *gender identity and expression* in campus nondiscrimination policies is important, the participants and I suggest college educators could approach diversity and inclusion work in different ways that may better recognize the dignity and worth of highly marginalized student populations. Spade (2015) offered one such strategy, which he termed the *trickle-up approach* to diversity and inclusion work. Rather than waiting for upper-level administrators to recognize and affirm the lives of trans* college students—a prospect that may be of little consequence in changing the material and psychic realities of transgender oppression on campus—trans* students, faculty, and staff should seek partnerships and coalitions with and among each other to create communities of support and promote self-efficacy and intragroup safety (Spade, 2015). Furthermore, trans* students can reach out to like-minded populations that may not be trans* but share similar goals and needs regarding safety and recognition on campus. As Spade wrote, such coalitions are centered as a way to

> build nonprofessional relationships that ground political practice and understanding in mutual care and trust. . . . This work prioritizes building leadership and membership on a "most vulnerable first" basis, *centering the belief that social justice trickles up, not down* [emphasis added]. . . . It is this space, where questions of survival and distribution are centered, where the well-being of the most vulnerable will not be compromised for promises of legal and media representation, where the difficult work of building participatory resistance led from the bottom up, is undertaken, where we can seek the emergence of deeply transformative trans resistance. (pp. 136–138)

For Spade (2015), creating a broad-based coalitional movement seeking justice on a most-vulnerable-first basis is a way to resist the seductive rhetoric of inclusion that often comes in the form of broad policy reforms, statements on inclusion and diversity made by upper-level administrators, or a college's or university's "commitment to diversity," which is often used throughout mission statements (Morphew & Hartley, 2006) and discussed across institutions of higher education (Ahmed, 2012), regardless of its actual veracity.

Approaching diversity and inclusion work on college and university campuses with a trickle-up approach would mean heeding the voices, needs, and experiences of those who are the most marginalized. This may mean recognizing who is not even present or visible on college campuses and what may be prohibiting that presence or visibility. It also means focusing time, attention, and energy on various intersections of identities that produce decreased life chances, particularly for trans* youth. In the context of higher education environments, this means educators should pay particular attention to the lives, experiences, and needs of trans* people of color, undocumented trans* people, trans* people living in poverty or who are homeless, and trans* people with disabilities, as these individuals invariably fall into the category of being the most vulnerable student populations. CU did not attend to such intersections of identities. By neglecting such important intersections, or by addressing them in ancillary or perfunctory ways, Micah, Jackson, Silvia, Derek, Adem, and BC faced decreased opportunities to succeed at CU. Indeed, the reality that almost half the study participants left CU, and not all of them came back, before obtaining a degree may itself be emblematic of educators' failure to prioritize students who are the most vulnerable. In this sense, taking a trickle-up approach to diversity and inclusion work not only might have had a positive impact on the study participants who left CU but also would invariably provide rights and privileges to other marginalized and vulnerable populations (e.g., people of color, working-class students, students with diverse sexualities, students with chronic illnesses). By focusing on the needs of the most vulnerable first as Spade (2015) suggested, rights will trickle up to those who also face marginalization, invisibility, and have yet to be recognized on college and university campuses.

Taking such a radically different approach to diversity and inclusion work on college and university campuses will likely take some patience and discussion. However, it is my contention that such a shift not only is necessary but also can often be tied to an institution's mission and values. If it is true that a commitment to diversity is common in mission statements (Morphew & Hartley, 2006) and discussed across institutions of higher education (Ahmed, 2012), then it would make sense to frame the trickle-up approach to diversity and inclusion work as a method for people to live such a commitment. Taking a trickle-up approach to diversity and social justice work also means asking hard questions regarding which populations are present or absent, visible or invisible, and targeted or welcome on college and university campuses. From here, educators can begin to frame educational initiatives, programmatic efforts, and support services for those whose access is the most limited.

The trickle-up approach is not always about making a massive shift in attitudes, behaviors, or approaches in student affairs practice. Indeed, many practitioners and offices already use this approach in their daily practice, even if they do not expressly define it as such. Strategies such as rethinking office hours to accommodate student schedules, promoting programming for rather than about highly marginalized student populations such as trans* students (Marine & Nicolazzo, 2014), and being vocal about the various ways systemic oppression negatively influences vulnerable populations on campus are positive steps toward taking a trickle-up approach to diversity and inclusion work. Although reorienting a person, an office, or an entire division of student affairs toward a trickle-up approach will not occur overnight, Spade's (2015) call is an essential shift to start making if student affairs educators take seriously their role of being "committed . . . to the cultivation of diversity" (Marine, 2011a, p. 1168).

## Reconceptualizing College Environments

There is a robust base of literature regarding higher education campus ecology and environments (e.g., Renn & Arnold, 2003; Renn & Patton, 2011; Renn & Reason, 2012; Strange & Banning, 2015) as well as a growing body of literature that focuses specifically on identity centers on college campuses, including Black cultural centers (Patton, 2010; Stewart, 2011) and LGBTQ centers (Marine & Nicolazzo, 2014). When combined with quantitative data sets such as that of Rankin, Weber, Blumenfeld, and Frazer (2010), it is clear a substantive depth of literature exists regarding how college environments influence the lives of those who live, learn, work, and play on campus.

Lesser known or focused on is how virtual spaces can expand educators' understanding of campus environments. Although virtual spaces are beginning to make an appearance in higher education literature (e.g., Kasch, 2013), they have yet to expand the way college educators think about notions of campus environments. For example, in applying the work of Bronfenbrenner (1993) on human ecology to college contexts, Evans, Forney, Guido, Patton, and Renn (2010) noted,

> Although Bronfenbrenner did not include computer-mediated contexts in which college students now experience "activities, roles, and interpersonal relations" (p. 16), in the twenty-first century it seems reasonable to include these contexts, which are not face-to-face settings, in the definition of *microsystems* [emphasis added] since they are sites where social, physical, and symbolic features may provoke or retard engagement with the environment, as described by Bronfenbrenner (1993). (p. 163)

Therefore, college educators must expand their notions of campus environments to include virtual spaces such as social media networks, online forums, video games, and video-sharing websites. When considering how the participants used virtual spaces to learn about themselves and their gender identities as well as successfully navigate the physical environment of CU, it is clear that virtual spaces were not merely a way for trans* students to pass time. In fact, in many ways, the participants lived online. For example, recalling the words of Jackson from Chapter 7, who stated, "I exist primarily on the

Internet, you know? That's pretty much my hometown," shows how important virtual spaces were for some participants. Furthermore, Megan talked about spending most of her youth inside, which she used to refer to being alone and playing video games in her room (Chapter 3). When she came to college, she discussed gaming as a way to reflect her identity as a woman, specifically by playing women video game characters. Therefore, for Megan, the act of playing video games became a way to practice her gender identity in a virtual space, which she was barred from doing in physical spaces because of the twin cultural realities of gender binary discourse and compulsory heterogenderism.

Moreover, the study participants and I continue to cultivate kinship through the Internet. In addition to providing a sense of connection during data collection, these relationships have increased in number and persist today. For example, Adem, who left CU and ended their participation in the study before its conclusion, has continually contacted me via social media networks, thereby maintaining a sense of connection and kinship. Similarly, Silvia, who decided to study abroad for the entire year after the study concluded, has continued to maintain contact through Instagram and e-mail. Therefore, these virtual spaces and computer-mediated contexts were important not only for participants to develop a sense of self but also in finding, connecting with, and maintaining bonds of kinship that persisted long after the official end to the study that brought us together in the first place.

In light of these data, college and university educators would be well advised to think through how expanding notions of campus environments may increase strategies for trans* students to navigate their campuses successfully. For example, in what ways could educators encourage gaming as a productive tool for exploring one's identities, particularly those identities students may be reticent to disclose because of a lack of safety, heightened vulnerability, or their own uncertainty? How might educators connecting with students via social networking platforms be a useful strategy for developing community as well as for connecting students to other people and resources outside campus? What are the benefits of seeing virtual spaces not just as a way to "meet students where they are at"—an often-used phrase by student affairs educators to denote how one should approach one's work—but as a tool to interact with them in a more private and potentially safer way? Building from this, how can such connections through virtual spaces begin to be understood as an important aspect of outreach beyond just inviting students to events and physical centers, which may involve certain risks or concerns? For example, recalling the experiences of Micah and Silvia as Black trans* collegians who felt some sense of ambivalence toward the overarching Whiteness of The Center, how might providing opportunities to connect through virtual space provide a way for them and other trans* collegians of color to connect without having to run the risk of facing racial microaggressions at The Center?

Moreover, participants talked at length of the importance of digital technologies and virtual spaces when beginning to explore their own trans* identities. However, most, if not all, of the educational programming at CU regarding diverse genders and sexualities occurred in physical settings (e.g., classrooms, clubs and organizations, and facilitated workshops). Therefore, a disconnect emerged between the ways trans* participants came to learn about their possible gendered futures and how practitioners educated others about those same possible gendered futures. Applying Raegan's reflection from Chapter 7 that "YouTube is the most comforting place, second to meeting trans* people in person," college educators should rethink educational programming efforts to align with where students are already going for such information. Although it is true participants sought physical spaces, such as TransActions, and that at least one participant (BC) made the decision to attend CU based on the existence of more inclusive physical spaces for trans* people, these environments were insufficient for trans* students' learning, developing, or feeling comfortable navigating their collegiate environments. Thus, educators should become adroit in their use of virtual space as a tool to connect with trans* college students, promote their learning and development, and encourage community building. In fact, this is even a part of the revised American College Personnel Association and National Association of Student Personnel Administrators' (2015) professional competencies document that details those competencies student affairs educators should base their practice on. The data from this study also align with another study on virtual space as a significant domain of kinship-building for trans* college students (Nicolazzo, Pitcher, Renn, & Woodford, in press), providing further impetus for college educators to give serious consideration to how virtual space and digital technologies can be used to promote trans* student success.

## Recommitting to Intersectional Praxis

Emanating from the critical legal scholarship of Kimberlé W. Crenshaw (1989, 1995), intersectionality has experienced somewhat of a renaissance in the field of higher education. As Jones (2014) stated, "Many in higher education were initially drawn to intersectionality because it emphasized linking identity to structures of privilege and oppression (Jones & Abes, 2013)" (p. xi). Despite this enthusiasm for using intersectionality as an analytical tool, Bowleg (2008) said, "Conducting and designing intersectionality research . . . poses a variety of thorny methodological challenges" (p. 312). Several higher education scholars have located such "thorny challenges" when discussing research with marginalized student populations (e.g., Stewart, 2010; Tillapaugh & Nicolazzo, 2014), a reflection that embodies Jones's claim that "higher education scholars have been relatively unsophisticated in the application of intersectionality because they overemphasized its identity applications" (p. xii). This aforementioned overemphasis on identity applications, or what Collins (2009) referred to as a "turn[ing] inward, to the level of personal identity narratives" (p. ix), overshadows the ways people navigate a social context marked by multiple interconnected systems of inequity.

Moving from the theoretical and methodological to the practical, student affairs educators at CU similarly struggled with what intersectionality looks like in practice. As some participants suggested, what educators heralded as intersectional programmatic efforts were merely stand-alone, cosponsored events between offices. However, as Micah suggested, "[We trans* people] are people period. Very, very diverse and very intersectional." Micah was saying that a commitment to intersectional praxis took more than individual programs focusing on two or more identities. In effect, this comment reflected what Bowleg (2008) wrote, specifically that Black + lesbian + woman ≠ Black lesbian woman. This sentiment was further emphasized by Micah's and Silvia's calling The Center a predominantly White space, and they struggled to reflect and discuss the complex realities of being a Black trans* person at CU, itself an institution with a deep history of racism and trans* erasure.

Higher education researchers and practitioners would be well advised to reflect students' lives in ways that honor the complexities of their experiences and the depth of their various social identities mediating their experiences at all times rather than just during specific programming efforts. In other words, higher education researchers and practitioners must recommit to intersectionality in a way that honors the core tenets of the analytical lens itself as well as the lives of the students they work alongside. To do so means first recommitting to understanding what intersectionality means, which has become muddled (Collins, 2009; Jones, 2014). Rather than resting on additive assumptions, intersectionality seeks to uncover the ways interlocking systems of oppression press on individuals to influence their (in)ability to navigate various social contexts (Bowleg, 2008). Researchers and practitioners should familiarize themselves with the various texts and exemplars of intersectionality (e.g., Jones & Abes, 2013; Mitchell, Simmons, & Greyerbiehl, 2014) present throughout the field of higher education.

Furthermore, it is imperative to review Crenshaw's (1989, 1995) foundational writing on intersectionality, as many reference her work without understanding its complexity or potency.

Researchers and practitioners must also give thought to understanding what intersectionality does; that is, they should have an awareness of what the intentions of intersectional approaches to research and practice are and move forward accordingly. As Micah's previous comment suggests, the intent of intersectional research and practice is not to discuss multiple identities for a limited amount of time as a part of an isolated, stand-alone program. Rather, intersectionality is a theoretical and analytical tool that describes how possibilities are expanded or prohibited to individuals based on their identities and the systems of privilege and power that shape their environments. For higher education practitioners, then, approaching one's work through an intersectional lens means interrogating the very structures that keep offices siloed and staffs unable to work together beyond onetime, stand-alone programs in the first place. It also means questioning why working alongside each other in more substantive ways may generate concerns, rooted in neoliberal ideology, about offices and budgets being collapsed into one another as a cost-saving measure.

Taking an intersectional approach to educational research and practice has the power to undo neoliberal ideology that keeps staffs in offices and departments from working together in more synergistic ways. It also has the power to create spaces in which researchers and practitioners recognize Micah's comment that he and other trans* students are complex people who all hold various, intersecting social identities. Thus, although the call to recommit oneself to intersectional praxis is rooted in the observation that as a field of higher education scholars and practitioners we have continually missed the mark, I agree with the variety of scholars I have cited in this book that we can do better. Indeed, we must do better not only for the future of intersectionality research and practice but also, more importantly, for the lives of the students we work with.

## Developing an Epistemology of Love

Describing what they termed an *epistemology of love* as a standpoint from which researchers could approach inquiry, Palmer and Zajonc (2010) asked,

> At first, love seems to have little to do with knowledge and our understanding of how it works, but if we set aside romantic love for the moment, is it not true that we come to know best that which we love most? (p. 94)

Palmer and Zajonc further suggested that such an epistemology of love was the "true heart of higher education" (p. 94), claiming that to approach educational praxis from a place of love had the potential ability to increase one's environment and connection with others. The unnecessary conflation between love as intimate personal connection and love as erotic or romantic desire is implicit in Palmer and Zajonc's comment. This conflation, although overly facile, has likely stood in the way of educators' discussing or embracing such an epistemology of love throughout their research and practice. Developing an epistemology of love in student affairs and higher education means seeing and hearing each other for who we are, which requires giving each other the agency to define who we are for ourselves as well as allowing each other to change and amend who we are or could be in the future. It is my contention that were we educational scholars and practitioners to embrace such an epistemology of love, we may very well be able to do research and create educational environments that increase possibilities (Butler, 2006) and life chances (Spade, 2015) for trans* students.

Speaking of the benefits of loving in community, hooks (2000) stated,

> Enjoying the benefits of living and loving in community empowers us to meet strangers without fear and extend to them the gift of openness and recognition. . . . Unlike other movements for social change that require joining organizations and attending meetings, *we can begin the process of making community wherever we are* [emphasis added]. (p. 143)

At first, the thought of extending loving kindness seems oversimplified, impossibly quixotic, or downright unimportant. However, hooks's (2000) notion of "living and loving in community" (p. 143) is precisely what the participants found through the development of kinship networks. It was also exactly what they desired but found lacking in other students, faculty, and staff as well as their environment at CU. Although I agree with hooks that living and loving in community can begin wherever we are, the overall lack of a love-in-community undergirded the manifestations of gender binary discourse and compulsory heterogenderism that engulfed CU's campus. Whereas making community can happen, as hooks's aforementioned comment suggested, without "joining organizations and attending meetings," the likelihood of community happening organically looks far less optimistic than her comment suggests.

As a final implication for research and practice, I suggest educators spend time thinking about how to cultivate an epistemology of love to apply to their work alongside students. Particularly for students with marginalized identities such as trans* students, love may be missing from their lives.

Because of the twin cultural realities of gender binary discourse and compulsory heterogenderism, trans* people are often forced to confront, navigate, and resist their lack of self-worth (Fisher & Freeland, 2015; Nicolazzo, 2014b). In reflecting on the connections and kinship that my study participants and I continue to develop, we have been able to create a counterstory to the negative, false, and nefarious perceptions that our trans*ness somehow marks us as weird, strange, or freaks. Raegan's words to me in Chapter 7 are particularly poignant, as they told me, "Half the reason I wanted to do this was because I wanted to get to know you." Thus, for Raegan, the possibility of being connected with me as another trans* person was a main motivating factor for reaching out and entering our research together. Even Tristan's telling me the one week out of the year he felt most comfortable was when he left CU to attend Creating Change, a conference attended by many people with diverse genders, was indicative of the importance and slipperiness of cultivating kinship (see Chapter 3).

As Magolda and Knight Abowitz (1997) stated, "Understanding community and achieving a sense of it in higher education is difficult—despite near universal endorsement of this ideal" (p. 267). The word *community* has in many respects become vacuous, largely because it is overused and misunderstood. However, cultivating community, or kinship, as the study participants and I have come to think of it, is a precious and highly prized value in higher education settings. More than just being important, the development and maintenance of kinship networks has the potential to radically reorganize the way trans* students experience and navigate their collegiate settings. Although the participants talked about their ability to develop kinship networks, there was a noticeable absence of discussion about cisgender students, faculty, and staff seeking to create and maintain similar kinship networks with them. I do not mean to suggest these partnerships were entirely absent. Two examples of ways non-trans* people created kinship networks with the participants in the study are Adem and Raegan dating cisgender partners and the not entirely trans* membership of groups such as TransActions. However, such connections were rare. In fact, the data indicate that the overarching cultural realities of gender binary discourse and compulsory heterogenderism at CU actively hindered cross-gender kinship formations.

Educators, particularly cisgender educators, should take it on themselves to find ways to cultivate, take part in, and infuse notions of "living and loving in community" (hooks, 2000, p. 143) throughout their daily practice. This means exploring the many ways connections between strangers are encouraged and discouraged. It also means addressing the myriad ways systemic privilege and oppression operate on campuses to influence such (dis)connections. Truly engaging in this kind of work means making a commitment to self-reflection, which may reveal how an individual is complicit in systemic trans* oppression. These realizations are never easy, desirable, or welcome. However, it behooves us all to take on this project if we are to embrace an epistemology of love that may very well increase possibilities for students being and doing trans* genders in college.

## In Their Own Words

In concluding this book, I believe it should end where the original study began—with the participants themselves. In the following, participants shared what they hoped students, faculty, and staff would do to work better alongside trans* people.

Kade: I think just education is the biggest thing. I think that a lot of people even that talk about trans* issues don't really have a great understanding of it. Like, it's [a] very textbook surface definition of what it means to be *trans\**. So one, if you're gonna discuss it in class, do your homework [chuckles]. Yeah. And then, just like with any group that you don't understand, just very basic kindergarten things like, don't say something that you wouldn't want said to you. Like, you wouldn't go asking some random person about their genitals, or really private things that you don't know, but with trans* people, it's totally cool [laughs sarcastically]. Yeah, so I just think general consideration is really important.

Megan: I would think if they were unsure of someone's gender, they could ask for their proper pronouns, and what name they want to be [called] . . . and that's about it, really. I mean, if you treat 'em as the gender they want to be treated as, then they'll be just fine with you.

Micah: I would tell people, honestly, I feel like I would sit them all in a room—faculty, staff, students, educators—everybody—the whole shebang. And just sit there and make sure they are well-mixed-up individuals, like, you're not always sitting next to someone that is just like you, and I would kinda do the look to your left, look to your right type [of thing], and [say], "You know, these are the people of your future. You're going to encounter these people every day. People who look like they're not—people aren't always gonna look like you. People aren't always gonna believe the same things that you believe." And my challenge would be, "Just look at yourself and say do you want to be the person in the middle who can't get along, that doesn't work well in this society because you are letting certain things create those walls." And [I'd say], "Now take those walls and tear 'em down. Do you think [the person next to you is] gonna do something that completely compromises who you are? If you can't say yes to that question, there is no reason why you can't sit down and have lunch with this person. Or you can't sit down and study with this person, or this person can't properly educate you about something. You just have to tear down those walls and not be so stuck in your own ways and your own binaries in which we were taught as a child because we are clearly progressing." We are a progressing society, this is America. And that would be my challenge, like, can you do those things?

Jackson:   I can't really think about policies that are bad necessarily; I'm just thinking of actually getting to know somebody as a person before . . . like, the most basic form of getting to know somebody as a person before you pass a judgment based on their gender expression or whatever.

  Um, I [also] think that it's important to bring up in curriculum. You know, when you bring up different . . . kinds of social issues that you don't ignore the trans* issues, because I feel like that's something that happens a lot, even within the gay community, you know? . . . I think a lot of issues with people being intolerant is people . . . growing up in a really homogenous area and not having really learned about other people. . . . And then if there is a way to influence policy in that way . . . you know?

Adem:   I would tell [the] administration to step up their game and get their shit together. They're just—in so many respects, they are lagging. I don't see it so much with the administration that I deal with on a daily or weekly basis, but . . . [pause] . . . I mean, and not even just in trans* respects, but as far as it goes in making it a welcoming and inclusive campus, like, what are you [administration] doing? [CU's president] can talk about diversity all he fucking wants, but at the end of the day, it's [CU's] just bigger. Bigger doesn't make it more diverse. Bigger doesn't make it better, bigger doesn't make it more welcoming, bigger doesn't make it more important; it's just bigger.

I close by sharing the words of BC. Although she likely does not know it, her cool dismissal of trans* oppression has been one of the most critical turning points for me as a trans* person. I often struggle as a trans* scholar who researches trans* resilience, especially when I am feeling less than resilient. However, during our first formal interview together, BC succinctly told me the very thing I have needed to hear—and often recall—over and over again. Whenever I have felt the creep of gender binary discourse, or I am feeling the press of compulsory heterogenderism, or I am exhausted from the labor of practicing trans* genders, I remember what BC told me. When my trans* kin share similar feelings, a result of the pernicious effects of trans* oppression, I tell them the same thing BC told me. Although BC made her comment in response to my anxieties about my first job search as a trans* person, which at the time was more than two years away, the words have turned into something of a mantra for me and my trans* kin. BC told me that regardless of where I went or what I was doing, I should always make sure to "just go in looking good."

# AFTERWORD

Practice, seeking to try over and over
Building my world anew
Filled with potential, hope/new disaster
Finding those who hold me
When me holding me is weighty, heavy
Seeing me as enough, my people
In a world where the body remains a problem

I am a Black Ghanaian/African American heterosexual cisgender man who holds a faculty position at Miami University. I am perhaps the least likely candidate to be writing this afterword. And perhaps it is likely that folks who hold my identities most need to read and digest the words Z Nicolazzo has poured throughout this book. I start with sharing my intersected identities to reinforce one important theme interwoven throughout this book—the importance of naming. Naming things that are hidden removes the veil and makes our biases and assumptions explicit.

I met Z during hir doctoral studies at Miami University, and I served on Z's dissertation committee. For some reasons unknown to me, Z has identified me as one of hir kin—as a person ze trusts, in whom ze confides, and with whom ze has built solidarity. And the feeling is mutual. Our relationship demonstrates the best of humanity—how one can build relationships across differences. Although a number of points resonated with me throughout Nicolazzo's book, I comment on two ideas I learned from reading it: the importance of resilience and kinship networks. I spend the remainder of this afterword discussing these points.

A strength of Nicolazzo's book is the way ze explicates the notion of resilience among trans* college students. The colloquial way in which we often talk about resilience is that someone gets up after being knocked down, keeps moving forward, or does not let obstacles stand in the way of their progress. We often frame resilience in a tough, hero mentality where one must persist against all odds. Nicolazzo's work is different here in that ze does not paint these trans* collegians as having some immutable strength but instead as imperfect, vulnerable human beings trying as best as they can to live as their full selves in a world not made for them, a world where the gender binary

161

persists and frames them as abnormal and thus doles out real consequences on their bodies through laws, policies, norms, and beliefs.

Using resilience as a verb, Nicolazzo effectively challenges resilience as something that one either possesses or does not. Seeing resilience as something one practices, Nicolazzo encourages readers to see how trans* collegians' resilience might shift depending on their situational context. Framing resilience in this way also places the onus squarely on postsecondary educators for creating contexts that enable trans* students to live as their full selves so they need not spend so much energy responding to contexts that challenge their very existence. Viewing resilience as a verb that one practices also enables readers to see how trans* collegians can adopt resilient strategies they can apply to other contexts or assert their agency and not visit contexts where practicing resilience is nearly impossible. What Nicolazzo reminds us, though, is that not visiting contexts is often a false choice, as trans* college students cannot remove themselves from some contexts that are harmful and oppressive, which is further evidence why educators must consistently and boldly examine their contexts and challenge the gender binary discourse that is so pervasive.

Another lesson I learned from reading Nicolazzo's book is the importance of kinship networks to trans* collegians. Notice the pluralization of network to imply that the study participants developed and maintained multiple kinship networks to aid in their abilities to navigate the compulsory heterogenderism and gender binary discourse that existed on their campuses. It is notable in Nicolazzo's findings that for some participants, kinship networks extended beyond trans*-only spaces. This point is important, as it calls on postsecondary educators who hold identities different from trans* students to work alongside them to develop these kinship networks. It also implies that trans* collegians may choose educators with identities different from their own as part of their kin. Because kinship networks are multifaceted and look different depending on the person, educators cannot be all things to all trans* students. Let me be clear: I am not suggesting that we absolve ourselves as educators from being advocates because, inevitably, some trans* collegians will not see us as their kin. I am contending that we not wrap our self-worth up in serving as good kin to trans* collegians, thereby placing the focus on being a good ally. Instead, we see ourselves as inherently flawed people, let go of our egos, and focus on our policies and practices and how our dominant identities, at times, preclude us from transforming environments so they are trans* inclusive.

A final point about kinship networks is the importance of participants in Nicolazzo's study having virtual spaces for these networks. Because the study participants sometimes lacked access to trans* kinship networks in their physical spaces, they often looked to social media as a platform for building these networks. These virtual spaces challenge some critiques of social media as a frivolous activity young people engage in without any real-world implications. On the contrary, these virtual spaces enabled trans* collegians to feel empowered, find solidarity, and practice resilience to navigate oppressive environments that persistently denied their existence.

I am deeply humbled that Z asked me to write this afterword. This book provoked a number of emotions, from sadness to anger to despair to hope to possibilities. I offer my own gratitude to the nine trans* collegians for sharing their stories with us, for reminding us that practicing resilience is a verb, and for pushing us to let go of our egos so we can see the ways we sometimes perpetuate the compulsory heterogenderism we seek to resist and transform. I urge readers to heed trans* college students' calls to uproot our policies and norms so they can live as the best versions of themselves in a world where that often seems impossible.

Stephen John Quaye
Associate Professor
Miami University
Oxford, Ohio
March 30, 2016

This glossary is intended to be a starting point in gaining more insight about trans* people, identities, and communities. In addition, I strongly suggest that readers see Stryker's (2008) glossary in her book *Transgender History* as well as the first double issue of *TSQ: Transgender Studies Quarterly*, titled "Postposttranssexual" (Currah & Stryker, 2014), which includes trans*-related terms.

## Agender

This is an identity signaling that one does not have, identify with, or align with any gender. Being agender does not mean people do not know their gender. Rather, it means not having or identifying with any gender.

## Cisgender

This term is used to identify nontrans* people. The prefix *cis* means "on this side" and is used to describe people who do not experience dissonance between their assigned sex at birth and its corresponding socially ascribed gender. However, Jourian (2015b) and Enke (2012) both cautioned against reifying a cis/trans* binary, as this oversimplified categorization misses the complexity of how gender maps across bodies, spaces, and times. Jourian's and Enke's insights are indeed reflected throughout this book, as multiple participants in the study (e.g., Adem, Micah, Raegan) often resisted easy gender categorizations that could be understood through the false cis/trans* binary.

## Compulsory able-bodiedness

A neologism created by McRuer (2006), compulsory able-bodiedness refers to the social discourses that reify able-bodied people, practices, and ideologies as supposedly normal. The term is multilayered as it describes acts, attitudes, and behaviors that manifest themselves on individual, institutional, and systemic levels.

## Compulsory heterogenderism

This is a neologism I created (Nicolazzo, 2015, 2016, in press) to describe how trans* people's genders are (mis)understood as sexualities. This happens as a result of people's reliance on sexuality-based stereotypes, which leads them to (mis)read trans* people's genders. As a result, trans* people's genders are erased and rendered culturally unknowable or impossible. This phenomenon also has the effect of making trans* people feel not trans* enough, as their trans*ness is continually questioned or not recognized.

## Critical trans politics

This critical theoretical perspective developed by Spade (2015) is invested in interrogating culturally embedded forms of trans* oppression and trans*; examines political strategizing grounded in intersectionality (Crenshaw, 1989, 1995); seeks to center on the voices, stories, and narratives of transgender and gender nonconforming people; and extends the value of polyvocality, or the foregrounding of multiple voices, to express many possible forms of resistance.

## Embodiment

This relates to the ways individuals may choose to morph their bodily representation either through biomedical modes or otherwise to mirror their internal gender identity or outward gender expression (e.g., someone born female taking injections to biomedically transition to a male sex; a drag king wearing a prosthetic penis to appear more masculine).

## Gender

This term describes the social discourse regarding how people identify, express, and embody the socially ascribed norms relating to their assigned sex at birth. Gender operates as a floating signifier for the ways individuals practice, do, or otherwise live in relation to these social norms. Precisely because of its ethereal status, gender has the ability to change and continues to change across time and context. Such (potential for) change, however, defies current social conceptualizations of the term in Western thought, which mark it as a naturalized, immutable fact that is always already tethered to one's assigned sex at birth.

## Gender binary

This is the false assumption that there are only two natural, immutable, and opposed genders (i.e., man and woman) that correspond with only two supposedly natural, immutable, and opposed sexes (i.e., male and female).

## Gender binary discourse

This term represents a constellation of words, phrases, actions, rules (written and unwritten), and social realities that regulate what are considered to be appropriate gender identities, expressions, and embodiments.

## Gender confirmation surgery

Pejoratively known as a sex change, this term relates to the multiple surgeries trans* people may elect to have to change how they embody their gender.

## Gender expression

This relates to one's outward expression of gender through cultural forms such as language, gestures, and artifacts (e.g., clothing, makeup). Similar to the discourse of gender, one's expression of gender may shift across time and space. However, these shifts do not mean one's gender expression is any less real or meaningful.

## Genderfuck

A gender identity, expression, or embodiment that denotes one's intentional blending, blurring, or otherwise fucking with socially ascribed gender norms. Genderfuck is an overtly political, highly confrontational, and intentionally confounding positionality that is intended to force others to confront their assumptions about gender.

## Gender identity

This relates to one's internal understanding of hir own gender. Quite literally, this term describes how one identifies one's gender, independent of how the individual expresses or embodies said identification. Similar to the discourse of gender, a person's identity may shift across time and space. However, these shifts do not mean one's gender expression is any less real or meaningful.

## Genderqueer

This term denotes how some people intentionally queer, or destabilize, their gender identity, expression, or embodiment. This term is similar to gender-fuck, but it could be understood to be less political, radical, or overt in orientation. In other words, where genderfuck is an attempt to radically shift public perceptions of gender, genderqueer is a more individual attempt to identify, express, or embody a positionality that is consonant with an individual's desires.

## Kinship networks

These close groups of peers recognize and honor trans* people's gender identities, expressions, and embodiments; provide a refuge from the cultural realities of gender binary discourse and compulsory heterogenderism; and act as a potential site from which trans* people can resist or push back against systemic trans* oppression if they so chose. Kinship networks are neither exclusively trans* (although they can be) nor singular in number, meaning individuals often have multiple kinship networks through which they move and obtain support. They exist on and off campus as well as in virtual spaces.

## Passing

This refers to the ability to be socially (mis)read as having a particular gender identity. Although some trans* people see passing as positive, it can also be a burden, or what trans* people feel they must do because of the threat or reality of violence. Passing can also be a positionality that is ascribed by others to an individual (e.g., "You pass as . . ."). Again, this has potentially positive and negative effects for trans* people, as the politics of passing are not easily discernable.

## Practices of resilience

This describes the strategies trans* people use to navigate college contexts that are entrenched in the twin cultural realities of gender binary discourse and compulsory heterogenderism. According to these strategies, resilience is a verb or an action people can (re)take as they cultivate effective strategies to promote and move toward their own success, however they define it.

## Proper pronouns

Sometimes called preferred gender pronouns, or PGPs, proper pronouns are those pronouns individuals choose to use and have used in reference to themselves. Pronouns can range in combinations and permutations, and people may even use multiple sets of pronouns in reference to themselves. Examples of pronouns include ze/hir; they/them/their (used in the singular); ze/zem/zir; she/her/hers; he/him/his. Some people may also use different pronouns, such as S or V. In this definition, I also use the modifier *proper* to suggest that there is nothing preferred about the pronouns people use to assert their dignity and humanity.

## Sex assigned at birth

This term describes the social discourse regarding how people are assigned to one of two supposedly natural, immutable sexes (i.e., male or female). Although some individuals are born as intersex, there is still intense pressure from medical practitioners to operate on intersex babies to modify their sex assignations so they align within the binary of male/female. This, then, has the effect of reifying the fallacious assumption of sex as a binary discourse.

## Trans*

This term refers to those who transgress the socially constructed discourse of how we identify, express, and embody our genders. The asterisk is borrowed from the symbol used for computer search functions that allow people to search for a certain prefix (e.g., trans-), resulting in a list of complete words using that prefix (Tompkins, 2014). In this sense, the asterisk is used to signal the expansiveness and constantly expanding communities of trans* people. There has been some debate about the use of the asterisk in trans* communities, however, and while it is out of the scope of this glossary to discuss these complexities, it should be noted that not all trans* people prefer it, use it, or agree with its use.

## Trans* feminine

This term denotes trans* people who identify, express, or embody feminine-of-center positionalities. Trans* feminine people may or may not move toward biomedically transitioning to a trans* woman.

## Trans* man

This term applies to trans* people who desire or are in the process of socially or biomedically transitioning (e.g., taking hormones, seeking gender confirmation surgeries). Not all people who identify as trans* men can or do transition. I have used the term in this book in relation to Kade, the study participant who identified as a trans* man, to illustrate this definition. It is also a reflection of how he named his own identity.

## Trans* masculine

This refers to trans* people who identify, express, or embody masculine-of-center positionalities. Trans* masculine people may or may not move toward biomedically transitioning to being a trans* man.

## Trans* oppression

This refers to a system of oppression that places at a disadvantage "people whose gender identity or expression do [*sic*] not conform to binary cultural norms and expectations" (Catalano & Griffin, 2016, p. 183). Using this term as an organizing principle for understanding the social asymmetry of gender enforcement and regulation requires that trans* people and their needs are acknowledged and centered in discussions. I have used this term throughout this book rather than using the term *genderism*, which operates as a critique of gender without necessarily centering on trans* people and our needs.

## Trans* woman

This applies to trans* people who desire or are in the process of socially or biomedically transitioning (e.g., taking hormones, seeking gender confirmation surgeries). Not all people who identify as trans* women can or do transition. I use the term in this book in relation to Megan and BC, who identified as trans* women, to illustrate this definition. It also illustrates how they named their own identies.

# APPENDIX

# Notes on Study Design

The data presented in this book were collected through an 18-month critical collaborative ethnographic study during the 2013–2014 and 2014–2015 academic years. I situated my research in a critical paradigm, which presupposes reality and truth as subjective and influenced through a system of sociopolitical power that privileges some while marginalizing others along the lines of social identity (Lather, 2006; Lincoln, Lynham, & Guba, 2011). Specifically, I used a particular strand of critical theory known as critical trans politics (CTP). Rather than falling for the illogical supposition that there is one answer to solving problems, Spade (2015) referred to the reality that trans* oppression is the result of multiple and intersecting forms of violence and the reinforcement of a dichotomous gender binary. As a theoretical perspective, CTP is invested in interrogating culturally embedded forms of trans* oppression and transphobia; examines political strategizing grounded in intersectionality (Crenshaw, 1989, 1995); centers on the voices, stories, and narratives of trans* and gender nonconforming people; and extends the value of polyvocality, or the foregrounding of multiple voices, to express many possible forms of resistance.

## Methodology: Critical Collaborative Ethnography

Critical collaborative ethnography is a branch of the broader tradition of critical inquiry. Critical theory is politically motivated (Carspecken, 1996; Kincheloe & McLaren, 1998) and oppositional in nature (E. Taylor, 1998). Critical collaborative ethnography rests on the notion of critical thought (Brookfield, 2012) as well as how privilege and power mediate one's multiple intersecting social identities and how, as a result, one navigates a social world riven with inequity (Crenshaw, 1989, 1995). Critical collaborative ethnography translates the political orientation of critical theory into the realm of ethnographic research. Echoing the writing of Thomas (1993), Bhattacharya (2008) defined the central aspect of *critical collaborative ethnography* as "refer[ring] to ethnographic practice that focuses on projects that challenge dominant hegemonic global structures at the intersection of race, gender, class, sexuality, and disability" (p. 305). By looking at the micro- and macrolevel systems of privilege and oppression, critical collaborative ethnography provided a lens through which the study participants and I interrogated the pervasiveness of cultural trans* oppression in the college environment. It also provided a platform for us to advocate for institutional reforms (Foley & Valenzuela, 2008), which is itself an essential component of any critically based research study.

The collaborative aspect of critical collaborative ethnography relates to working alongside participants rather than doing research on or about them (Bhattacharya, 2008). Entering into a collaborative research relationship with other individuals means we all took part in constructing and making sense of our shared reality (Lykes, 1989). This process involved the development of close, trusting relationships (Foley & Valenzuela, 2008) rooted in a shared sense of solidarity in the research itself (Lykes, 1989). Collaboration also required continued negotiation between me and the research participants. As Brettell (1993) noted, "The [participant] is never always right and . . . the ethnographer . . . is sometimes wrong" (p. 16). Therefore, the collabora- tive nature of my study served as a way to check constantly the negotiation of power as well as whose voice and analysis was forwarded throughout the research process.

## Research Questions and Data Collection

Given the extended time participants and I were collecting data, we used various methods for collection, each of which was tied to at least one, if not multiple or all, of my research questions, which were as follows: (a) What are the cultural gender norms confronting trans* college students?; (b) How are these cultural gender norms manifested and enforced?; (c) How do trans* college students confront, navigate, resist, and/or push back against these cul- tural gender norms?; (d) What role do coalitions among students, faculty, and staff on campus play in the formation and/or maintenance of individual and/ or group-based trans* resiliency, if any?; and (e) How do participants define and make sense of resiliency as they navigate their gendered cultural context?

In answering these questions, and pursuant to critical collaborative eth- nographic methodology, I used the following methods for data collection: participant observation (Emerson, Fretz, & Shaw, 2001; Wolcott, 2008) in which participants and I met 2 to 3 days per week over the course of our 18 months together; document analysis (Wolcott, 2008), which included online documents, campus postings, newspaper articles, and CU policies;

ethnographic interviewing (Heyl, 2001; O'Reilly, 2005, 2009; Wolcott, 2008), which included one formal recorded interview with each participant each semester of their involvement, lasting anywhere from 45 to 90 minutes; and participant narrative summaries (Tillapaugh, 2012), which included prompts participants were asked to respond to once a semester for each semester of their involvement.

## Goodness Criteria

In accordance with O'Reilly's (2005) suggestion of spending at least a year in the field, I spent 18 months doing fieldwork for this study. Spending a year and a half at CU allowed the strange to become familiar and the familiar to become strange (Magolda & Ebben Gross, 2009; O'Reilly, 2005). Spending an extended amount of time in the field allowed me to gain a more complete understanding of CU and to contemplate the various meanings of my experiences as a researcher instead of making quick assessments without the full context. My 18 months in the field also allowed me to build trust with the participants and other stakeholders across campus (Lincoln & Guba, 1985). Additionally, the variety of methods I employed for data collection ensured that my prolonged engagement was meaningful.

Similar to my prolonged time in the field collecting data, our use of multiple data collection methods allowed me to triangulate the data, thereby increasing the trustworthiness and credibility of my findings. Rather than just using one data collection method, the four I chose to employ (i.e., participant observation, document analysis, ethnographic interviewing, and participant narrative summaries) provided me with ample data for me to draw credible conclusions. Moreover, I relied on three peer reviewers who offered their perspectives on my data and conclusions through peer debriefing sessions. I also conducted multiple member checks throughout the research process to garner further information and insight into trans* college student resilience. In conducting periodic member checks, I invited all research participants to review and provide feedback on the research process each semester of their involvement. Additionally, I provided all research participants with transcripts of their personal interviews and their individual narrative summaries. I then invited participants to provide clarification and feedback about what I had provided them with and asked them what aspects of the culture at CU they thought might be illuminating to the research study that I should explore in more depth.

Member checks also served as a way for participants and me to deepen our shared understanding regarding my research questions. In this way, member checks served as an important springboard to the *thick description* (Geertz, 1973) I provided when I wrote the results of our research. Geertz stated, "Doing ethnography is like trying to read (in the sense of 'construct a reading of') a manuscript—foreign, faded, full of ellipses, incoherencies, suspicious emendations, and tendentious commentaries" (p. 10). In response to this, Geertz said the aim of ethnographic texts was "to draw large conclusions from small, but very densely textured facts; to support broad assertions about the role of culture in the construction of collective life by engaging them exactly with complex specifics" (p. 28). These very densely textured facts and complex specifics are invoked in the notion of thick description. My time in the field, along with the various methods of data collection, allowed me to develop thick descriptions of the culture of trans* students and their resilience in confronting, navigating, and resisting the trans* oppression inherent in the higher education environment where they found themselves. In turn, this thick description enhanced the credibility of my study, analysis, and findings.

## Possibilities and Challenges of Collaborative Methodologies

As I and T.J. Jourian (Jourian & Nicolazzo, 2016) have written about previously, there is significant liberatory potential when using collaborative and participatory methodologies alongside trans* populations. These methodologies provide not only an opportunity for trans* people to take part in writing their own counterstories and to have more control over their (self-)representations but also allow a more equitable and transparent research process. However, suggesting a study is collaborative has a number of challenges. How collaborative a study is may vary widely. For example, for the present study, participants did not help construct the study design, decide on research questions, or participate in writing this book. However, participants did take part in data analysis and were consulted throughout the research process when I ran into challenges or had questions related to the writing process. Furthermore, the relationships between participants and me exceeded traditional participant/interviewer relationships, as suggested by Bhattacharya (2008). Relationships with participants were highly reciprocal, rooted in deep connection and trust (Foley & Valenzuela, 2008), and embodied a sense of shared solidarity (Lykes, 1989). Despite this, I often wondered how collaborative the study needed to be to substantiate it as a collaborative study in the first place.

I also worried about participants' time in crafting and doing collaborative research. I did not want to ask too much of participants, given their already demanding schedules. However, I also did not want to presume the participants could not make good choices for themselves about how, when, and to what extent they participated in our study. The negotiation of too much or not enough involvement was consistently on my mind throughout the 18 months we worked together. Although I am not sure I ever negotiated the question of time and involvement as best I could have (or should have), any guilt I felt about heaping too much work on them was assuaged when the participants expressed sadness about the research study ending and then kept in touch after the study concluded. In fact, the lasting relationships I still have with many of these participants is a major benefit of collaborative research itself and may indeed signal its efficacy as the chosen methodology for the present study. Far from being hyperbolic, I can honestly say the relationships I have kept with several participants have been some of the most meaningful, inspiring, and honest relationships I have constructed in my adult life. I have remained close with these young adults as they graduated or moved on from CU and am anticipating with great zeal hearing about the great things they do throughout their lives.

## Possibilities and Challenges of Resiliency Research

Along with the possibilities and challenges associated with the collaborative nature of the research design, doing affirmative, resilience-based research itself posed several conundrums for me. Taking a resilience-based approach served as an important counterstory to the overwhelming deficit-based rhetoric surrounding trans* lives in educational research as well as in the social imaginary. However, I worried that focusing heavily on resilience and success might overshadow the pain, frustration, and fear some participants shared (and I myself felt) at times throughout our working together. I often felt trapped in an either/or binary where we as trans* people could be either resilient or weak, successful or failures, visible and accounted for or immaterial and impossible. Furthermore, I worried that if I tried to create a more complex tapestry of trans* lives—as the data indeed suggest—it might be too hard, murky, or confusing to follow. I did not want to do an injustice to the stories and experiences of the nine people who spent the better part of a year and a half working alongside me, but I also did not want their experiences to be lost because of readers' inability to follow the complexity of their emotional and material lives.

Although this study resulted in much more data than could ever be represented in this book, I feel I have been able to do justice to the participants who shared so much of themselves with me. I did not shy away from describing difficult moments, nor did I stray from sharing their many incredible successes. Just as all other people, the participants in this study lived lives that were sometimes contradictory. They experienced pain alongside pleasure, fear alongside possibility, and kinship alongside alienation. At the end of my research process, I now know that what participants and I were searching for all along was not mere resilience or success; we were searching for raw experience and to have our counterstories heard. So perhaps, in the end, resilience and success may not have been particular points of arrival, but they came through the process and practice of our being alongside one another and searching together.

## Study Boundaries and Transferability

Far from attempting to compensate for some supposed lack of validity or ability to generalize the findings to broader contexts (themselves standards of postpositivist and quantitative research, which I never intended to take on), I do find it important to offer some suggestions for how readers may transfer findings from this study. I also find it important to acknowledge the ways this study was framed as a reminder of what the study—and, by extension, the findings—was and was not. I start by describing the study boundaries and then move into a discussion about the questions readers may want to consider when attempting to transfer the study findings to various contexts.

### *Boundaries*

Although I was intentional about choosing CU for fieldwork, I am also cognizant that only two of the participants were Black. I had no participants who identified as Latinx, American Indian/Indigenous/Native American/First Nation, or Asian American/Desi/Pacific Islander. This lack of racial and ethnic representation was limiting, as the participants did not reflect the racial and ethnic makeup of the wider, national trans* population. Furthermore, although participants certainly did not have large amounts of disposable income (in fact, BC left CU before obtaining a degree because of her need to work to earn money), the very reality of their being in college signaled a particular socioeconomic status that many trans* people may never achieve. In fact, Grant and colleagues (2011) found that trans* people were four times more likely to make $10,000 or less annually, which was not a reality for the participants (or myself). However, in a related and eerily similar statistic, Grant and colleagues found that less than half (45%) of trans* people aged 18 to 24 were in school. Although all participants began our study in school, four of the nine left CU during data collection. In other words, a little more than half the students participating in the study (all of whom were 18–24 at the time) were on track to complete their college education, closely aligning with Grant and colleagues' finding. Although one participant (BC) did eventually return to CU, and another (Jackson) began attending Stockdale State, and I talked with others about the possibility of their doing the same, the confluence between Grant and colleagues' data and the study participants is worrisome. Specifically, it highlights just how overwhelming, pervasive, and nefarious gender binary discourse and compulsory heterogenderism are on college campuses as well as how these twin cultural realities may foreclose opportunities for trans* collegians.

Furthermore, I was able to be at CU only 2 to 3 days a week for the 18 months of fieldwork. Although I was able to see, experience, and listen a lot, I missed much because of the limited time I was able to spend on campus. Although the time I spent on campus was significant, it sometimes felt like it was not enough. For example, participants sometimes told me they had been waiting to tell me things or share stories about particular experiences they had. I wonder what it would have been like being with them when they were having those experiences, and I think that had I been able to do so, it would likely have resulted in a richer set of data. I do not intend for this to represent a flaw in participants' memories but more so a realization that although I spent much time on campus, it sometimes felt like I could not be as present as I (or several participants) would have liked me to be. This also illustrates the closeness of the kinship networks we were able to create and our desire to be with and alongside each other whenever possible.

Finally, I was expressly concerned with trans* students rather than the meaning that faculty or staff (trans*-identified or otherwise) made of trans* students' experiences. Marine (2011a) has studied the thoughts of administrators at women's colleges regarding trans* students, and although there is still room for additional scholarship on how faculty and staff understand gender transgression on college campuses, this was not something I attended to for the present inquiry. Thus, when interpreting and transferring the results of this study, readers should take care not to assume what participants and I found relates in any way to faculty and staff.

## *Transferability*

Mertens (2015) stated, "In qualitative research, the burden of transferability is on the reader to determine the degree of similarity between the study site and the receiving context" (p. 271). However, it strikes me as important to mention several things readers should consider when they attempt to transfer the results of the present study to their own educational contexts. First, it bears repeating that the city of Stockdale has a history of racial tension and anti-LGBTQ legislation. Because campuses are microcosms of their environments, it is fair to suggest that Stockdale's history influenced the cultural understandings of gender on CU's campus. Readers in different sociocultural contexts or locations without such a tenuous history of racism, trans* oppression, and homophobia may want to consider how their unique historical context may differ from Stockdale's and, thus, how their campus context may also diverge from that of CU.

Second, it is also worth noting that understanding one's cultural environment enough to recognize when, how, and if the findings and implications of the present study may transfer takes time. For example, the findings and implications of this study took more than two and a half years to develop, 18 months of which consisted of prolonged engagement with participants in the field. Fully understanding one's culture is a study in time and patience. Likewise, determining the transferability of the present study to other contexts may also require similar amounts of time and patience. Despite the neoliberal push to do more with fewer resources and in less time, embodied in the notions of heightened productivity and efficiency that are becoming increasingly popular throughout higher education, I suggest slowing down in determining how, when, or even if the findings and implications from the present study can be transferred to various contexts. The twin cultural realities of gender binary discourse and compulsory heterogenderism along with the other findings participants and I developed are complex. As a result, they demand complex solutions. It would be disingenuous, risky, and unethical to assume one could easily or quickly transfer the findings and implications from this study to other contexts without having a handle on the way gender mediates students' experiences in other contexts. Thus, I advise exercising caution and practicing prudence when determining the transferability of the present study. Also, in reflecting the communal nature of the present study, I suggest determining the transferability of the findings and implications in community with trans* students. This will not only center on the voices of those of us who are often overlooked, forgotten, or told we do not exist but also empower trans* people to take the lead in determining how change is implemented in their own collegiate environments.

# REFERENCES

Abes, E. S. (2011). Exploring the relationship between sexual orientation and religious identities for Jewish lesbian college students. *Journal of Lesbian Studies, 15*(2), 205–225.

Abes, E. S., & Jones, S. R. (2004). Meaning-making capacity and the dynamics of lesbian college students' multiple dimensions of identity. *Journal of College Student Development, 45,* 612–632.

Abes, E. S., & Kasch, D. (2007). Using queer theory to explore lesbian college students' multiple dimensions of identity. *Journal of College Student Development, 48*(6), 619–636.

Ablow, K. (2011). *J. Crew plants the seeds for gender identity.* Retrieved from www .foxnews.com/health/2011/04/11/j-crew-plants-seeds-gender-identity

Adam, B. D. (1978). *The survival of domination: Inferiorization and everyday life.* New York, NY: Elsevier.

Ahmed, S. (2006). *Queer phenomenology: Orientations, objects, others.* Durham, NC: Duke University Press.

Ahmed, S. (2010). *The promise of happiness.* Durham, NC: Duke University Press.

Ahmed, S. (2012). *On being included: Racism and diversity in institutional life.* Durham, NC: Duke University Press.

Alexander, J., & Yescavage, K. (2003). *Bisexuality and transgenderism: InterSEXions of the others.* Binghamton, NY: Harrington Park Press.

American College Personnel Association & National Association of Student Personnel Administrators. (2015). *Professional competency areas for student affairs practitioners.* Washington, DC: Author.

André, A., & Chang, S. (2006). "And then you cut your hair": Genderfucking on the femme side of the spectrum. In Mattilda (Ed.), *Nobody passes: Rejecting the rules of gender and conformity* (pp. 254–269). Berkeley, CA: Seal Press.

Anzaldúa, G. (2007). *Borderlands/La frontera* (3rd ed.). San Francisco, CA: Aunt Lute Books.

Astin, A. W. (1993). *What matters in college: Four critical years revisited.* San Francisco, CA: Jossey-Bass.

Baker, S. S., Cox, K., Cox, M., Dean, D., & Tsou, S.-C. (Producers), & Baker, S. S. (Director). (2015). *Tangerine* [Motion picture]. United States: Duplass Brothers Productions.

Barnett, R., & Rivers, C. (2004). *Same difference: How gender myths are hurting relationships, our children, and our jobs.* New York, NY: Basic Books.

Beauchamp, T. (2013). Artful concealment and strategic visibility: Transgender bodies and U.S. state surveillance after 9/11. In S. Stryker & A. Z. Aizura (Eds.), *Transgender studies reader 2* (pp. 46–55). New York, NY: Routledge.

Beemyn, B. (2003). Serving the needs of transgender college students. *Journal of Gay and Lesbian Issues in Education, 3*(1), 33–49.

Beemyn, B. (2005). Making campuses more inclusive of transgender students. *Journal of Gay and Lesbian Issues in Education, 3*(1), 77–88.

Beemyn, B., Curtis, B., Davis, M., & Tubbs, N. J. (2005). Transgender issues on college campuses. *New Directions for Student Services, 111*, 49–60.

Beemyn, B., Domingue, A., Pettitt, J., & Smith, T. (2005). Suggested steps to make campuses more trans-inclusive. *Journal of Gay and Lesbian Issues in Education, 3*(1), 89–95.

Beemyn, B., & Rankin, S. (2011). *The lives of transgender people.* New York, NY: Columbia University Press.

Bell, D. (1989). Racism: A prophecy for the year 2000. *Rutgers Law Review, 42*(93), 93–108.

Bell, L. A. (2007). Theoretical foundations for social justice education. In M. Adams, L. A. Bell, & P. Griffin (Eds.), *Teaching for diversity and social justice* (2nd ed., pp. 1–14). New York, NY: Routledge.

Between the Lines Staff. (2014). *Suspect in Tiffany Edwards' murder turns himself in.* Retrieved from www.pridesource.com/article.html?article=66832

Bhattacharya, H. (2008). New critical collaborative ethnography. In S. N. Hesse-Biber & P. Leavy (Eds.), *Handbook of emergent methods* (pp. 303–322). New York, NY: Guilford Press.

Bilodeau, B. (2005). Beyond the gender binary: A case study of two transgender students at a midwestern research university. *Journal of Gay and Lesbian Issues in Education, 3*(1), 29–44.

Bilodeau, B. L. (2009). *Genderism: Transgender students, binary systems and higher education.* Düsseldorf, Germany: VDM Verlag.

Bilodeau, B. L., & Renn, K. A. (2005). Analysis of LGBT identity development models and implications for practice. *New Directions for Student Services, 111*, 25–40.

Bochner, A. P., & Ellis, C. (1996). In C. Ellis & A. P. Bochner (Eds.), *Composing ethnography: Alternative forms of qualitative writing* (pp. 13–45). Walnut Creek, CA: AltaMira Press.

Boldly Go. (2013, February 8). Trans normativity [Web log post]. Retrieved from boldlygo.co/trans-normativity

Bonchev, D., & Rouvray, D. H. (2005). Preface. In D. Bonchev & D. H. Rouvray (Eds.), *Complexity in chemistry, biology, and ecology* (pp. vii–xiv). Boston, MA: Springer.

Bornstein, K. (1994). *Gender outlaw: On men, women, and the rest of us.* New York, NY: Vintage Books.

Born This Way Foundation. (n.d.). *Our mission.* Retrieved from bornthiswayfoundation.org

Bourdieu, P. (2002). *Outline of a theory in practice* (R. Nice, Trans.). Cambridge, UK: Cambridge University Press. (Original work published 1977)

Bowleg, L. (2008). When Black + lesbian + women ≠ Black lesbian woman: The methodological challenges of qualitative and quantitative intersectionality research. *Sex Roles, 59*(5/6), 312–325.

Boylan, J. F. (2003). *She's not there: A life in two genders.* New York, NY: Broadway Books.

Brettell, C. B. (1993). Introduction: Fieldwork, text, and audience. In C. B. Brettell (Ed.), *When they read what we write: The politics of ethnography* (pp. 1–24). Westport, CT: Bergin & Garvey.

Bronfenbrenner, U. (1993). The ecology of cognitive development: Research models and fugitive findings. In R. H. Wozniak & K. W. Fischer (Eds.), *Development in context: Acting and thinking in specific environments* (pp. 3–14). Mahwah, NJ: Erlbaum.

Brookfield, S. D. (2012). *Teaching for critical thinking: Tools and techniques to help students question assumptions.* San Francisco, CA: Jossey-Bass.

Burns, C. (2011). *Fact sheet: LGBT discrimination in higher education financial aid.* Retrieved from www.americanprogress.org/issues/lgbt/news/2011/08/24/10163/ fact-sheet-lgbt-discrimination-in-higher-education-financial-aid

Butler, J. (2004). *Undoing gender.* New York, NY: Routledge.

Butler, J. (2006). *Gender trouble: Feminism and the subversion of identity.* New York, NY: Routledge.

Califia, P. (2003). *Sex changes: The politics of transtrans\* oppression* (2nd ed.). San Francisco, CA: Cleis Press.

Calton, J. M., Cattaneo, L. B., & Gebhard, K. T. (2015). Barriers to help seeking for lesbian, gay, bisexual, transgender, and queer survivors of intimate partner violence. *Trauma, Violence, & Abuse.* Advanced online publication. doi:10.1177/1524838015585318

Campbell, K. M. (2011). The road to S.B. 1070: How Arizona became ground zero for the immigrants' rights movement and the continuing struggle for Latino civil rights in America. *Harvard Latino Law Review, 14*, 1–21.

Campus Pride. (n.d.-a). *Frequently asked questions.* Retrieved from www.campusprid eindex.org/faqs/index

Campus Pride. (n.d.-b). *Welcome to the new Campus Pride index.* Retrieved from www.campusprideindex.org

Cantor, D., Fisher, B., Chibnall, S., Townsend, R., Lee, H., Bruce, C., & Thomas, G. (2015). *Report on the AAU campus climate survey on sexual assault and sexual misconduct.* Washington, DC: Association of American Universities. Retrieved from www.aau.edu/uploadedFiles/AAU_Publications/AAU_Reports/Sexual_ Assault_Campus_Survey/AAU_Campus_Climate_Survey_12_14_15.pdf

Carmel, T., Hopwood, R., & dickey, l. m. (2014). Mental health concerns. In L. Erickson-Schroth (Ed.), *Trans bodies, trans selves: A resource for the transgender community* (pp. 305–332). New York, NY: Oxford University Press.

Carspecken, P. F. (1996). *Critical ethnography in educational research: A theoretical and practical guide.* New York, NY: Routledge.

Cass, V. C. (1979). Homosexual identity formation: A theoretical model. *Journal of Homosexuality, 4*, 219–235.

Cass, V. C. (1984). Homosexual identity formation: Testing a theoretical model. *Journal of Sex Research, 20,* 143–167.

Catalano, D. C. J. (2014). *Welcome to guyland: Experiences of trans\* men in college* (Doctoral dissertation). Retrieved from http://scholarworks.umass.edu/dissertations_2/60/

Catalano, D. C. (2015a). Beyond virtual equality: Liberatory consciousness as a path to achieve trans\* inclusion in higher education. *Equity & Excellence in Education, 48*(3), 418–435.

Catalano, D. C. J. (2015b). "Trans enough?": The pressures trans men negotiate in higher education. *TSQ: Transgender Studies Quarterly, 2*(3), 411–430.

Catalano, D. C. J. (in press). Resisting coherence: Trans men's experiences and the use of grounded theory methods. *International Journal of Qualitative Studies in Education.*

Catalano, D. C. J., & Griffin, P. (2016). Sexism, heterosexism, and trans\* oppression. In M. Adams, L. A. Bell, D. J. Goodman, & K. Y. Joshi (Eds.), *Teaching for diversity and social justice* (3rd ed., pp. 183–211). New York, NY: Routledge.

Catalano, C., McCarthy, L., & Shlasko, D. (2007). Transgender oppression curriculum design. In M. Adams, L. A. Bell, & P. Griffin (Eds.), *Teaching for diversity and social justice* (2nd ed., pp. 219–245). New York, NY: Routledge.

Catalano, C., & Shlasko, D. (2013). Transgender oppression: Introduction. In M. Adams, W. J. Blumenfeld, C. Castañeda, H. W. Hackman, M. L. Peters, & X. Zúñiga (Eds.), *Readings for diversity and social justice* (3rd ed., pp. 425–431). New York, NY: Routledge.

Chaffee, K., Davis, C., Smith, L., & Walsh, M. (2013). *Miami university makes strides toward acceptance of gay students.* Retrieved from wyso.org/post/miami-university-makes-strides-toward-acceptance-gay-students#stream/0

Chalabi, M. (2014). Why we don't know the size of the transgender population [Web log post]. Retrieved from www.fivethirtyeight.com/features/why-we-dont-know-the-size-of-the-transgender-population.

Clare, E. (2001). Stolen bodies, reclaimed bodies: Disability and queerness. *Public Culture, 13*(3), 359–365.

Clare, E. (2003). Gawking, gaping, staring. *GLQ: A Journal of Lesbian and Gay Studies, 9*(1/2), 257–261.

Clare, E. (2015). *Exile and pride: Disability, queerness, and liberation* (3rd ed.). Durham, NC: Duke University Press.

Collins, P. H. (2009). Forward: Emerging intersections—building knowledge and transforming institutions. In B. T. Dill & R. E. Zambrana (Eds.), *Emerging intersections: Race, class, and gender in theory, policy, and practice* (pp. vii–xiii). New Brunswick, NJ: Rutgers University Press.

Conrad, P. (2012, March 21). Male student files discrimination charge. *Journal-News.* Retrieved from www.middletownjournal.com/news/news/local/miami-student-files-discrimination-charge/nNYtH

Conron, K. J., Scott, G., Stowell, G. S., & Landers, S. J. (2012). Transgender health in Massachusetts: Results from a household probability sample of adults. *American Journal of Public Health, 102*(1), 118–122. doi:10.2105/AJPH.2011.30031

Cooper, T. (2012). *Real man adventures.* San Francisco, CA: McSweeney's Books.

Corbin, J., & Strauss, A. (2008). *Basics of qualitative research* (3rd ed.). Thousand Oaks, CA: Sage.

Crenshaw, K. (1989). Demarginalizing the intersection of race and sex: A Black feminist critique of antidiscrimination doctrine, feminist theory, and antiracist politics. *University of Chicago Legal Forum, 140,* 139–167.

Crenshaw, K. W. (1995). Mapping the margins: Intersectionality, identity politics, and violence against women of color. In K. Crenshaw, N. Gotanda, G. Peller, & K. Thomas (Eds.), *Critical race theory: The key writings that formed the movement* (pp. 357–383). New York, NY: The New Press.

Currah, P. (2006). Gender pluralisms under the transgender umbrella. In P. Currah, R. M. Juang, & S. Prince Minter (Eds.), *Transgender rights* (pp. 3–31). Minneapolis: University of Minnesota Press.

Currah, P., & Stryker, S. (2014). Postposttransexual: Key concepts for a twenty-first-century transgender studies. *TSQ: Transgender Studies Quarterly, 1*(1/2).

Currah, P., & Stryker, S. (2015). Introduction. *TSQ: Transgender Studies Quarterly, 2*(1), 1–12.

D'Augelli, A. R. (1994). Identity development and sexual orientation: Toward a model of lesbian, gay, and bisexual development. In E. J. Trickett, R. J. Watts, & D. Birman (Eds.), *Human diversity: Perspectives on people in context* (pp. 312–333). San Francisco, CA: Jossey-Bass.

Davis, A. Y. (2016). *Freedom is a constant struggle: Ferguson, Palestine, and the foundation of a movement.* Chicago, IL: Haymarket Books.

Davis, E. C. (2008). Situating "fluidity": (Trans)Gender identification and the regulation of gender diversity. *GLQ: A Journal of Lesbian and Gay Studies, 15*(1), 97–130. doi:10.1215/10642684-2008-020.

de Laine, M. (2000). *Fieldwork, participation and practice: Ethics and dilemmas in qualitative research.* Thousand Oaks, CA: Sage.

Dilley, P. (2005). Which way out? A typology of non-heterosexual male collegiate identities. *The Journal of Higher Education, 76,* 56–88.

Dugan, J. P., Kusel, M. L., & Simounet, D. M. (2012). Transgender college students: An exploratory study of perceptions, engagement, and educational outcomes. *Journal of College Student Development, 53*(5), 719–736.

Dunn, J. (1999, March 18). Rolling Stone style: Hip-hop. *Rolling Stone.* Retrieved from www.rollingstone.com/culture/features/rs-style-19990318

Duran, A., & Nicolazzo, Z. (in press). Exploring the ways trans* collegians navigate academic, romantic, and social relationships. *Journal of College Student Development.*

Dusenbery, M. (2013). What about the guys who do fit the "gay stereotype"? *Atlantic.* Retrieved from www.theatlantic.com/sexes/archive/2013/05/what-about-the-guys-who-do-fit-the-gay-stereotype/276407

Dzmura, N. (2010). *Balancing on the mechitza: Transgender in Jewish community.* Berkeley, CA: North Atlantic Books.

Ekins, R., & King, D. (2006). *The transgender phenomenon.* Thousand Oaks, CA: Sage.

Elia, J. P., & Yep, G. A. (2012). Sexualities and genders in an age of neoterrorism. *Journal of Homosexuality, 59*(7), 879–889.

Emerson, R. M., Fretz, R. I., & Shaw, L. L. (2001). Participant observation and fieldnotes. In P. Atkinson, A. Coffey, S. Delamont, J. Lofland, & L. Lofland (Eds.), *Handbook of ethnography* (pp. 352–368). Thousand Oaks, CA: Sage.

Enke, A. F. (2012). The education of little cis: Cisgender and the discipline of opposing bodies. In A. Enke (Ed.), *Transfeminist perspectives in and beyond transgender and gender studies* (pp. 60–77). Philadelphia, PA: Temple University Press.

Evans, N. J., Forney, D. S., Guido, F. M., Patton, L. D., & Renn, K. A. (2010). *Student development in college: Theory, research, and practice* (2nd ed.). San Francisco, CA: Jossey-Bass.

Evans, N. J., & Wall, V. A. (1991). *Beyond tolerance: Gays, lesbians, and bisexuals on campus.* Lanham, MD: University Press of America.

Fassinger, R. E. (1998). Lesbian, gay, and bisexual identity and student development theory. In R. L. Sanlo (Ed.), *Working with lesbian, gay, bisexual, and transgender college students: A handbook for faculty and administrators* (pp. 13–22). Westport, CT: Greenwood Press.

Fausto-Sterling, A. (1985). *Myths of gender: Biological theories about women and men.* New York, NY: Basic Books.

Fausto-Sterling, A. (2000). *Sexing the body: Gender politics and the construction of sexuality.* New York, NY: Basic Books.

Feinberg, L. (1998). *Trans liberation: Beyond pink or blue.* Boston, MA: Beacon Press.

Fergus, S., & Zimmerman, M. A. (2005). Adolescent resilience: A framework for understanding healthy development in the face of risk. *Annual Reviews of Public Health, 26*, 399–419. doi:10.1146/annurev.publhealth.26.021304.144357

Fine, M., Weis, L., Weseen, S., & Wong, L. (2003). For whom? Qualitative research, representations, and social responsibilities. In N. K. Denzin & Y. S. Lincoln (Eds.), *The landscape of qualitative research: Theories and issues* (2nd ed., pp. 167–207). Thousand Oaks, CA: Sage.

Fisher, K. (Producer), & Freeland, S. (Director). (2015). *Her story* [Web series]. Retrieved from https://www.youtube.com/channel/UCw2Mg0PoxZkAHAzDi abWr9A/feature

Foley, D., & Valenzuela, A. (2008). Critical ethnography: The politics of collaboration. In N. K. Denzin & Y. S. Lincoln (Eds.), *The landscape of qualitative research* (3rd ed., pp. 287–310). Thousand Oaks, CA: Sage.

Foucault, M. (1990). *The history of sexuality: Volume 1: An introduction* (R. Hurley, Trans.). New York, NY: Vintage Books. (Original work published 1976)

Foucault, M. (1995). *Discipline and punish* (A. Sheridan, Trans.). New York, NY: Vintage Books. (Original work published 1975)

Fried, I. (2000). It's a long journey, so bring an extra set of clothes. In K. Howard & A. Stevens (Eds.), *Out and about on campus: Personal accounts by lesbian, gay, bisexual and transgendered college students* (pp. 14–22). Los Angeles, CA: Alyson Books.

Gagné, P., Tewksbury, R., & McGaughey, D. (1997). Coming out and crossing over: Identity formation and proclamation in a transgender community. *Gender & Society, 11*(4), 478–508.

Ganesan, V., & Swenson, A. (2010). Prop 107 ends Affirmative Action in Arizona. *Student Free Press.* Retrieved from http://www.studentfreepress.net/archives/4572

Garfinkel, H. (2006). Passing and the managed achievement of sex status in an "intersexed" person. In S. Stryker & S. Whittle (Eds.), *The transgender studies reader* (pp. 58–93). New York, NY: Routledge.

Garner, T. (2015). Becoming. *TSQ: Transgender Studies Quarterly, 1*(1/2), 30–32.

Gates, G. J. (2011). *How many people are lesbian, gay, bisexual, and transgender?* Retrieved from williamsinstitute.law.ucla.edu/wp-content/uploads/Gates-How-Many-People-LGBT-Apr-2011.pdf

Geertz, C. (1973). *The interpretation of cultures.* New York, NY: Basic Books.

Gilbert, M. A. (2009). Defeating bigenderism: Changing gender assumptions in the twenty-first century. *Hypatia, 24*(3), 93–112.

Gilson, E. (2011). Vulnerability, ignorance, and oppression. *Hypatia, 26*(2), 308–332.

Giroux, H. A. (2015). Democracy in crisis, the specter of authoritarianism, and the future of higher education. *Journal of Critical Scholarship on Higher Education and Student Affairs, 1*(1), 101–113.

Giroux, H. A., & Searls Giroux, S. (2004). *Take back higher education: Race, youth, and the crisis of democracy in the post–civil rights era.* New York, NY: Palgrave Macmillan.

Gossett, R. (2015). *"What are we defending?": Reina's talk at the INCITE! COV4 conference.* Retrieved from www.reinagossett.com/what-are-we-defending-reinas-talk-at-the-incite-cov4-conference

Grace, L. J. (2014). Transgender dysphoria blues. On *Transgender dysphoria blues* [CD]. Elkton, FL: Total Treble Studios.

Grant, J. M., Mottet, L. A., Tanis, J., Harrison, J., Herman, J. L., & Keisling, M. (2011). *Injustice at every turn: A report of the national transgender discrimination survey.* Washington, DC: National Center for Transgender Equality and National Gay and Lesbian Task Force.

Gray, A. (2000). Wearing the dress. In K. Howard & A. Stevens (Eds.), *Out and about on campus: Personal accounts by lesbian, gay, bisexual and transgendered college students* (pp. 83–92). Los Angeles, CA: Alyson Books.

Greenaway, E. T. (2001). *Girls will be boys.* Retrieved from www.alternet.org/story/11017

Greene, R. R., Galambos, C., & Lee, Y. (2003). Resilience theory: Theoretical and professional conceptualizations. *Journal of Human Behavior in the Social Environment, 8*(4), 75–91.

Gupton, J. T. (2015). Engaging homeless students in college. In S. J. Quaye & S. R. Harper (Eds.), *Student engagement in higher education: Theoretical perspectives and practical approaches for diverse populations* (2nd ed., pp. 221–236). New York, NY: Routledge.

Halberstam, J. (1998). Transgender butch: Butch/FTM border wars and the masculine continuum. *GLQ: A Journal of Lesbian and Gay Studies, 4*(2), 287–310.

Halberstam, J. (2005). *In a queer time and place: Transgender bodies, subcultural lives.* New York: New York University Press.

Halberstam, J. J. (2012). *Gaga feminism: Sex, gender, and the end of normal.* Boston, MA: Beacon Press.

Hale, C. J. (1998). Consuming the living, dis(re)membering the dead in the butch/
FTM borderlands. *GLQ: A Journal of Lesbian and Gay Studies, 4*(2), 311–348.

Haller, B. A. (2006). Promoting disability-friendly campuses to prospective students: An analysis of university recruitment materials. *Disability Studies Quarterly,
26*(2). Retrieved from http://dsq-sds.org/article/view/673/850

Hanhardt, C. B. (2013). *Safe space: Gay neighborhood history and the politics of violence.* Durham, NC: Duke University Press.

Haper, G. W., & Schneider, M. (2003). Oppression and discrimination among lesbian, gay, bisexual, and transgender people and communities: A challenge for community psychology. *American Journal of Community Psychology, 31*(3/4), 243–252.

Hardiman, R., & Jackson, B. (2007). Conceptual foundations for social justice education. In M. Adams, L. A. Bell, & P. Griffin (Eds.), *Teaching for diversity and
social justice* (2nd ed., pp. 35–66). New York, NY: Routledge.

Harvey, D. (2007a). *A brief history of neoliberalism.* New York, NY: Oxford University Press.

Harvey, D. (2007b). Neoliberalism and creative destruction. *Annals of the American
Academy of Political and Social Science, 610,* 22–44.

Hayes, J. A., Chun-Kennedy, C., Edens, A., & Locke, B. D. (2011). Do double
minority students face double jeopardy? Testing minority stress theory. *Journal of
College Counseling, 14,* 117–126.

Henderson, E. F. (2014). Bringing up gender: Academic abjection? *Pedagogy, Culture
& Society, 22*(1), 21–38.

Henderson, E. F. (2015). *Gender pedagogy: Teaching, learning and tracing gender in
higher education.* Basingstoke, UK: Palgrave Macmillan.

Henning-Stout, M., James, S., & Macintosh, S. (2000). Reducing harassment of
lesbian, gay, bisexual, transgender, and questioning youth in schools. *School
Psychology Review, 29*(2), 180–191.

Heyl, B. S. (2001). Ethnographic interviewing. In P. Atkinson, A. Coffey, S. Delamont, J. Lofland, & L. Lofland (Eds.), *Handbook of ethnography* (pp. 369–383).
Thousand Oaks, CA: Sage.

Hill, D. B. (2003). Gendersim, transphobia, and gender bashing: A framework for
interpreting anti-transgender violence. In B. C. Wallace & R. T. Carter (Eds.),
*Understanding and dealing with violence: A multicultural approach* (pp. 113–136).
Thousand Oaks, CA: Sage.

hooks, b. (2000). *All about love: New visions.* New York, NY: Harper Perennial.

Human Rights Watch. (2001). *Hatred in the hallways: Violence and discrimination
against lesbian, gay, bisexual, and transgender students in U.S. schools.* New York,
NY: Author.

Inckle, K. (2015). Debilitating times: Compulsory ablebodiedness and White privilege in theory and practice. *Feminist Review, 111,* 42–58.

Jackson, A. Y., & Mazzei, L. A. (2012). *Thinking with theory in qualitative research:
Viewing data across multiple perspectives.* New York, NY: Routledge.

Jacoby, B. (2015). Engaging commuter and part-time students. In S. J. Quaye & S.
R. Harper (Eds.), *Student engagement in higher education: Theoretical perspectives*

*and practical approaches for diverse populations* (2nd ed., pp. 289–305). New York, NY, Routledge.

Jaschik, S. (2014). Duke asks the question. *Inside Higher Ed.* Retrieved from www .insidehighered.com/news/2014/09/02/duke-u-adds-voluntary-admissions-question-sexual-orientation-and-gender-identity

Jones, S. R. (2014). Forward. In D. Mitchell, Jr., C. Y. Simmons, & L. A. Greyer-biehl (Eds.), *Intersectionality & higher education: Theory, research, & praxis* (pp. xi–xiv). New York, NY: Peter Lang.

Jones, S. R., & Abes, E. S. (2013). *Identity development of college students: Advancing frameworks for multiple dimensions of identity.* San Francisco, CA: Jossey-Bass.

Jones, S. R., Torres, V., & Arminio, J. (2006). *Negotiating the complexities of qualitative research in higher education: Fundamental elements and issues* (2nd ed.). New York, NY: Routledge.

Jourian, T. J. (2014). Trans*forming authentic leadership: A conceptual framework. *Journal of Critical Thought and Praxis, 2*(2), Article 8.

Jourian, T. J. (2015a). Evolving nature of sexual orientation and gender identity. *New Directions for Student Services, 152,* 11–23. doi:10.1002/ss.20142

Jourian, T. J. (2015b). Queering constructs: Proposing a dynamic gender and sexuality model. *Educational Forum, 79*(4), 459–474.

Jourian, T. J. (2016). *"My masculinity is a little love poem to myself": Trans*masculine college students' conceptualizations of masculinities* (Doctoral dissertation). Retrieved from ecommons.luc.edu/luc_diss

Jourian, T. J., & Nicolazzo, Z. (2016). Bringing our communities to the research table: The liberatory potential of collaborative methodological practices. *Educational Action Research.*

Jourian, T. J., Simmons, S. L., & Devaney, K. (2015). "We are not expected": Trans* educators (re)claiming space and voice in higher education and student affairs. *TSQ: Transgender Studies Quarterly, 2*(3), 431–446.

Kasch, D. M. (2013). *Social media selves: College students' curation of self and others through Facebook* (Unpublished doctoral dissertation). University of California, Los Angeles.

Kincheloe, J. L., & McLaren, P. L. (1998). Rethinking critical theory and qualitative research. In N. K. Denzin & Y. S. Lincoln (Eds.), *The landscape of qualitative research: Theories and issues* (pp. 260–299). Thousand Oaks, CA: Sage.

Krovetz, M. L. (1999). A key element for supporting youth at-risk. *Clearing House, 73*(2), 121–123.

Kuh, G. D., Hu, S., & Vesper, N. (2000). "They shall be known by what they do": An activities-based typology of college students. *Journal of College Student Development, 41*(2), 228–244.

Kuh, G. D., & Whitt, E. J. (1988). *The invisible tapestry: Culture in American colleges and universities* (ASHE-ERIC Higher Education Report No. 1). Washington, DC: Association for the Study of Higher Education.

Lane, R. (2009). Trans as bodily becoming: Rethinking the biological as diversity, not dichotomy. *Hypatia, 24*(3), 136–157.

Lane, R. (2016). Reading trans biology as a feminist sociologist. *TSQ: Transgender Studies Quarterly, 3*(1/2), 185–191.

Lather, P. (2006). Paradigm proliferation as a good thing to think with: Teaching research in education as a wild profusion. *International Journal of Qualitative Studies in Education, 19*(1), 35–57.

Lie, A. (2002). Passing realities. In J. Nestle, C. Howell, & R. Wilchins (Eds.), *Genderqueer: Voices beyond the sexual binary* (pp. 166–170). Los Angeles, CA: Alyson Books.

Lincoln, Y. S., & Guba, E. G. (1985). *Naturalistic inquiry.* Beverly Hills, CA: Sage.

Lincoln, Y. S., Lynham, S. A., & Guba, E. G. (2011). Paradigmatic controversies, contradictions, and emerging confluences, revisited. In N. K. Denzin & Y. S. Lincoln (Eds.), *The Sage handbook of qualitative research* (pp. 97–128). Thousand Oaks, CA: Sage.

Lombardi, E. L., Wilchins, R. A., Priesing, D., & Malouf, D. (2001). Gender violence: Transgender experiences with violence and discrimination. *Journal of Homosexuality, 42*(1), 89–101.

Lykes, M. B. (1989). Dialogue with Guatemalan Indian women: Critical perspectives on constructing collaborative research. In R. K. Unger (Ed.), *Representations: Social constructions of gender* (pp. 167–185). Amityville, NY: Baywood.

MacKenzie, G. O. (1994). *Transgender nation.* Bowling Green, OH: Bowling Green State University Popular Press.

Madison, D. S. (2012). *Critical ethnography: Method, ethics, and performance* (2nd ed.). Los Angeles, CA: Sage.

Magolda, P., & Knight Abowitz, K. (1997). Communities and tribes in residential living. *Teachers College Record, 99*(2), 266–310.

Magolda, P. M., & Ebben Gross, K. (2009). *It's all about Jesus! Faith as an oppositional collegiate subculture.* Sterling, VA: Stylus.

Marine, S. B. (2011a). "Our college is changing": Women's college student affairs administrators and transgender students. *Journal of Homosexuality, 58,* 1165–1186. doi:10.1080/00918369.2011.605730

Marine, S. B. (2011b). Stonewall's legacy: Bisexual, gay, lesbian, and transgender students in higher education. *ASHE Higher Education Report, 37*(4).

Marine, S. B. (in press-a). Changing the frame: Queering access to higher education for trans* students. *International Journal of Qualitative Studies in Higher Education.*

Marine, S. B. (in press-b). For Brandon, for justice: Naming and ending sexual violence against trans* college students. In J. C. Harris & C. Linder (Eds.), *Critical perspectives on sexual violence on college campuses: Centering historically marginalized student voices.* Sterling, VA: Stylus.

Marine, S. B., & Nicolazzo, Z (2014). Names that matter: Exploring the tensions of campus LGBTQ centers and trans* inclusion. *Journal of Diversity in Higher Education, 7*(4), 265–281.

Mattilda (Ed.). (2006a). *Nobody passes: Rejecting the rules of gender and conformity.* Berkeley, CA: Seal Press.

Mattilda. (2006b). Reaching too far: An introduction. In Mattilda (Ed.), *Nobody passes: Rejecting the rules of gender and conformity* (pp. 7–19). Berkeley, CA: Seal Press.

Mazzei, L. A. (2013, July). *Posthuman enactments of vibrant data.* Keynote plenary presented at the Summer Institute of Qualitative Inquiry, Manchester Metropolitan University, Manchester, UK.

McBeth, S. (1993). Myths of objectivity and the collaborative process in life history research. In C. B. Brettell (Ed.), *When they read what we write: The politics of ethnography* (pp. 145–162). Westport, CT: Bergin & Garvey.

McRuer, R. (2006). *Crip theory: Cultural signs of queerness and disability.* New York: New York University Press.

Mertens, D. M. (2015). *Research and evaluation in education and psychology: Integrating diversity with quantitative, qualitative, and mixed methods* (4th ed.). Thousand Oaks, CA: Sage.

Miller, R. A. (in press). "My voice is definitely strongest in online communities": Students using social media for queer and disability identity-making. *Journal of College Student Development.*

Mitchell, D., Jr., Simmons, C. Y., & Greyerbiehl, L. A. (Eds.). (2014). *Intersectionality & higher education: Theory, research, & praxis.* New York, NY: Peter Lang.

Mock, J. (2014). *Redefining realness: My path to womanhood, identity, love, & so much more.* New York, NY: Atria Books.

Montgomery, S. (2002). Twenty passings. In J. Nestle, C. Howell, & R. Wilchins (Eds.), *Genderqueer: Voices beyond the sexual binary* (pp. 238–246). Los Angeles, CA: Alyson Books.

Morphew, C. C., & Hartley, M. (2006). Mission statements: A thematic analysis of rhetoric across institutional type. *The Journal of Higher Education, 77,* 456–471.

Mulé, N. J., Ross, L. E., Deeprose, B., Jackson, B. E., Daley, A., Travers, A., & Moore, D. (2009). Promoting LGBT health and wellbeing through inclusive policy development. *International Journal for Equity in Health, 8*(18). doi:10.1186/1475-9276-8-18

Nakamura, K. (1998). Transitioning on campus: A case studies approach. In R. L. Sanlo (Ed.), *Working with lesbian, gay, bisexual, and transgender college students: A handbook for faculty and administrators* (pp. 179–187). Westport, CT: Greenwood Educators Reference Collection.

Namaste, V. K. (2000). *Invisible lives: The erasure of transsexual and transgendered people.* Chicago, IL: University of Chicago Press.

Namaste, V. K. (2006). Genderbashing: Sexuality, gender, and the regulation of public space. In S. Stryker & S. Whittle (Eds.), *The transgender studies reader* (pp. 584–600). New York, NY: Routledge.

National Center for Education Statistics. (1999). *An institutional perspective on students with disabilities in postsecondary education.* Washington, DC: U.S. Government Printing Office.

National Center for Transgender Equality. (2016, May 13). HHS issues regulations banning trans health care discrimination [Web log post]. Retrieved from www.transequality.org/blog/hhs-issues-regulations-banning-trans-health-care-discrimination

New, J. (2015, September 25). The "invisible" one in four. *Inside Higher Ed.* Retrieved from www.insidehighered.com/news/2015/09/25/1-4-transgender-students-say-they-have-been-sexually-assaulted-survey-finds

Nicolazzo, Z (2014a). Celluloid marginalization: Pedagogical strategies for increasing students' critical thought through the multiple (re)readings of trans* subjectivities in film. *Journal of LGBT Youth, 11*(1), 20–39.

Nicolazzo, Z (2014b). Identity as inquiry: Living and researching from the borderlands. In R. N. Brown, R. Carducci, & C .R. Kuby (Eds.), *Disrupting qualitative inquiry: Possibilities and tensions in educational research.* (pp. 205–226). New York, NY: Peter Lang Press.

Nicolazzo, Z (2015). *"Just go in looking good": The resilience, resistance, and kinship-building of trans* college students* (Doctoral dissertation). Retrieved from www.ohiolink.edu/etd

Nicolazzo, Z (2016, February 11). My exhaustion with the "do better" illogic [Web log post]. Retrieved from http://znicolazzo.weebly.com/trans-resilience-blog/-my-exhaustion-with-the-do-better-illogic

Nicolazzo, Z (2016). "Just go in looking good": The resilience, resistance, and kinship-building of trans* college students. *Journal of College Student Development, 57*(5), 538–556.

Nicolazzo, Z (in press). Compulsory heterogenderism: A collective case study. *NASPA Journal About Women in Higher Education.*

Nicolazzo, Z, & Marine, S. B. (2015). "It will change if people keep talking": Trans* students in college and university housing. *Journal of College and University Student Housing, 42*(1), 160–177.

Nicolazzo, Z, Marine, S. B., & Galarte, F. J. (2015). Trans*formational pedagogies [Special issue]. *TSQ: Transgender Studies Quarterly, 2*(3).

Nicolazzo, Z, Pitcher, E., Renn, K. A., & Woodford, M. (in press). An exploration of trans* kinship as a strategy for student success. *International Journal of Qualitative Studies in Education.*

Nicolosi, J. (1997). *Reparative therapy of male homosexuality.* Northvale, NJ: Jason Aronson.

O'Reilly, K. (2005). *Ethnographic methods.* New York, NY: Routledge.

O'Reilly, K. (2009). *Key concepts in ethnography.* Los Angeles, CA: Sage.

Orleck, A. (2005). *Storming Caesars Palace: How Black mothers fought their own war on poverty.* Boston, MA: Beacon Press.

Palmer, P. J., & Zajonc, A. (2010). *The heart of higher education: A call to renewal.* San Francisco, CA: Jossey-Bass.

Pascoe, C. J. (2007). *Dude, you're a fag: Masculinity and sexuality in high school.* Berkeley: University of California Press.

Patton L. D., & Simmons, S. (2008). Exploring complexities of multiple identities of lesbians in a Black college environment. *Negro Educational Review, 59*(3/4), 197–215.

Patton, L. (2010). *Cultural centers in higher education: Perspectives on identity, theory, and practice.* Sterling, VA: Stylus.

Patton, L. D., & Catching, C. (2009). "Teaching while Black": Narratives of African American student affairs faculty. *International Journal of Qualitative Studies in Education, 22*(6), 713–728.

Pérez-Peña, R. (2013, February 12). College health plans respond as transgender students gain visibility. *New York Times.* Retrieved from www.nytimes.com/2013/02/13/education/12sexchange.html?_r=0

Pitcher, E. N. (2015). *Re-conceptualizing gender equity: Voices and experiences of trans\* faculty.* Paper presented at the annual meeting of the American Education Research Association, Chicago, IL.

Pitcher, E. N. (2016a). *Being and becoming professionally other: Understanding how organizations shape trans\* academics' experiences* (Unpublished doctoral dissertation). Michigan State University, East Lansing.

Pitcher, E. N. (2016b, April). *Trans\* academics' perspectives about informal practices that create supportive, neutral, or hostile academic workplaces.* Paper presented at the annual meeting of the American Education Research Association, Washington, DC.

Planas, R. (2012). *Arizona official considers targeting Mexican American studies in university.* Retrieved from latino.foxnews.com/latino/politics/2012/03/28/arizona-official-considers-targeting-mexican-american-studies-in-university

Puar, J. K. (2007). *Terrorist assemblages: Homonationalism in queer times.* Durham, NC: Duke University Press.

Pusch, R. S. (2005). Objects of curiosity: Transgender college students' perceptions of the reactions of others. *Journal of Gay & Lesbian Issues in Education, 3*(1), 45–61. doi:10.1300/J367v03n01_06

Putnam, R. D. (2001). *Bowling alone: The collapse and revival of American community.* New York, NY: Simon & Schuster.

Quart, A. (2008, March 16). When girls will be boys. *New York Times.* Retrieved from www.nytimes.com/2008/03/16/magazine/16students-t.html?_r=0

Rabodeau, T. (2000). Finding my place in the world, or which bathroom should I use today? In K. Howard & A. Stevens (Eds.), *Out and about campus: Personal accounts by lesbian, gay, bisexual and transgendered college students* (pp. 172–180). Los Angeles, CA: Alyson Books.

Rankin, S., & Beemyn, G. (2012). Beyond the binary: The lives of gender-nonconforming youth. *About Campus, 17*(4), 2–10.

Rankin, S., Weber, G., Blumenfeld, W., & Frazer, S. (2010). *2010 state of higher education for lesbian, gay, bisexual & transgender people.* Charlotte, NC: Campus Pride.

Renn, K. A. (2007). LGBT student leaders and queer activists: Identities of lesbian, gay, bisexual, transgender, and queer identified college student leaders and activists. *Journal of College Student Development, 48,* 311–330.

Renn, K. A. (2010). LGBT and queer research in higher education: The state and status of the field. *Educational Researcher, 39*(2), 132–141. doi:10.3102/0013189X10362579

Renn, K. A., & Arnold, K. D. (2003). Reconceptualizing research on peer culture. *The Journal of Higher Education, 74*(3), 261–291.

Renn, K. A., & Patton, L. D. (2011). Campus ecology and environments. In J. H. Schuh, S. R. Jones, S. R. Harper, & Associates (Eds.), *Student services: A handbook for the profession* (5th ed., pp. 242–256). San Francisco, CA: Jossey-Bass.

Renn, K. A., & Reason, R. D. (2012). *College students in the United States: Characteristics, experiences, and outcomes.* San Francisco, CA: Jossey-Bass.

Rich, A. (1980). Compulsory heterosexuality and lesbian existence. *Signs, 5*(4), 631–660.

Richards, J. (2016, February 1). Her Story's *Jen Richards on why LGBT people need to tell their own stories* (S. Kabango, interviewer). Retrieved from www.cbc.ca/radio/q/schedule-for-monday-february-1-2016-1.3428312/her-story-s-jen-richards-on-why-lgbt-people-need-to-tell-their-own-stories-1.3428391

Ridner, S. L., Frost, K., & LaJoie, A. S. (2006). Health information and risk behaviors among lesbian, gay, and bisexual college students. *Journal of the American Academy of Nurse Practitioners, 18*(8), 374–378.

Rogers, J. (2000). Getting real at ISU: A campus transition. In K. Howard & A. Stevens (Eds.), *Out and about campus: Personal accounts by lesbian, gay, bisexual and transgendered college students* (pp. 12–18). Los Angeles, CA: Alyson Books.

Rothman, L. (2012, November 1). A cultural history of mansplaining. *Atlantic.* Retrieved from www.theatlantic.com/sexes/archive/2012/11/a-cultural-history-of-mansplaining/264380

Rubin, G. (2006). Of catamites and kings: Reflections on butch, gender, and boundaries. In S. Stryker & S. Whittle (Eds.), *The transgender studies reader* (pp. 471–479). New York, NY: Routledge.

Rubin, G. S. (2011). The traffic in women: Notes on the "political economy" of sex. In G. S. Rubin (Ed.), *Deviations: A Gayle Rubin reader* (pp. 33–65). Durham, NC: Duke University Press.

Rubin, H. (2003). *Self-made men: Identity and embodiment among transsexual men.* Nashville, TN: Vanderbilt University Press.

Sanlo, R. (2004). Lesbian, gay, and bisexual college students: Risk, resiliency, and retention. *Journal of College Student Retention, 6*(1), 97–110.

Schaffer, A. (2012). *If your baby girl might be born with a small penis.* Retrieved from www.slate.com/articles/double_x/doublex/2012/08/intersex_babies_should_you_treat_their_condition_with_prenatal_drugs_.html

Schilt, K., & Westbrook, L. (2009). Doing gender, doing heteronormativity: "Gender normals," transgender people, and the social maintenance of heterosexuality. *Gender & Society, 23*(4), 440–464.

Sedgwick, E. K. (2008). *Epistemology of the closet.* Berkeley: University of California Press.

Seelman, K. L., Walls, N. E., Costello, K., Steffens, K., Inselman, K., Montague-Asp, H., & Colorado Trans on Campus Coalition. (2012). *Invisibilities, uncertainties, and unexpected surprises: The experiences of transgender and gender non-conforming students, staff, and faculty at universities & colleges in Colorado.* Denver, CO: Colorado Trans on Campus.

Serano, J. (2007). *Whipping girl: A transsexual woman on sexism and the scapegoating of femininity.* Berkeley, CA: Seal Press.

Serano, J. (2013). *Excluded: Making feminist and queer movements more inclusive.* Berkeley, CA: Seal Press.

Sharp, J. (Producer), & Pierce, K. (Director). (1999). *Boys don't cry* [Motion picture]. United States: Fox Searchlight Pictures

Simmons, S. L. (2016). *"I am because we are": A portrait of trans\*postsecondary educators' experiences in higher education* (Doctoral dissertation). Retrieved from http://ecommons.luc.edu/luc_diss/

Singh, A. A., Hays, D. G., & Watson, L. S. (2011). Strength in the face of adversity: Resilience strategies of transgender individuals. *Journal of Counseling & Development, 89*, 20–27.

Sloop, J. M. (2000). Disciplining the transgendered: Brandon Teena, public representation, and normativity. *Western Journal of Communication, 64*(2), 165–189.

Snorton, C. R. (2009). "A new hope": The psychic life of passing. *Hypatia, 24*(3), 77–92.

Solórzano, D. G., & Yosso, T. J. (2002). Critical race methodology: Counter-storytelling as an analytical framework for education research. *Qualitative Inquiry, 8*(1), 23–44.

Soto, S. K., & Joseph, M. (2010). Neoliberalism and the battle over ethnic studies in Arizona. *Thought & Action: NEA Higher Education Journal, 26*, 45–56.

Spade, D. (2008). Fighting to win. In M. B. Sycamore (Ed.), *That's revolting! Queer strategies for resisting assimilation* (pp. 47–53). New York, NY: Soft Skull Press.

Spade, D. (2010). Be professional! *Harvard Journal of Law & Gender, 33*(1), 71–84.

Spade, D. (2015). *Normal life: Administrative violence, critical trans politics, and the limitations of law* (2nd ed.). Durham, NC: Duke University Press.

Stainburn, S. (2013, July 30). The gay question: Check one. *New York Times.* Retrieved from www.nytimes.com/2013/08/04/education/edlife/more-college-applications-ask-about-sexual-identity.html?_r=0

Steigerwald, F., & Janson, G. R. (2003). Conversion therapy: Ethical considerations in family counseling. *Family Journal, 11*(1), 55–59. doi:10.1177/1066480702238473

Steinmetz, K. (2014, May 29). The transgender tipping point. *Time.* Retrieved from time.com/135480/transgender-tipping-point

Stewart, D. L. (2010). Researcher as instrument: Understanding "shifting" findings in constructivist research. *Journal of Student Affairs Research and Practice, 47*(3), 291–306.

Stewart, D. L. (Ed.). (2011). *Multicultural student services on campus: Building bridges, re-visioning community.* Sterling, VA: Stylus.

Stewart, D-L. (in press). Transversing the gender DMZ: An autoethnographic exploration of non-binary genderqueer transmasculine identity in higher education. *International Journal of Qualitative Studies in Education.*

Stieglitz, K. A. (2010). Development, risk, and resilience of transgender youth. *Journal of the Association of Nurses in AIDS Care, 21*(3), 192–206. doi:10.1016/j.jana.2009.08.004

Stotzer, R. L. (2009). Violence against transgender people: A review of United States data. *Aggression and Violent Behavior, 14,* 170–179. doi:10.1016/j.avb.2009.01.006

Strange, C. C., & Banning, J. H. (2015). *Designing for learning: Creating campus environments for student success* (2nd ed.). San Francisco, CA: Jossey-Bass.

Stryker, S. (2008). *Transgender history.* Berkeley, CA: Seal Press.

Stryker, S., & Whittle, S. (Eds.). (2006). *The transgender studies reader.* New York, NY: Routledge.

Sue, D. W. (2010a). *Microaggressions and marginality: Manifestation, dynamics, and impact.* Hoboken, NJ: Wiley.

Sue, D. W. (2010b). *Microaggressions in everyday life: Race, gender, and sexual orientation.* Hoboken, NJ: Wiley.

Sylvia Rivera Law Project. (2007). *"It's war in here": A report on the treatment of transgender and intersex people in New York, NY state men's prisons.* New York, NY: Sylvia Rivera Law Project.

Tatum. B. D. (2013). The complexity of identity: "Who am I?" In M. Adams, W. J. Blumenfeld, C. Castañeda, H. W. Hackman, M. L. Peters, & X. Zúñiga (Eds.), *Readings for diversity and social justice* (3rd ed.) (pp. 6–9). New York, NY: Routledge.

Taylor, E. (1998). A primer on critical race theory. *Journal of Blacks in Higher Education, 19,* 122–124.

Taylor, K. (2012). Discussing diversity: Lawyer rules actions of Miami officials non-discriminatory. *The Miami Student, 40*(6). Retrieved from issuu.com/miamistuent/docs/09-07-12/1

Teich, N. M. (2012). *Transgender 101: A simple guide to a complex issue.* New York, NY: Columbia University Press.

Thomas, J. (1993). *Doing critical ethnography.* Newbury Park, CA: Sage.

Tierney, W. G. (1993). *Building communities of difference: Higher education in the twenty-first century.* Westport, CT: Bergin & Garvey.

Tillapaugh, D. W. (2012). *Toward an integrated self: Making meaning of the multiple identities of gay men in college* (Unpublished doctoral dissertation). University of San Diego, CA.

Tillapaugh, D., & Nicolazzo, Z (2014). Backward thinking: Exploring the relationship among intersectionality, epistemology, and research design. In D. Mitchell, Jr., C. Y. Simmons, & L. A. Greyerbiehl (Eds.), *Intersectionality & higher education: Theory, research, & praxis* (pp. 111–122). New York, NY: Peter Lang.

Tompkins, A. (2014). Asterisk. *TSQ: Transgender Studies Quarterly, 1*(1/2), 26–27.

Transgender Law Center. (2014). *Victory: Cincinnati, OH, agrees to transition-related care for employees!* Retrieved from transgenderlawcenter.org/archives/11071

Tuchman, G. (2009). *Wannabe u: Inside the corporate university.* Chicago, IL: University of Chicago Press.

Valentine, D. (2007). *Imagining transgender: An ethnography of a category.* Durham, NC: Duke University Press.

Van Breda, A. D. (2001). *Resilience theory: A literature review.* Retrieved from vanbreda.org/adrian/resilience/resilience_theory_review.pdf

Villenas, S., & Deyhle, D. (1999). Critical race theory and ethnographies challenging the stereotypes: Latino families, schooling, resilience and resistance. *Curriculum Inquiry, 29*(4), 413–445.

Wall, V. A., & Evans, N. J. (Eds.). (1999). *Toward acceptance: Sexual orientation issues on campus.* Lanham, MD: University Press of America.

Warner, M. (1999). *The trouble with normal: Sex, politics, and the ethics of queer life.* Cambridge, MA: Harvard University Press.

Weston, K. (1991). *Families we choose: Lesbians, gays, and kinship.* New York, NY: Columbia University Press.

Whittle, S. (2006). Foreword. In S. Stryker & S. Whittle (Eds.), *The transgender studies reader* (pp. xi–xvi). New York, NY: Routledge.

Wilchins, R. (2002a). It's your gender, stupid. In J. Nestle, C. Howell, & R. Wilchins (Eds.), *Genderqueer: Voices from beyond the sexual binary* (pp. 23–32). Los Angeles, CA: Alyson Books.

Wilchins, R. (2002b). Queerer bodies. In J. Nestle, C. Howell, & R. Wilchins (Eds.), *Genderqueer: Voices from beyond the sexual binary* (pp. 33–46). Los Angeles, CA: Alyson Books.

Wilkins, A. C. (2008). *Wannabes, Goths, and Christians: The boundaries of sex, style, and status.* Chicago, IL: University of Chicago Press.

Wolcott, H. F. (2008). *Ethnography: A way of seeing* (2nd ed.). New York, NY: AltaMira Press.

Wolff, S. (1995). The concept of resilience. *Australian & New Zealand Journal of Psychiatry, 29*(4), 565–574.

Worley, J. (2011). "Street power" and the claiming of public space: San Francisco's "vanguard" and pre-Stonewall queer radicalism. In E. A. Stanley & N. Smith (Eds.), *Captive genders: Trans embodiments and the prison industrial complex* (pp. 41–56). Oakland, CA: AK Press.

Yoshino, K. (2006). *Covering: The hidden assault on our civil rights.* New York, NY: Random House.

Young, I. M. (1990). *Justice and the politics of difference.* Princeton, NJ: Princeton University Press.

# ABOUT THE AUTHOR

**Z Nicolazzo** is an assistant professor of adult and higher education and a faculty associate in the Center for the Study of Women, Gender, and Sexuality at Northern Illinois University, DeKalb. Z has a BA in philosophy from Roger Williams University (2004); an MS in college student personnel from Western Illinois University (2006); and a PhD in student affairs in higher education, with a graduate certificate in women's, gender, and sexuality studies from Miami University (2015). Z's research agenda is focused on mapping gender across college contexts, with particular attention to trans* collegians, and the intersections of race, gender, sexuality, and disability. Prior to becoming a faculty member, Z worked as a full-time student affairs professional in the areas of residence life, sexual violence prevention, and fraternity and sorority life. Readers can follow Z on hir website (znicolazzo .weebly.com) or on Twitter (@trans_killjoy).

## Also available from Stylus

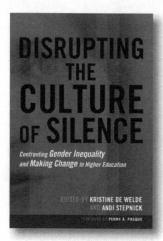

**Disrupting the Culture of Silence**

*Confronting Gender Inequality and Making Change in Higher Education*

Edited by Kristine De Welde and Andi Stepnick
Foreword by Penny A. Pasque

"Engagingly written and rich in formal data and telling anecdotes, this sociologically smart collection will be an important tool for graduate students and faculty confronting what remains a male-biased system of higher education. The editors draw on their own interviews with women in many academic disciplines and enlist other researchers and activists to provide a rich and deep look at gendered experiences in academia today. Commendably, the editors give strong representation to women of color, disabled women, and lesbians in defining how 'women' experience (and overcome) diverse challenges. Variations among disciplines and between institutions are also highlighted. The beauty of the volume emerges most in its telling details: e.g., the problematic idea that 'just say no' to service work is a feasible organizational strategy; the value in changing policy rather than seeking ad hoc accommodations; the self-contradictory advice about when in an academic career to have a baby. Excellent bibliography and list of disciplinary and other extra-university resources for change make this book an invaluable resource for all faculty or students looking for insight into strategies for real inclusivity. . . . Highly recommended."—*Choice*

22883 Quicksilver Drive
Sterling, VA 20166-2102

Subscribe to our e-mail alerts: www.Styluspub.com